ROAD TRIPS IN THE USA

ROAD TRIPS IN THE USA

50 ADVENTURES ON THE OPEN ROAD

PREVIOUS PAGE Driving through the Badlands in South Dakota

OPPOSITE Crossing over San Francisco's Golden Gate Bridge

CONTENTS

FEATURES

Mr. D'z
ROUTE
66
ROOT BEER
ROUTE
66
DINER
KINGMAN
ARIZONA
MR D'Z
ROUTE 66
Diner
Mr. D'z
HISTORIC ROUTE
66
TEXAS 54
5384
ROUTE 66 DINER

INTRODUCTION

I drive, therefore I am.

OK, so Descartes didn't quite put it that way, but if he'd been American, he probably would have. For better or worse, cars are an integral part of the American identity, and driving is practically shorthand for national traits like independence, individualism, and the pioneer spirit.

So, sure, you could travel the country by plane or train or bus, but to really get under its skin, you need to drive. That means partaking in the great American tradition that is the road trip. There's a reason why it's featured in so many iconic movies—there's no better feeling than packing a cooler, stuffing the glove compartment full of maps, and hitting the highway.

To fuel your next journey, we've compiled some of the country's best drives in *Road Trips in the USA*. The routes here carry you through all 50 states and range from multi-week coast-to-coast epics to short spins that take just a few hours but leave long-lasting impressions. You'll find classic drives like Route 66 and the Blue Ridge Parkway but also lesser-known journeys such as Vermont Route 100 and Beartooth Highway, along with themed trips that explore the legacies of the Civil Rights Movement and the nation's musical heritage. We've also shone the spotlight on some road trip icons that may warrant further exploration, from eerie ghost towns to roadside Muffler Men. Follow the routes as we've presented them here, or use them as inspiration to chart your own course. After all, on a road trip where you go is up to you. What you discover, well, that's up to the road.

So, sure, you could travel the country by plane or train or bus, but to really get under its skin, you need to drive.

OPPOSITE Vintage cars parked by Mr. D'z diner, on Route 66

ABOVE RIGHT The winding road by Diablo Lake, Washington

RIGHT Admiring the red-rock landscape in Utah

PREPARING FOR YOUR ROAD TRIP

ICON KEY

ACCOMMODATIONS

DETOUR

FACT

GREAT VIEW

HIKE

MUSEUM

PHOTO OP

PIT STOP

WILDLIFE

While there's plenty to be said for jumping in your car and hitting the open road, advance planning will ensure you make the most of each and every road trip. To help you prepare, we've put together some handy pointers.

PLANNING A ROAD TRIP

To plan a successful road trip, you'll need to consider everything from where you want to go and what kind of distance you'll cover, right down to the specific details surrounding car insurance, gas stops, and accommodations (especially in rural locations). For safety, plan regular stops to avoid becoming tired behind the wheel and check the weather in advance—some roads are inaccessible in winter months. If you're looking to complete a multistate route, it's worth remembering that laws and speed limits vary state by state.

CHOOSING YOUR VEHICLE

If you have your own vehicle, there's little stopping you—though do check road conditions before setting off to make sure you won't need a 4WD. Renting a car is generally a simple task, though companies often only rent to drivers over 21 years old, and most impose a daily surcharge on drivers under the age of 25. Major rental agencies include Enterprise, Budget, Hertz, and Avis, and you'll find rental centers at airports, in cities, and even in mid-sized towns.

Driving an EV is a great way to minimize your road trip's environmental impact, but it does require a bit more planning. Though the country's EV infrastructure is improving, charging stations remain far less common than gas stations. PlugShare, ChargePoint, and Electrify America are all helpful apps for finding charging points.

DOCUMENTS AND INSURANCE

International drivers will need a valid driver's license from their home country and an International Driving Permit, to avoid complications. Both documents should be in your possession whenever you're driving. If driving your own vehicle, keep your vehicle registration and insurance documents in the car or have digital versions on your phone; if renting, do the same with the contract and any other rental documents.

Nearly all states require drivers to have car insurance, including international travelers. Overseas visitors planning to rent a vehicle can easily purchase car insurance from the rental agency. Should you get in an accident or find yourself in a situation that is hazardous or involves injuries, dial 911 for emergency assistance. If your vehicle breaks down or has a mechanical issue, move off the road or into the emergency lane, turn on your hazard lights, and call for roadside assistance. Some states have their own roadside assistance hotlines, as do many insurance companies and car rental agencies. Alternatively, you can call a local towing company.

Health care in the U.S. is good but expensive. Overseas visitors should secure comprehensive medical travel insurance before arrival.

RULES OF THE ROAD

The legal driving age varies by state, ranging from 16 to 18 years old. Speed limits can also vary by state but, broadly speaking, the maximum is around 70 mph (110 km/h) on Interstates and major multilane highways, 55 mph (90 km/h) on two-lane highways, and 25 mph (40 km/h) in cities and residential areas. Always pay attention to the posted limit and keep an eye out for tolls, which typically appear on Interstates and major highways. Stop signs should also be adhered to.

Though cell phones can be useful for navigation, texting while driving is banned in almost every state. Rules also apply to drinking—the blood alcohol content limit in the U.S. is 0.08 percent, except in Utah, where it's 0.05 percent. Under no circumstances should you drive under the influence of drink or drugs.

ROAD CONDITIONS

U.S. roads are typically well maintained, especially Interstates and major highways, though adverse weather can present complications. Winter weather in mountainous areas can make travel difficult or impossible, and climate change is increasingly creating hazards like wildfires and flash floods. If you're unsure of road conditions along your route, check online before heading out. State department of transportation websites and social media feeds are also reliable sources of information on road closures, accidents, and anything else that might impact your drive.

USEFUL WEBSITES

E-ZPass Skip the lines with this pre-paid electronic tolling system, most commonly used in the Eastern U.S. and Midwest. *www.e-zpassiag.com*

GasBuddy A must for U.S. road trips, this app locates nearby gas stations and notifies you about deals. *www.gasbuddy.com*

NPS app The best source for real-time conditions within national parks, with updates on road closures, long entry lines, and weather advisories. *www.nps.gov/index.htm*

what3words This locations app helps 911 teams find people in emergencies, especially those in rural areas. *www.what3words.com*

TOP Driving toward the sunset with the top down

ABOVE Colorful shop signs along Route 66, Oklahoma

EXPLORE

THE ROAD TRIPS

1. Denali Highway
2. Richardson Highway
3. O'ahu Circle Island Drive
4. Hāna Highway
5. Olympic Peninsula Loop
6. Cascade Loop Scenic Byway
7. Oregon Coast Highway 101
8. Volcanic Legacy Scenic Byway
9. Napa Valley's Silverado Trail
10. Yosemite National Park
11. Pacific Coast Highway
12. Southern Pacific
13. Extraterrestrial Highway
14. Highway 50: The Loneliest Road
15. Hells Canyon Scenic Byway
16. Going-to-the-Sun Road
17. America's National Park Highway
18. Beartooth Highway
19. Grand Teton to Yellowstone
20. The Mighty 5
21. Trail of the Ancients
22. High Road to Taos
23. Trail Ridge Road
24. Texas Hill Country
25. Nebraska Highway 2
26. Badlands Loop Scenic Byway
27. Black Hills Loop
28. Lewis and Clark Trail
29. Great River Road
30. North Shore Scenic Drive
31. Oregon Trail
32. Route 66
33. Lake Michigan Circle Tour
34. Kentucky Bourbon Trail
35. Natchez Trace Parkway
36. Blues Trail
37. Civil Rights Trail
38. Blue Ridge Parkway
39. Civil War Trail
40. Overseas Highway
41. TransAmerica Trail
42. Midland Trail Scenic Byway
43. Outer Banks Scenic Byway
44. Lincoln Highway
45. Atlantic Coast Trail
46. Lake Champlain Byway
47. Vermont Route 100
48. Kancamagus Highway
49. New England Lighthouse Trail
50. Maine's Route 1

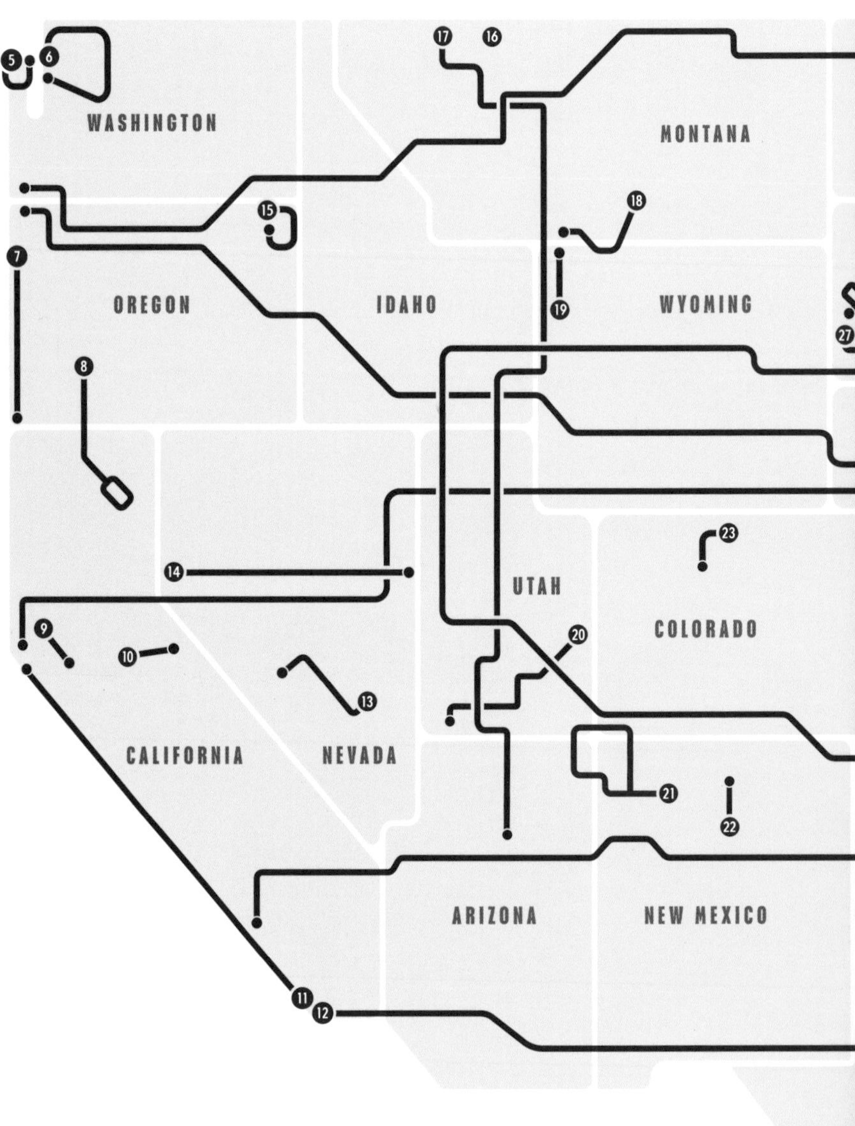

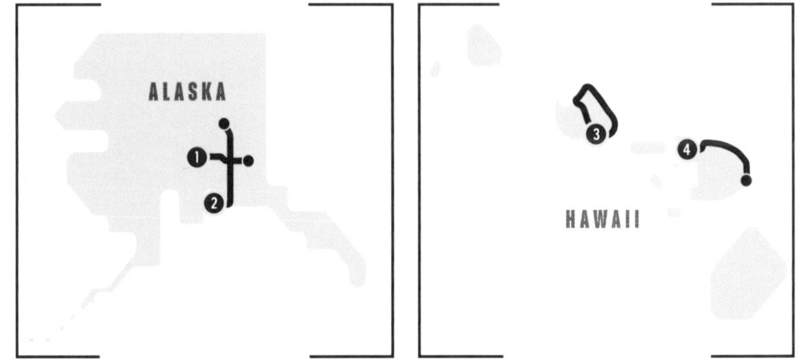

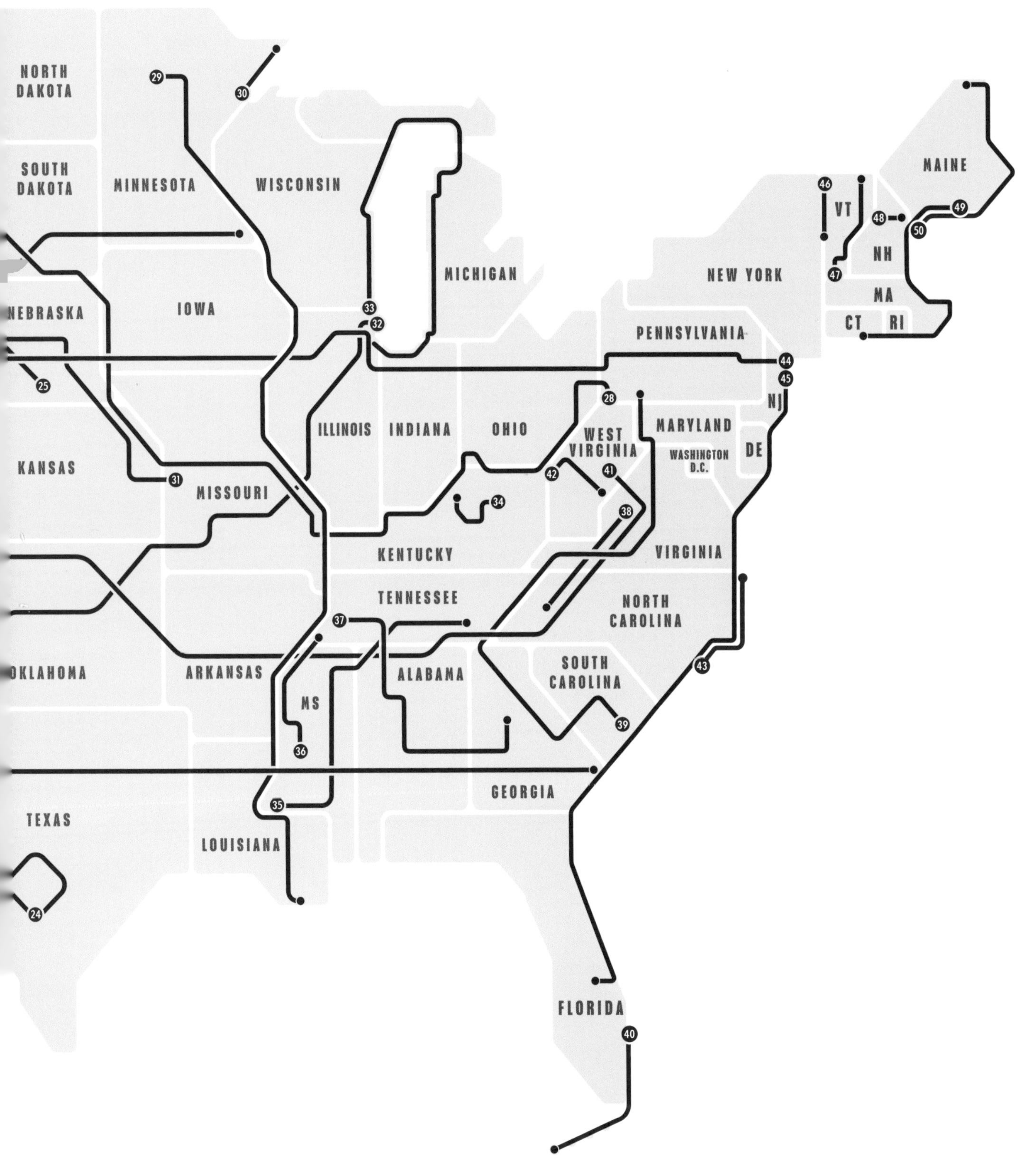
NORTH DAKOTA
SOUTH DAKOTA
MINNESOTA
WISCONSIN
MICHIGAN
NEW YORK
MAINE
VT
NH
MA
CT
RI
NEBRASKA
IOWA
PENNSYLVANIA
NJ
KANSAS
ILLINOIS
INDIANA
OHIO
WEST VIRGINIA
MARYLAND
WASHINGTON D.C.
DE
MISSOURI
KENTUCKY
VIRGINIA
TENNESSEE
NORTH CAROLINA
OKLAHOMA
ARKANSAS
MS
ALABAMA
SOUTH CAROLINA
GEORGIA
TEXAS
LOUISIANA
FLORIDA
24
25
28
29
30
31
32
33
34
35
36
37
38
39
40
41
42
43
44
45
46
47
48
49
50

DENALI HIGHWAY

START/FINISH
Paxson, Alaska/ Cantwell, Alaska

DISTANCE
135 miles (215 km)

DURATION
1–2 days

ROAD CONDITIONS
Mainly gravel

THE BEST TIME TO GO
Summer or early fall to avoid road closures

OPPOSITE A moose and her calf crossing the icy Denali Highway at sunrise

Alaska is synonymous with the wild, and few road trips underline its rugged spirit like the Denali Highway. The winding route scythes through the mountains and glaciers of the Alaska Range, with sweeping views at every turn.

Denali Highway, also known as Alaska Route 8, is a "highway" in name alone. Mostly a gravel track, with speeds restricted to 55 mph (90 km/h), it's best suited to a 4WD vehicle if adventurous detours are on the agenda. You could drive it in four hours, but why rush? This is the ideal route to take your foot off the pedal, not least because the majority of the highway runs above the tree line, offering stunning panoramic views.

Two towns (although this is stretching the definition of "town") anchor either end of the road: Paxson and Cantwell. Begin your journey in tiny Paxson, if only so you're driving *toward* Mount Denali: North America's tallest mountain makes for a supremely photogenic end point.

TUNDRA AND TRAILS

Leaving Paxson, it's a quick climb into an imposing sweep of tundra. By the time you reach mile 6, you'll be intimately aware of the mountains of the Alaska Range, an ever-present companion on the journey. A pull-off leads to Sevenmile Lake, which would grace the cover of many a tourism brochure in the Lower 48. Here, it's just another blue expanse, surrounded by seasonal blueberry bushes.

Back on the main road, pull off at mile 13 for views of more stunning lakes—as many as 40 in clear conditions. This is also a spectacular spot to snap some peaks: the Wrangell mountains, including Mount Wrangell itself, the northernmost active volcano in the Pacific Rim.

Moving on, you reach the Tangle Lakes: at mile 20, slip on some rubber boots (it can get wet), and hike the

PAXSON

SEVENMILE LAKE
Follow the gravel pull-off to enjoy stunning views of this serene lake.

6 MILES

MOUNT WRANGELL
This volcano was named by the Russians after Baron Ferdinand Petrovich von Wrangel.

13 MILES

THE SWEDE MOUNTAIN TRAIL

The strenuous climb is rewarded with views of Tangle Lakes and the Alaska Range.

20 MILES

LANDMARK GAP

Feel the sky bear down on you while navigating the tundra trails here.

25 MILES

MACLAREN SUMMIT

It's not heaven, but you're pretty close at over 4,000 ft (1,220 m) high.

37 MILES

Swede Mountain trail. It's a short route, but strenuous, with some 1,500 ft (455 m) of altitude gain. Your reward, though, is fantastic views.

By now, you'll have picked up a sense of immense space and emptiness, but in fact this area was, prior to European contact, a relatively thriving population center. Tangle Lakes is home to over 500 early prehistoric archeological sites. What brought humans here? Largely, good hunting: retreating glaciers left deep cuts that made natural tracks for migrating caribou. One famous example is Landmark Gap, where you'll find a web of foot trails into the high tundra that provide even more breathtaking vistas. On clear days, you may be able to spot caribou (although their numbers have declined in recent years).

More awesome views await at Maclaren Summit, at 4,086 ft (1,226 m) the second-highest highway pass in the state, with a vision of blasted tundra that defies description. Hiking the child-friendly Maclaren Summit Trail will bring you even closer to this rugged, wind-carved backdrop.

GEOLOGICAL WONDERS

As the road descends, keep an eye out for palsas—mounds with a permanently frozen peat core, a common feature of subarctic landscapes. You'll also see countless tiny lakes dotting the marshy mire, formed by melting permafrost. After around 40 miles (70 km), there's a chance to pause for breath—or even a cozy stay—at the Maclaren River Lodge, which has fed and sheltered hunters and travelers for half a century. In that time it's also brought Wi-Fi to the wilderness.

As glaciers recede, they leave their detritus behind, forming stony piles known as moraines. One of the most notable in the state is the wonderfully dubbed Crazy Notch, a looming ridge formed by the Maclaren Glacier, which you'll spot at mile 46.

If you don't feel like shelling out for a place to crash, continue on for 10 miles

MOUNT MCKINLEY

Denali's name comes from a local Athabaskan language, and is based on the word for "big" or "high." For too many years, however, it was called Mount McKinley, named for the U.S. presidential candidate (later president) William McKinley by a gold prospector in 1896. The official name change occurred in 2015, to the approval of Alaskans across political stripes.

56 MILES

CLEARWATER CREEK WAYSIDE

One of the most scenic places to camp on a drive full of hyperbolic scenery.

80 MILES

SUSITNA RIVER

The bridge over the river carries you deeper into the wilds of Interior Alaska.

END

CANTWELL

(15 km) until you reach the informal campsite at Clearwater Creek Wayside. The grounds, situated along a necklace of lakes and marshes, attract waterfowl and caribou. Otherwise, hit the road to soak up more geological wonders at mile 59 as the highway mounts the spine of an esker, an elevated riverbed transformed by a retreating glacier into a spaghetti-ish ridge of gravel and silt.

ON TO DENALI

The Denali Highway keeps rolling on, through alpine tundra, permafrost lakes, and peat marsh, keeping you permanently at the edge of your seat. The air is fresh, too. At mile 80, watch it rising from the whirlpools of the Susitna River–a spectacular, and dangerous, set of rapids. From here, it's 15 miles (25 km) to an unmarked and underrated side road with an epic panorama of the colossal, snowcapped Alaska Range; you may well be the only visitor.

By mile 124, your adventurous soul is reaching its quest's end as the highway's namesake–the 20,310-ft (6,190-m) Mount Denali–looms in the distance. Motor on, to finish in "busy" Cantwell (population: 200), or continue on the gloriously paved Parks Highway to Denali National Park, to get spine-tinglingly close to this most majestic of peaks.

RIGHT Eskers, ancient riverbeds, near mile 59

BELOW Camping in Denali National Park

OPPOSITE A herd of migrating Nelchina caribou

RICHARDSON HIGHWAY

Fairbanks
Valdez

START/FINISH
Fairbanks, Alaska/ Valdez, Alaska

DISTANCE
370 miles (595 km)

DURATION
2–3 days

ROAD CONDITIONS
Well paved; detours might require off-road vehicles

THE BEST TIME TO GO
Summer or early fall for the best weather

When it comes to raw beauty, no state ticks off so many superlatives as Alaska. Taking in mountains and glaciers, wildlife and waterfalls, the Richardson Highway arrows into the heart of the Last Frontier's most dramatic scenery.

Penetrating the rugged interior of Southcentral Alaska, the Richardson Highway was the first major road built in the U.S.'s largest state. Driving it provides an encounter with nature that will leave you wide-eyed, as you cruise past saw-toothed mountains, taiga woods, black bogs, and rushing white rivers on your way south to the Gulf of Alaska.

The ideal road trip begins in Fairbanks, a former Gold Rush town that's grown to become the state's second-largest city. Stop by Morris Thompson Cultural and Visitors Center for insights into Alaska's culture and folkways, particularly those of Native Alaskans, who make up 15 percent of its population. On the edge of town, the University of Alaska Museum of the North is a deep dive into Alaska's unique environment and ecology, and a great primer on everything you're about to encounter on your journey.

Sitting just south of the Arctic Circle, Fairbanks boasts a haul of "northern-most" locations in the U.S. (Catholic school, synagogue, Walmart, Starbucks, and so on.) It's also the country's center for northern lights tourism, and if you're here between late August and late April, you'll have a chance of catching the show before you leave.

BAUBLES AND BISON

But leave you must. Head east on Alaska Route 2 and almost immediately you'll be wrapped in the thick woods of the interior. For fans of kitsch, North Pole, about 15 miles (25 km) southeast, is an essential stop. Forever festive, the town has leaned all the way in on being a

OPPOSITE The highway leading to Mount Moffitt, in the Alaska Range

FAIRBANKS

START

FAIRBANKS
Begin your trip in the state's second-largest city and a hub of northern lights tourism.
0 MILES

NORTH POLE
It's not the real North Pole, but it's a quick stop for some Christmas kitsch.
15 MILES

THE ALASKA RANGE OVERLOOK

One of those roadside pullovers where the views will make all of your friends jealous.

65 MILES

DELTA JUNCTION

Tuck into a delicious bison burger at Buffalo Center Drive-In.

96 MILES

DONNELLY CREEK

You'll find few more impressive campsites in the entire country than this one.

123 MILES

TRANS-ALASKA PIPELINE

You can drive the Richardson in about 7 hours, whereas it takes oil two weeks to travel the Trans-Alaska Pipeline from Valdez to Prudhoe Bay.

12-month Christmas hub, complete with a Santa house and street names such as Mistletoe Lane and Reindeer Alley. Look out for moose as you drive on—these massive beasts are regularly seen lumbering by the highway—and after 65 miles (105 km), pull over at the Delta River and Alaska Range Overlook for unbound views of the Alaska Range; keep a sharp eye for bears, caribou, and more moose down on the riverbed.

About 95 miles (165 km) southeast of Fairbanks you'll reach Delta Junction, a small town with wild bison roaming the area. They're on the menu at the town's Buffalo Center Drive-In, where heaped burgers are brought straight to your car. The floats and sundaes are also worth writing home about.

ABOVE Lupins in bloom by the side of the Richardson Highway

VALLEY OF WONDER

Delta Junction marks your southward turn, as the Richardson becomes Alaska Route 4. Beyond Fort Greely (a launch site for antiballistic missiles), you might consider pitching up at Donnelly Creek, a recreation area famed for its location amid whispering pines, views of the Alaska Range, and proximity to porcupines and moose. Keeping on south, the next stretch of the highway envelopes you in feral beauty as you pass rushing rivers and milky streams, the mountains rising around you like the jawline of an ancient dragon. If you've company, you'll want to switch who's behind the wheel—it's impossible to keep your eyes just on the road in this magnificent slice of northerly Eden.

Keep venturing south, the Rainbow Ridge soaring to the east, and pass through tiny Paxson. You'll motor by the ruins of roadhouses and often spy the gray Trans-Alaska Pipeline: this 48-inch- (120-cm) wide, 800-mile- (1,290-km-) long steel tube carries oil from the Arctic Circle, meandering its way (just like you) to Valdez. Some 250 miles (400 km) south of Fairbanks, the road rolls into Glennallen, the first real "town" since Delta Junction. You'll want to refuel here, in every sense of the word.

Happily, the natural beauty of the Richardson is far from finished. As

you continue your drive south on Alaska Route 4, you'll notice in the distance the ice-encrusted volcanoes of the Wrangell Mountains, protected as part of the enormous Wrangell-St. Elias National Park and Preserve. Though often obscured by cloud cover, these dramatic peaks will accompany you for most of the rest of the trip.

GLACIER TO GULF

Richardson Highway eventually swings west and, 335 miles (540 km) south of Fairbanks, passes by Worthington Glacier. Although this mighty landmark has shrunk in size in recent years, the landscape around here—and the nearby Thompson Pass—remains breathtaking: a wild, lunar stretch of rocky alpine plains, ocher grass, wind-scoured gullies, and sheer cliff faces.

About 15 miles (25 km) on, you pass Horsetail Falls, fed by milky snowmelt, and then it's onto Valdez, your final stop. The northernmost ice-free port in the U.S., this artsy town on the Gulf of Alaska somehow holds all the beauty of the trip in microcosm: in the mirror sheen of Valdez Glacier Lake, the bobbles of ice floating in the Gulf, and, behind, the mountains piercing the big blue sky. It's the ideal place to park up, have a beer, and congratulate yourself on navigating a piece of rugged paradise.

TOP The dramatic ice fields of Worthington Glacier

ABOVE Valdez Harbor, at the end of your journey

WRANGELL-ST. ELIAS NATIONAL PARK

Soak up views of the Wrangell Mountains from the road.

255 MILES

THOMPSON PASS

Take the loop trail here to come face to face with an alpine tundra ecosystem.

335 MILES

VALDEZ

End your journey in this beautiful entrepôt of artists and outdoor types.

370 MILES

END

VALDEZ

O'AHU CIRCLE ISLAND DRIVE

START/FINISH
Honolulu, Hawaii/ Honolulu, Hawaii

DISTANCE
115 miles (185 km)

DURATION
1–2 days

ROAD CONDITIONS
Paved; a mix of expressways and local two-lane roads

THE BEST TIME TO GO
Winter, to see the best North Shore waves

OPPOSITE Aerial view of the highway skirting the looming Koko Crater

You'll be tempted to drive this one barefoot. The O'ahu Circle Island Drive is over a hundred miles of pure aloha, carrying you from lively Honolulu to roadside shrimp trucks, epic surf breaks, tropical beaches, and back again.

Unless you're a local, every O'ahu drive starts in Honolulu, Hawaii's capital and a microcosm of all that makes this complex state so captivating. A swing through the city will set you up nicely for your trip: the Bishop Museum, Chinatown's wet markets, and Waikīkī for mai tais on the sand are good for starters, but there's plenty more to explore if you've got the time.

ALONG THE SOUTHEAST SHORE

When you're ready to drive the island, secure a generous supply of provisions at Leonard's, a beloved purveyor of *malasadas* (Portuguese donuts, often filled with coconut or macadamia cream) since 1952, and head east on Interstate H-1. Just off the highway is the unmissable Diamond Head, a 760-ft- (232-m-) high volcanic crater formed by an eruption 300,000 years ago.

Soon after Diamond Head, H-1 becomes Hawaii Route 72. In O'ahu's southeastern corner, it arrives at Hanauma Bay, one of those places that's so lovely it makes you feel Hawaii isn't quite real. Formed inside a volcanic cone and protected by a 7,000-year-old coral reef, it's a famous snorkeling destination, filled with parrotfish and Hawaii's state fish, the *humuhumunukun ukuapua'a*. Two miles (3 km) beyond is Sandy Beach. The gorgeous golden expanse is a favorite of no less than Honolulu native and ex-president Barack Obama, who is known to body-surfs here. Unless you're a professional, though, it's best to stay on dry land—Sandy's nickname is Break Neck Beach.

HONOLULU

DIAMOND HEAD
Military bunkers, a lighthouse, and epic views await at the summit of this volcanic crater.

6 MILES

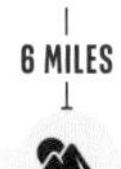

HANAUMA BAY
Snorkel inside a volcanic cone amid tropical fish and an ancient coral reef.

15 MILES

ABOVE Byodo-In Temple, shadowed by lush peaks

RIGHT The pointed islet of Mokoli'i, rich in legendary tales

OPPOSITE Surfers riding the gnarly Banzai Pipeline

UP THE WINDWARD COAST

Continue on Route 72 before turning west on Route 61. After two miles (3 km), you can head north on Route 83 to complete the circle, but stay on 61 to take in the Nu'uanu Pali State Wayside. From atop the 1,200-ft (366-m) ridge, enjoy views of windward O'ahu and then look straight down. That's the long trip hundreds of O'ahuan warriors took in 1795, when the troops of Kamehameha the Great chased them over the edge during his conquest of the island.

Back on Route 83, drive north through Kāne'ohe to reach Byodo-In Temple, a handsome replica of an 11th-century temple in Uji, Japan. When the Ko'olau peaks behind it are wrapped in clouds and the sunlight hits its vermillion walls... well, that's why haikus were invented. About 10 minutes later, the road approaches the coast. Look offshore and you'll spot Mokoli'i. Legend says the conical islet is the tail of a lizard spirit dispatched by the goddess Hi'iaka.

For the next few miles you're squeezed between the glistening ocean and the crumpled green walls of the Ko'olau Range. About half an hour from Mokoli'i, Lā'ie is home to the large Polynesian Culture Center, where staff demonstrate the traditions of various Polynesian nations. Around 2.5 miles (4 km) past Lā'ie, Kahuku is one of several towns on

NU'UANU PALI STATE WAYSIDE

Gaze out over the near-vertical Ko'olau Range on O'ahu's spectacular windward side.

32 MILES

BYODO-IN TEMPLE

Get a photo of yourself ringing the three-ton brass bell at this Buddhist temple.

43 MILES

KAHUKU

Near the island's northern tip, this town is famous for its shrimp trucks.

67 MILES

82 MILES

HALE'IWA

Snack on shave ice from Matsumoto's as you browse shops and art galleries.

105 MILES

PEARL HARBOR NATIONAL MEMORIAL

Memorials honor those killed in the December 7, 1941 attack.

END

HONOLULU

O'ahu's northeast coast known for their shrimp trucks. Giovanni's started the craze back in 1993 and still serves rice and plump shrimp marinated in olive oil and garlic from a graffitied truck, but you won't go wrong wherever you stop.

THE NORTH SHORE AND BEYOND

Round O'ahu's northern tip and you're soon driving along the Seven-Mile Miracle, the closest thing surfing has to a Holy Land. Subdued in summer, this sacred stretch of coast awakens in winter, when some of the world's most epic waves hurtle toward shore, including the Banzai Pipeline, arguably the sport's most legendary break. Between November and March, expect the area's beaches to be filled with elite surfers preparing to compete in the World Surf League Championship Tour.

Midway down the Miracle, on the southern edge of Pūpūkea, is the Waimea Valley, a sacred historical site containing a shrine dedicated to Ku'ula, the Hawaiian god of fishing, and Hale Iwi, the House of Bones, likely a 17th-century burial temple. A short trail leads to Waimea Falls, which pours into a natural pool where you can swim.

Four miles (6.5 km) after the Waimea Valley, you'll come to Hale'iwa, the North Shore's biggest town. It's easy to find yourself pausing your road trip here to shop for 'ukuleles, coconut peanut butter, and prints from local artists. Hale'iwa's one obligatory, must-do, non-negotiable stop is Matsumoto's, for what many claim is the best shave ice on the island.

The last stretch of the drive is rather anticlimactic, as Route 99 turns into an urban highway that feels more weekday commute than tropical road trip. Just west of Honolulu, Pearl Harbor National Memorial commemorates Japan's 1941 attack on the U.S. Pacific Fleet through exhibits and memorials to the ships and sailors that were lost. After you've paid your respects, step back outside and let the Hawaiian sunshine restore the good vibes as Interstate H-1 carries you back into Honolulu.

SHAKA ORIGINS

The shaka, the thumb-and-little-finger-out hand gesture you see in Hawaii, originated on O'ahu's north coast. In the early 20th century, Hamana Kalili crushed three middle fingers in mill machinery. Reassigned to a security role on a train, he'd wave off kids trying to hop aboard. They stole the hand gesture to let other train-jumpers know Kalili wasn't around, and the shaka was born.

HĀNA HIGHWAY

START/FINISH
Kahului, Hawaii/ Hāna, Hawaii

DISTANCE
55 miles (90 km)

DURATION
4–8 hours

ROAD CONDITIONS
Paved; frequent blind bends, narrow shoulders, and single-lane bridges

THE BEST TIME TO GO
Year-round; expect congestion in summer

OPPOSITE Aerial view of Maui's winding Hāna Highway

The Hāna Highway runs away from the resorts and into wild Hawaii. With more than 600 curves and something to see around every one—from volcanic headlands to jungle waterfalls—the road insists you slow down to Maui time.

When you're ready to leave your poolside cabana for a more authentic Hawaii, the Hāna Highway is waiting. Its 50 magical miles (80 km) run through remote northeastern Maui, one of the most unspoiled parts of the state. At its end is the peaceful hamlet of Hāna. Rich in history and little changed in decades, it's the resort towns' antithesis.

The Hāna Highway was a rough, one-lane gravel road when first completed in 1926. Today, it's a smooth paved highway, though not without its navigational challenges: roughly 620 turns (many of them blind), dozens of single-lane bridges, extremely narrow shoulders, and endless distracting views. It's also atop many Maui to-do lists, and you may find yourself in traffic jams, especially around popular sights.

SURF'S UP

The drive begins on Hawaii Route 36 in Kahului, Maui's main town, which grew with the sugar industry in the 19th century. The first miles are featureless and flat but in the distance the slopes of Haleakalā, an active shield volcano that forms eastern Maui, promise adventure.

Seven miles (11 km) from Kahului is Pā'ia, one of those delightfully eccentric towns Hawaii does so well, with New Age vibes and colorful independent stores. On its east side is Ho'okipa Beach, where sea turtles and monk seals sometimes hang out and surfers ride the North Shore swells. When the surf is up—usually in winter—Hahana Road, 5 miles (8 km) east from Ho'okipa, makes for a gnarly detour. It terminates at a cliff overlooking Pe'ahi

KAHULUI

START

PĀ'IA

In between its beaches, laid-back Pā'ia offers galleries, yoga studios, and vegan eats.

7 MILES

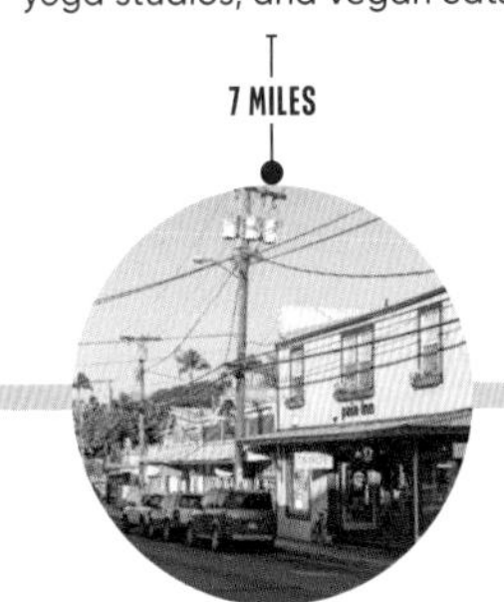

HO'OKIPA BEACH

Watch surfers catch barrels, and spot turtles at sunset, on Ho'okipa's golden sands.

10 MILES

TWIN FALLS
Easily accessible, this string of cascades is a picturesque early highlight of the drive.

20 MILES

EUCALYPTUS TREES
It's not graffiti: the colorful streaks on these rainbow eucalyptus trees are natural.

24 MILES

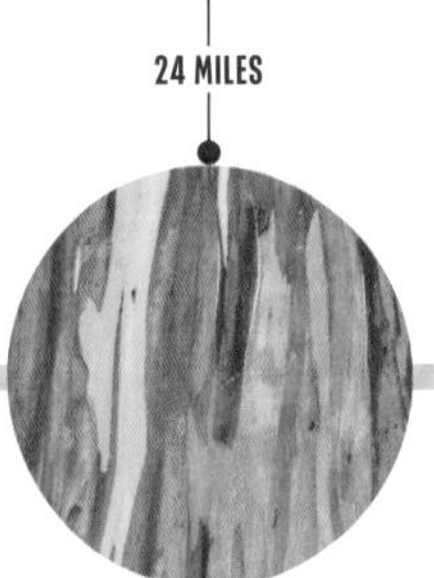

WAIKAMOI RIDGE TRAIL
Loop through thickets of ancient trees and lush ferns on this easy nature trail.

27 MILES

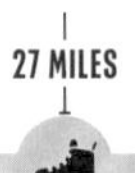

(Jaws) surf break, which, in any given year, produces some of the largest surfable waves on the planet.

INTO THE INTERIOR

Just past Pā'ia, Route 36 turns away from the coast and heads inland, eventually becoming Route 360. Here, the mile markers restart from zero and the Road to Hāna really begins. Almost immediately, you're enveloped in greenery, with thickly vegetated slopes coming right up to the road's edge. The first highlight is Twin Falls, a grouping of more than two cascades, in fact, including one that pours off the roof of a shallow cavern into a pool. Across Waipio Stream, the highway meanders like a river. Ferns press up against your car, and tropical flowers provide pops of color. Even those are outdone by a grove of eucalyptus trees at mile 7. As the trees shed their outer layer, their green inner bark changes to brilliant shades of yellow, orange, lime, and purple, making them look as if they've just returned from some sort of rave.

Just past mile 9, the Waikamoi Ridge Trail offers a great opportunity to see Maui's flora up close. The short pathway winds past lobster claw-like heliconia and kukui trees; listen closely and you may hear an *'amakihi*, a bright yellow species of Hawaiian honeycreeper.

Every now and then along the route, a little stand selling coconuts, smoothies, and shaved ice will pop up. Almost all of them sell fresh banana bread, the Hāna Highway's signature snack. Aunty Sandy's, on the Ke'anae Peninsula, and Halfway to Hāna, just after it, offer two of the best loaves on the drive.

It can be hard to appreciate Maui's full feral beauty from the car, but past the peninsula, a lookout at Wailua Valley State Wayside Park offers perspective. North lies the Pacific, blue and infinite, while to the south is the Ko'olau Gap, connecting Haleakalā's uplands with the coast in an unbroken swath of green.

EXTEND YOUR TRIP

The Hāna Highway doesn't actually end at Hāna. It continues clockwise around the island before becoming Hawaii Route 31, the Pi'ilani Highway, just past the village of Kipahulu. Continue until 31 becomes 37, which cuts north across Maui's interior and brings you back to Kahului.

47 MILES

NĀHIKU MARKETPLACE

Fuel up on barbecue and banana bread and score souvenirs at this welcome stop.

50 MILES

WAI'ĀNAPANAPA STATE PARK

A beach, forest, and grottoes are just a few of the state park's manifold charms.

END

HĀNA

But just when it feels you've disappeared into arcadia, civilization! At mile 29 is Nāhiku Marketplace, a collection of alfresco eateries serving Maui specialties like kalua pork tacos and fried fish. After your meal, pop into Nāhiku Gallery for local art and souvenir T-shirts.

END OF THE HIGHWAY

You're now approaching Hāna's outskirts, where the road irons out its kinks and the jungle foliage thins. Around mile 31, Ulaino Road leads to sprawling Kahanu Garden, whose collection focuses on plants integral to Hawaiian culture. The garden's highlight, though, is the hulking Pi'ilanihale Heiau, the largest *heiau* (place of worship) in all Polynesia.

Before Hāna Town, a final diversion brings you to Wai'ānapanapa State Park, a Shangri-La concentrate of Maui's charms. Amid its modest proportions are a native hala forest, a sea arch, a bird sanctuary, lava rock formations, underwater grottoes, a black-sand beach, and pools that turn red from tiny *'opae'ula* shrimp. Note you must make a reservation to visit the park.

With a final turn of the road, you reach Hāna. Once the center of a kingdom encompassing the entire island, it's now a sleepy outpost at the far edge of Maui and a thoroughly soothing place to while away a few days.

ABOVE Ordering fresh banana bread at a roadside stall

RIGHT The curving Hāna Highway

OPPOSITE Filming surfers catching giant waves at Pe'ahi

OLYMPIC PENINSULA LOOP

Port Townsend ▸ Port Townsend

START/FINISH
Port Townsend, Washington/Port Townsend, Washington

DISTANCE
460 miles (740 km)

DURATION
3 days

ROAD CONDITIONS
Paved, isolated roads; snowy at higher elevations

THE BEST TIME TO GO
July for blossoming lavender and wildflowers

OPPOSITE Shadows stretching across the winding road and mountainous Hurricane Ridge

Unplug from modern life and venture around the perimeter of the pristine Olympic National Park, where remote saltwater shores, the bluest of glacial lakes, and great tracts of primeval rainforest await.

Your journey unfolds, and later finishes, in the charming Victorian seaport of Port Townsend. Dotted with old-fashioned lampposts and lined with waterfront cafés, its historic downtown district is the perfect place to sit back and people watch. Miles of sandy beaches and Indigenous trails also offer you a chance to soak up local history and spy swooping bald eagles—an excellent introduction to this nature-packed drive.

Grab your car keys and drive southwest, joining Highway 20. You'll soon skirt past Discovery Bay, named after Captain George Vancouver's ship that brought the British explorer to the region in 1792. Then it's north onto Highway 101 (the main highway for the length of the loop) to Sequim, an agricultural community adorned by no fewer than nine lavender farms. By mid-July the blossoms saturate the landscape in a purple haze. If time allows, it's well worth a wander around the aromatic fields. Though it's unlikely you'll spot a reptile here, you may spy a snake-like formation 6 miles (10 km) north at Dungeness Spit. Shaped like a serpent's head preparing to strike, it's the longest natural sandspit in the U.S.

WEST TO LAKE CRESCENT

Continue on the highway westbound, passing farmsteads and roadside diners, and you'll soon get to the city of Port Angeles, situated in the rain shadow of the Olympic Mountains alongside the glistening Salish Sea. From here it's a winding, 45-minute drive through tunnels and woodlands up to your first slice of

PORT TOWNSEND

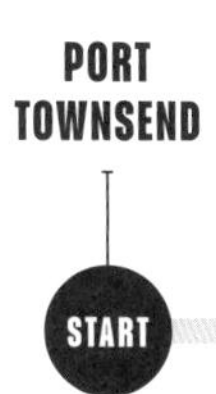

PORT TOWNSEND
Stop by the Jefferson Museum, Tommyknocker's Cornish Pasty shop, and the Pourhouse pub.

0 MILES

SEQUIM
If it's late summer, take the time to wander around the softly scented lavender fields.

31 MILES

73 MILES

HURRICANE RIDGE

Take in outstanding 360-degree views of emerald valleys and jagged, snowy peaks.

111 MILES

LAKE CRESCENT

Paddleboat rentals are available at the lake's century-old lodge.

173 MILES

FORKS

Visit the sites mentioned in the *Twilight* book series, and pick up souvenirs at Forks Outfitters.

RIGHT Jagged rock formations standing tall at Rialto Beach

OPPOSITE Walking through the moss-laden Hoh Rain Forest

VICTORIAN ROOTS

Port Townsend grew from a maritime settlement in the 1850s to a gateway city in the 1890s on speculation of becoming the main railroad terminus of the Pacific Northwest. Seattle was chosen instead, but Port Townsend was left with impressive Victorian-era public buildings and private residences that have been superbly preserved.

Olympic National Park–centerpiece of the entire peninsula–at the visitor center for Hurricane Ridge. On a clear day, you can see Vancouver Island, Canada, in the distance.

After allowing yourself enough time to take in the epic vistas, head west toward the pocket-sized Lake Sutherland. Though it's tempting to stop at this sapphire jewel, stay on the road for a few minutes more to reach its larger neighbor: Lake Crescent. Enveloped by forested hills, this tranquil lake is the perfect place for a quick dip or paddle, with water so clear you'll be able to see the glistening scales of rainbow trout and kokanee. If you prefer to stay dry, tighten your laces and hike the 2-mile (3-km) out-and-back Marymere Falls Trail, snapping a photo by the waterfall.

BEARS, BEACHES, AND BOOKS

After a hearty breakfast drive west along Lake Crescent's southern shores, exiting the park. Keep your eyes peeled on the road for black bears who like to cross the asphalt at a moment's notice. After a steady climb, the highway begins its gradual descent through a quiet stretch of densely grown forest with the Sol Duc River by your side. Take a coastal detour to Rialto Beach where the low hanging fog and graveyard of giant, washed-up tree trunks create a haunting atmosphere. Time the tide right and you can walk through a natural rock arch called Hole-in-the-Wall, chiseled out by the powerful surf.

Back behind the wheel, drive through Forks, an old timber town that gained fame as the setting for American author Stephenie Meyer's *Twilight* series and subsequent films. Merchandise secured, motor on to Upper Hoh Road to another

In the moisture-laden, temperate Hoh Rain Forest, towering Sitka spruce and western red cedar are draped in clumps of mosses and lichens, and tall, dewy ferns clog the undergrowth.

park visitor center: here, in the moisture-laden, temperate Hoh Rain Forest, towering Sitka spruce and western red cedar are draped in clumps of mosses and lichens, and tall, dewy ferns clog the undergrowth.

An hour southwest, exchange leafy forests for red-hued sand and sculptural driftwood at Ruby Beach. Dig your toes into the sand and look across the ocean to Destruction Island, the site of deadly 18th-century conflicts between European sailors and Indigenous Americans.

RETURN TO PORT TOWNSEND

Continuing south, the highway weaves inland to Lake Quinault, set within more mild rainforest and home to record-breaking Douglas fir (the tallest reaching 302 ft/90 m). Venture into the wilderness by walking the old logging road trail on the lake's north shore, or motor north to Hoodsport where more sublime nature awaits. Set on the sandy banks of the Hood Canal, a narrow fjord of the Puget Sound, Hoodsport is the gateway to Staircase, an area with impressive trails.

Back in the car, break up the final stretch of the drive by dining at Hama Hama Oyster Saloon—a local favorite serving fresh oysters—before completing the final 50 miles (80 km) back to Port Townsend. This time, though, you'll be visiting with far more memories, and miles, under your belt from this epic loop.

HOH RAIN FOREST

This vast rainforest is the domain of bobcats, cougars, and spotted owls.

205 MILES

STAIRCASE

Follow the 2-mile (3-km) Staircase Rapids Loop Trail under giant trees.

392 MILES

END

PORT TOWNSEND

CASCADE LOOP SCENIC BYWAY

START/FINISH
Everett, Washington/ Whidbey Island, Washington

DISTANCE
440 miles (705 km)

DURATION
4–6 days

ROAD CONDITIONS
Well-maintained paved roads; some congestion in popular areas

THE BEST TIME TO GO
Late spring to early fall, before snow-related road closures

OPPOSITE The Methow River, flowing through the Methow Valley

Capturing the stunning natural beauty of the Pacific Northwest, this drive takes you from the coast to the North Cascades' alpine peaks and back. Stop for wine tasting, lakeside picnics, and fun nights in small towns.

The rugged Cascade Loop Scenic Byway weaves a leisurely path through Washington's forested northwestern corner, passing sparkling alpine lakes and imperious, snowcapped peaks along the way. This is a journey of plunging canyons and mighty cascades, bookended by the mountains to the east and west.

SNOHOMISH TO SKYKOMISH

The drive dives straight into this dramatic scenery. Heading southeast on Highway 2 from the lively town of Everett, nestled on the shores of Puget Sound, you enter the salmon-rich wetlands of the Snoqualmie Wildlife Area—a popular birding destination, with numerous trails. Not long out of Everett's city limits, Snohomish comes into view, a town embellished with historical buildings —some of which date back to the 1860s—that recall its prosperous agrarian past. Pull into 1st Street, on the banks of the Snohomish River, to browse for vintage pottery in its antique shops (there are more than a dozen on 1st Street alone). If you need a caffeine hit before the next stretch of road, pop into Looking Glass Coffee for an espresso served in a 1910 heritage hall.

As you continue onward along Highway 2, the road disects emerald woods and crosses gravel river beds. Farther in the distance, on the southern horizon, looms the massive hulk of Mount Rainier, streaked with glaciers.

As the road climbs upward, it intersects with the Skykomish River,

EVERETT

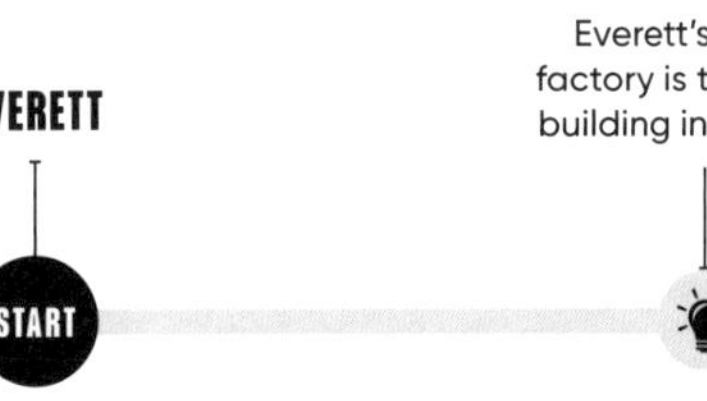

BOEING EVERETT
Everett's Boeing factory is the largest building in the world.

SNOHOMISH
The Snohomish people had settlements in the region for more than 12,000 years.

10 MILES

Stretch your legs on the Iron Goat Trail, a lush, leafy (and possibly haunted) 6-mile (10-km) hike that loops around an abandoned railroad.

TOP Big Chief Mountain, Stevens Pass ski area

ABOVE Turnwater Canyon in North Cascades National Park

OPPOSITE A rolling vineyard near the town of Chelan

which was plied by steamboats until the 1910s. After driving across an old army-green bridge, the hamlet of Index will appear on the left. Avid rock climbers are drawn to sheer cliffs here for some of the best granite climbing in the state.

Farther along the highway is the Espresso Chalet café, with an unmissable life-size statue of Bigfoot out in front. Even if you don't want to pose for a selfie, it's worth stopping to see—and hear—the Bridal Veil Falls, which thunder down from Lake Serene at the east wall of Mount Index. The falls can be reached via a 4-mile (6.5-km) out-and-back trek. Alternatively, drive 15 minutes farther, past the village of Skykomish, to stretch your legs on the Iron Goat Trail, a lush, leafy (and possibly haunted) 6-mile (10-km) hike that loops around an abandoned railroad. Hop on a caboose rail car, peek inside derelict tunnels, and look out for rusted pieces of track—relics being gradually reclaimed by the wilderness since a deadly avalanche occurred here in 1910.

ALONG THE WENATCHEE RIVER

Back on the road, you'll crest the forested Stevens Pass, home to a ski resort in winter and a bike park in summer. The highway then pitches

ESPRESSO CHALET

Grab a coffee with Bigfoot before hiking to nearby Bridal Veil Falls.

39 MILES

IRON GOAT TRAILHEAD

The first 3 miles (5 km) of this trail are accessible flat-packed gravel at a level grade.

61 MILES

103 MILES

LEAVENWORTH

Don't miss Oktoberfest for plenty of Bratwurst and beer, held in October.

114 MILES

CASHMERE

Near Cashmere lies Enchantment Lakes, home to hundreds of alpine lakes.

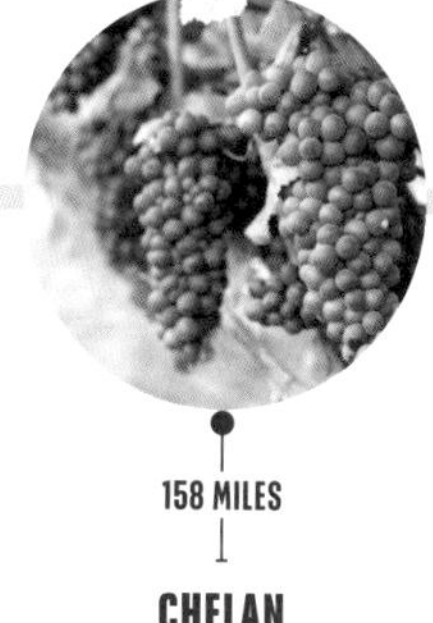

158 MILES

CHELAN

Here in October? Stomp grapes with the locals during the Lake Chelan Crush Festival.

down through the narrow, steep-sided Tumwater Canyon, sharing the curves with the fast, boulder-laden Wenatchee River. Vivid orange alders and fiery red maples pepper the evergreens that line its banks. Park at a pullout, breathing in the cool crisp air, and look out for schools of wild chinook salmon in the bubbling water; they spawn from mid-September through October.

The highway soon opens up to the wide Wenatchee River Valley, where the once quiet rail and timber town of Leavenworth has been transformed–taking advantage of its spectacular mountain backdrop–into a fairytale Bavarian-themed village. Come evening, crowds spill out onto the heated courtyard of München Haus for pretzels, sausages, and German-style brews. For a bird's-eye view of the village, head up to the arid-looking Peshastin Pinnacles, a series of sandstone spires that rise to heights of up to 200 ft (60 m). The vista takes in groves of stocky trees heavy with plump green pears, and neat rows of leafy vines brimming with purple grapes.

After leaving Leavenworth (and its delicious Bratwursts) behind, motor toward the town of Cashmere, where the locally beloved Aplets & Cotlets confectionery is made. Similar in style to Turkish delight, it's an ideal snack for the road.

BIGFOOT

Tales of large and hairy humanoids living in the wilds are common around the globe, like the Yeti of the Himalayas and the Sasquatch of Canada. The story of Bigfoot is no different, with legends existing within Indigenous folklore for centuries. The creature is said to have been spotted in the Cascade Mountains, but any real evidence has yet to be found.

WEAVING TO WINTHROP

Highway 2 follows the Wenatchee River for 20 minutes or so, through another valley filled with apple, pear, and cherry trees, before reaching its confluence with the Columbia River at Sunnyslope. You turn north here, along the scenic 97 Alt. highway, a former 19th-century wagon route that runs parallel to Highway 2 the other side of the Columbia River. Within an hour, you'll reach the southern shores of sparkling, cobalt-blue Lake Chelan and its eponymous community town. Clusters of lakeside cabins fronted with boat docks fan west from the resort and ribbons of vineyards and orchards sprinkle the slopes of the surrounding hills. During the summer months, the lake buzzes with activity: waterskiing, boating, snorkeling, fishing, and windsurfing. If time allows, swap the car for a passenger ferry and board

WINTHROP

Winthrop was once a camp for trappers and miners before becoming a themed town.

218 MILES

ROSS LAKE RECREATION AREA

Diablo and Ross lakes are both the result of dams built in the 1930s to supply hydroelectricity.

284 MILES

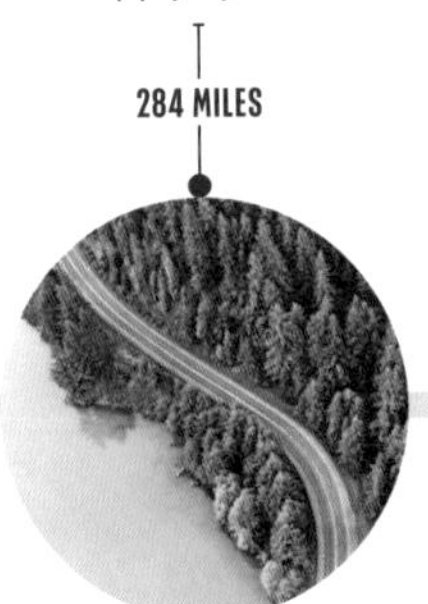

the *Lady of the Lake* to tour its otherwise unreachable wooded shoreline. Back behind the wheel, continue to Winthrop, about an hour's drive north on 97 Alt. along the Columbia River and then on to Highway 153. As the road takes you along the Methow Valley (pronounced "met-how"), roughly following the Methow River through dry, sage-covered hills and vales stippled with fragrant ponderosa pine, the craggy North Cascades peaks begin to appear in the foreground.

A good place to hunker down for the night, the tiny Old West-style town of Winthrop greets you with wooden, false-fronted establishments and frontier-style signage. Soak up the ambience along the boardwalk that shadows the shops and cafés downtown, listening to the creaks of the wooden planks (now you'll wish you brought your cowboy boots). After browsing the paintings and sculptures by local artists in the Winthrop Gallery, settle down with a glass of local wine at Three Fingered Jack's Saloon—the oldest legal saloon in the state.

INTO THE MOUNTAINS

Rise early and continue northwest, passing quiet meadows and pastures. As you leave the valley, you'll climb toward Washington Pass, reaching an altitude of 5,477 ft (1,669 m). At this point, the windscreen fills with cinematic views of the massive granite spires of Liberty Bell and Early Winters. Luckily, there's a lookout rest area nearby to give you more time to admire these beauties.

More spectacular views await beyond the pass in the form of the adjacent Diablo and Ross lakes, each a sparkling shade of blue. You've now reached the Ross Lake Recreation Area, part of the larger North Cascades National Park, which has a host of hiking trails that beckon you to stay awhile.

Continue west on the highway, skirting Diablo Lake's southern arm and heading through a section of remote forest that's home to moose and grizzly bears. Soon, the lofty peaks of the North Cascades

EXTEND YOUR TRIP

The San Juan Islands can be seamlessly tacked onto a Cascade Loop trip by taking a ferry from the city of Anacortes: daily services run to each of the four main islands. Porpoises and pods of orcas can often be seen just offshore and sea lions frequent the rock coves. Biking adventures, locally sourced seafood, and overnight stays in snug cabins are all the more reasons to linger.

355 MILES

SKAGIT VALLEY

During April and May, the whole of Skagit Valley is painted in a riot of flowering tulips.

FIDALGO ISLAND

This island is named after Spanish cartographer and explorer Salvador Fidalgo.

440 MILES

WHIDBEY ISLAND

Explore historic Admiralty Head Lighthouse, on the island's southern shores.

WHIDBEY ISLAND

give way to the rolling hills and golden fields of the Skagit Valley. The highway heads for Sedro-Woolley, a small city with logging and railroad origins set on the banks of the Skagit River, with views of the snowy hulk of Mount Baker standing sentinel to the north. If time allows, pay a visit to the stately home of Willowbrook Manor, just outside the city, where you can arrange bike tours of the area, complete with tea and scones.

BACK TO THE COAST

Half an hour on from Sedro-Woolley, you hit the coast once more, crossing over the Swinomish Channel to forested Fidalgo Island. At its northern tip is the maritime community of Anacortes, a former salmon cannery town. From its busy harbor, ferries depart for neighboring isles, boats head out on whale-watching tours, and kayakers paddle off to nearby coves. Bypass the bustle and head south to Whidbey Island, stopping at the 1930s Deception Pass Bridge to snap some incredible seascapes. Then continue on to reach Whidbey, your final destination. It's a memorable place to end a memorable trip. Finish with a feast of local Penn Cove mussels, raising a glass to the 400-plus miles of spectacular northwestern scenery now behind you. From Clinton, you can hop on a ferry back to Everett if you wish to complete the loop.

ABOVE The town of La Conner in the Skagit Valley

LEFT Sea-kayaking off Whidbey Island

OPPOSITE Emporium General Store in Winthrop

OREGON COAST HIGHWAY 101

Astoria

Brookings

START/FINISH
Astoria, Oregon/ Brookings, Oregon

DISTANCE
340 miles (545 km)

DURATION
4–5 days

ROAD CONDITIONS
Well-maintained paved roads; expect foggy, rainy conditions

THE BEST TIME TO GO
July, for the summer sun and visibility

OPPOSITE Enjoying the ocean views at a coastal lookout on Oregon Coast Highway 101

Unfurling like a ribbon down Oregon's Pacific seaboard, this windswept coastal road reveals a dizzying hit list of steep, craggy headlands and misty lighthouse scenes, with plenty of cheery seaside towns en route.

Awash with natural beauty, the Oregon Coast Highway is the unsung hero of the West Coast, often overlooked for warmer waters and Californian sunshine. It's a slower drive, too, not least because you'll want to pull over and take in the rugged scenery at every opportunity.

Founded in 1811 as a humble fur-trading post, Astoria is the oldest American settlement west of the Rocky Mountains—and your starting point. Cruising through downtown, among the restored heritage buildings you'll notice the handsome Italianate Liberty Theatre, constructed in 1925 as a symbol of the city's rebirth after a devastating fire. There's a smattering of candy-colored Victorian gingerbread homes up in the hills, although it's the impressive 4-mile (6.5-km) Astoria-Megler Bridge that really steals the spotlight. Opened in 1966, it's the longest continuous truss bridge on the continent.

TO CANNON BEACH

Leaving Astoria behind, Highway 101 gravitates southwest toward the Pacific. Before long, the site of Fort Clatsop arrives on your left. Dating back to 1805, this intriguing attraction marks the halfway point of the trailblazing Lewis and Clark Expedition (p133).

The highway sails past several seaside communities, often shrouded in morning fog, before entering a swath of evergreen forest. Ancient spruce and cedar groves are concealed within, providing refuge for Roosevelt elk. Sneak views of the glistening ocean as the road approaches Ecola State Park.

ASTORIA

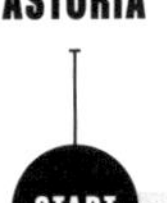

ASTORIA

Check out the remains of the 1906 British shipwreck in Fort Stevens State Park.

0 MILES

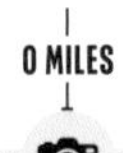

ECOLA STATE PARK

Take the Tillamook Head Trail to see Terrible Tilly, an 1880s lighthouse with a spooky past.

25 MILES

This forested headland is graced with a variety of walking trails that lead out to misty coves. At low tide, the driftwood-strewn beaches are perfect for exploring tidepools that teem with marine life.

Next, it's back on the road down to Cannon Beach, a charming seaside town and home to one of Oregon's most iconic sights: Haystack Rock. Protruding out of the Pacific's cool blue waters, this 235-ft- (70-m-) tall monolith is an ideal backdrop for an evening beach picnic around the cozy glow of a bonfire. Spend the night in a four poster at the century-old Cannon Beach Hotel, lulled to sleep by breaking waves.

RIGHT A bald eagle; the birds are common along the coast

BELOW Haystack Rock, its base shrouded in sea mist

OPPOSITE Boats at Coos Bay, near the end of your journey

SEA LIONS AND SAND DUNES

In the morning, continue south, taking in exceptional coastal views, before following the highway inland to Tillamook Creamery for a refreshing scoop or two of ice cream. A detour west from here will take you on the breathtaking Three Capes Scenic Route to the sea stacks, caves, and towering sand dune at Cape Kiwanda. But Highway 101 continues south to Newport, a lovely town with an attractive Art Deco bridge and plenty of interesting marine activity. It's well known for its resident sea lions—boisterous, barking creatures easily viewed from a safe distance just above. As the night settles in, tuck under a duvet at an inn along Newport's Nye

CANNON BEACH

Pick up a bonfire kit in town, then head to the beach for roasted marshmallows.

27 MILES

TILLAMOOK CREAMERY

This farmer-owned dairy cooperative offers guided tours on the art of cheese-making.

65 MILES

NEWPORT

The Oregon coast is chock-full of graceful bridges including Newport's Yaquina Bay Bridge.

164 MILES

Beach, where rows of treasure-filled boutiques and vintage vacation cottages overlook miles of sandy beach.

Come morning it's time to find a sight you'll have seen on plenty of Newport postcards: the stunning view of the picturesque, classic white-and-red Heceta Head Lighthouse from 1894. Out on a high bluff, it's best captured from the highway pullout, about a mile and a half farther south. Then it's on to the cream-hued, shifting landscape of the Oregon Dunes National Recreation Area. This otherworldly 40-mile (65-km) stretch of coastal sand dunes is one of the largest such expanses in the world, with some of the dunes topping 500 ft (150 m) in height. They provided much of the inspiration for American author Frank Herbert's science-fiction classic, *Dune*, and can be explored on foot, by buggy, or, most uniquely, on a sandboard.

With expansive views of the rippling dunes, and tufts of tall sea grass swaying in the wind, the drive continues to the city of Coos Bay, set in a naturally protected harbor. Founded as a camp of shipwreck survivors in the 1850s, the city has a rich maritime past, best explained at the Coos History Museum. Work up an appetite strolling along the downtown boardwalk and poking around the antique shops, then join the locals at the Fishermen's Seafood Market for fresh fish tacos.

SCREEN TIME

If the scenery at Ecola State Park feels familiar, it's because it was used as a film site for the cult-classic movie *The Goonies*, as well as *Kindergarten Cop*, *Point Break*, *Free Willy*, and *Twilight*.

SOUTH TO BROOKINGS

Continue your southward journey to stunning Samuel H. Boardman State Scenic Corridor, a 12-mile (20-km) stretch of Highway 101 best explored at a leisurely pace. The highlights awaiting you include the multiple sea stacks of Arch Rock rising out of the fog, the milky-turquoise waters of Thunder Rock Cove, and the moss-and-mushroom-lined path to Whaleshead Beach, where shorebirds such as plovers race across the long slip of sand.

Wrap up your trip in Brookings, a laid-back former timber town on the bay of the Chetco River. Stroll along the boardwalk, and then park yourself at Harris Beach with your eyes on the oblong Bird Island, a sanctuary for the rare tufted puffin. Watch as the sun dips below the horizon in hues of gold, peach, and rose. It's a suitably dreamy end for a memorable trip.

VOLCANIC LEGACY SCENIC BYWAY

Chemult

Mineral

START/FINISH
Mineral, California/ Chemult, Oregon

DISTANCE
460 miles (740 km)

DURATION
5–7 days

ROAD CONDITIONS
Paved; wintry conditions can be hazardous in mountainous areas; some sites only accessible via gravel or dirt roads

THE BEST TIME TO GO
July to October (some roads close between November and June)

OPPOSITE Driving the Volcanic Legacy Scenic Byway through Crater Lake National Park

Linking two national parks and taking in steaming fumaroles, frigid glaciers, and snowcapped volcanoes, the Volcanic Legacy Scenic Byway is a drive of fire and ice. It's also a reminder not just of the land's beauty but also its ferocity.

It's easy to think of the earth as inert. Stable. Unchanging. But of course it's really a slow-moving machine, and in certain places its subterranean gears show through, reminding you of the creative and destructive power the planet possesses.

The land along the Volcanic Legacy Scenic Byway is one of those places. Running from Lassen Volcanic National Park in northern California to Crater Lake National Park in southern Oregon, the byway passes active volcanoes and fascinating remnants of past eruptions. Its southernmost segment is a large loop through and around the forbidding wilderness of Lassen Volcanic National Park, and to do the full drive you'll have to double up on California State Route 89, the journey's most astonishing—and potentially dangerous—section.

THE SOUTHERN LOOP

Starting in the village of Mineral, take Route 36 east through cedar and fir forests to Chester, a base for camping, boating, and fly-fishing in and around Lake Almanor. (Traveling with kids? Get guaranteed laughs by pointing out Butt Mountain off to the south.) Loop around the lake and rejoin 36 at Westwood, before taking Route 44 up through Lassen National Forest to Old Station.

Turn south on Route 89 and follow it into Lassen Volcanic National Park, a contradictory realm of wildflower-filled mountain meadows and boiling pits of mud. The park contains all four types of volcanoes: cinder cones, composite volcanoes, shield volcanoes, and lava

MINERAL

START

CHESTER
Boat, camp, fly-fish, or just soak up the serene setting of peaceful Lake Almanor.

27 MILES

WESTWOOD
The world's largest pine lumber mill once stood in this old logging town.

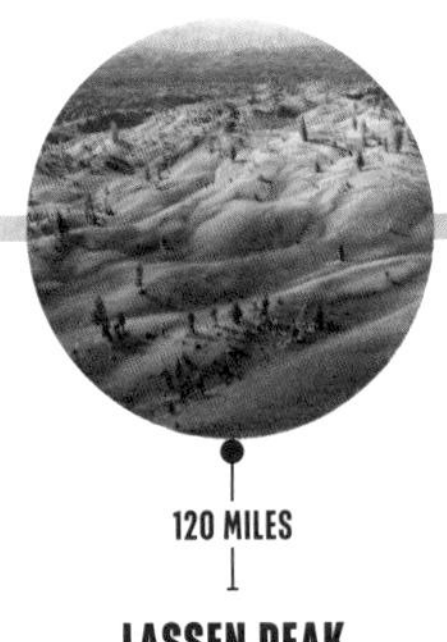

120 MILES

LASSEN PEAK

This active volcano shot ash 30,000 ft (9 km) into the air when it last erupted, in 1917.

126 MILES

SULPHUR WORKS

Hold your nose and get up close to boiling mudpots and hissing fumaroles.

207 MILES

BURNEY FALLS

This was Teddy Roosevelt's favorite waterfall, and it'll probably be yours, too.

MOUNT SHASTA

Mount Shasta is the source of numerous legends. The Indigenous Shasta people say that the Great Spirit created the mountain and then used it to climb down from the heavens. Another legend claims that a lost civilization of advanced beings live in a secret city hidden within the volcano.

ABOVE A boardwalk leading past fumaroles at Bumpass Hell

OPPOSITE ABOVE Beautiful Crater Lake, at sunrise

OPPOSITE BELOW A reflection of Mount Shasta

domes. Among these is Lassen Peak, a 10,456-ft (3,187-m) massif, which last erupted between 1914 and 1917, blasting out steam and molten rock high into the air. The U.S. Geological Survey rates its current threat potential as "very high." Interestingly, you drive right over it, switchbacking up to just below its summit. A 2.5-mile (4-km) hiking trail can take you all the way to the top.

The way down offers encounters with the region's geothermal wonders. A mile (1.5 km) from the Lassen Peak parking lot is the trailhead to Bumpass Hell (more kid laughs!), 16 acres (6.5 hectares) of noxious fumaroles, boiling springs, and seething steam that reaches 322°F (161°C). Further along and immediately adjacent to the road is Sulphur Works, a bubbling pit of mud and sulfuric fumes that could be the devil's hot tub.

To complete the southern loop, follow Route 89 back to Mineral, then return the way you came to Old Station.

CAVES, WATERFALLS, AND CINDER CONES

Heading north, you'll come to the Subway Cave lava tubes, remnants of an underground river of lava that flowed here less than 20,000 years ago. Six miles (10 km) past the intersection with Route 299 is Burney Falls, which President Theodore Roosevelt called the "Eighth Wonder of the World." That's overstating things, but only just. Twin central cascades plunge 129 ft (39 m) into

TULE LAKE SEGREGATION CENTER
Learn about one of the country's more shameful chapters at this World War II internment camp.

LAVA BEDS NATIONAL MONUMENT
Medicine Lake Volcano has left hundreds of lava tube caves and cinder cones here.

UPPER KLAMATH LAKE
A haven for wildlife, this is the largest freshwater lake west of the Rocky Mountains.

CHEMULT

a fan-shaped pool, while on either side of them, lacy white rivulets trickle down a rock wall draped in ferns.

Around the point Route 89 passes through the town of McCloud, and then merges with Interstate 5, you'll catch your first glimpse of Mount Shasta, a towering stratovolcano that last erupted around 1200 BCE. Its upper reaches hold 10 glaciers, including Whitney Glacier, the longest in California. The city of Mount Shasta, suitably, has big mountain energy, and you'll find crystal shops promising connection "with your Eternal Guides" and businesses selling quantum fluctuation resonators here.

When I-5 reaches the city of Weed, exit and take U.S. 97 northeast through the Butte Valley, a high desert plateau more reminiscent of southern Wyoming than California. Just before the Oregon border is a byway spur that leads to the town of Tulelake. This was the site of the Tule Lake Segregation Center, the largest of the detention camps that the government used to imprison Japanese Americans—without charge or trial—during World War II.

West of Tulelake, Hill Road leads to Lava Beds National Monument, where Indigenous rock art shares space with cinder cones and close to 700 lava tube caves. The formations are the product of the adjacent Medicine Lake Volcano—still active after half a million years.

NORTH TO CRATER LAKE

Crossing into Oregon, you'll cruise along vast Upper Klamath Lake before heading north to Fort Klamath and Crater Lake National Park, just 25 miles (40 km) from Chemult and journey's end. Completely surrounded by the steep walls of the caldera, Crater Lake feels protected from the outside world, like somewhere you can only access through a magic portal. The tranquility is deceiving. Some 7,700 years ago, a vent opened on the slope of Mount Mazama, and 12 cubic miles (50 cubic km) of molten lava escaped. Its magma gone, the mountain then collapsed on the empty chamber, leaving a vast caldera. Over hundreds of years, rain and snow filled the depression, creating the lake you see today—a legacy, like everything on this elemental drive, of the region's turbulent past.

NAPA VALLEY'S SILVERADO TRAIL

Calistoga ▸ Napa

START/FINISH
Calistoga, California/
Napa, California

DISTANCE
40 miles (65 km)

DURATION
1–2 days

ROAD CONDITIONS
Well-maintained two-lane roads

THE BEST TIME TO GO
August–October, for harvest season

OPPOSITE The verdant, rolling vineyards lining the Napa Valley region

With so many glasses of crisp wine to sample, this drive might require a fierce round of rock, paper, scissors to secure the passenger seat. But rest assured, if you are the designated driver, the stunning views are just as satisfying.

This scenic trip through California wine country follows a road with 19th-century roots. The historic Silverado Trail, established in 1852, was once the main thoroughfare for miners and fortune hunters seeking to strike it rich on the silver deposits in the hills.

Wine production started in the region in the 1870s, though an insect infestation followed by prohibition meant that the industry was little known outside of California for nearly 100 years. The main transformation took place in the 1970s, when local wines won top marks in a blind tasting competition, triumphing against more established producers from France and Italy. Now the region is the undisputed wine capital of the U.S.

GEYSERS AND CASTLES

Start your journey in Calistoga, a quaint little town known for its geothermal springs and, of course, wine. It's a five-minute drive to the outskirts of town to see Old Faithful Geyser of California, a well-photographed natural wonder that, like its namesake in Yellowstone National Park, erupts unswervingly: expect rainbow mist every 15–30 minutes. Set in serene surroundings, it's an ideal spot to enjoy a caffeinated brew before setting off on your vineyard tour.

After joining Highway 128, and returning through Calistoga, you might feel like you've traveled back in time as you cruise past Castello di Amorosa. Surrounded by grapevines, this stone castle could easily be mistaken for a medieval stronghold, but it was actually built in 1994 by winemaker Dario Sattui in honor of his Italian heritage.

CALISTOGA

OLD FAITHFUL GEYSER

Marvel at the majesty of this natural wonder on the outskirts of Calistoga.

1 MILE

CASTELLO DI AMOROSA

Travel back in time to 14th-century Italy at this replica castle.

7 MILES

HITTING THE TRAIL

It's soon time to join up with the Silverado Trail proper, which runs parallel to Highway 128. Continue past the "Welcome to Napa Valley" sign, before heading northeast across Bale Lane and the shaded Napa River, home to river otters, endangered fall-run chinook salmon, and clapper rail birds. Following the road as it winds through rolling hills, countless wineries will tempt you along the way, but keep driving until you reach Rombauer Vineyards, and you won't be disappointed. Just 10 minutes outside of Calistoga, this family-run vineyard sits on top of a small hill, surrounded by a copse of trees with vineyards down below. The lush landscape here makes it a particularly delightful location to stretch your legs, and snap some photos before heading toward the tasting room to put your nose and tastebuds to the test. For a unique experience, book a cave tour along with your tasting—the door to the caves is shaped like a giant wine cask.

Looking to pair some food with all this wine? The Napa region won't leave you hungry. If budgets allow, follow the road for 4 miles (6.5 km) and treat yourself to the locally leaning menu at five-star Meadowood Hotel's upscale restaurant, with ingredients sourced from Meadowood's own farm and other nearby food purveyors. Alternatively, explore the food and wine offerings in

NAPA VALLEY

Stop for a pic with the Napa Valley sign, or simply wave as you breeze by.

8 MILES

ROMBAUER VINEYARDS

Learn about the winemaking process, taste delicious wines, and take a tour of the caves.

13 MILES

MEADOWOOD HOTEL

Sip on crisp, local wine while enjoying seasonal produce at this five-star resort.

17 MILES

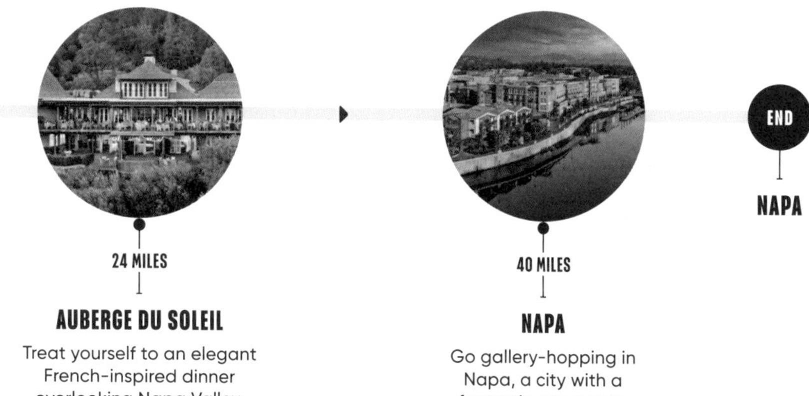

the nearby town of St. Helena, an effortless blend of rustic wine country and California chic, with ample opportunities for an additional spot of retail therapy. St. Helena is also home to the Robert Louis Stevenson Museum, dedicated to the Scottish writer who honeymooned for two months in the area. The trip inspired Stevenson's 1883 travel memoir, *The Silverado Squatters*.

Though the Silverado Trail is fairly short, and can easily be completed in a single day, the sheer number of wineries and other attractions in the area warrant an overnight stay. Traveling 5 miles (8 km) beyond St. Helena will bring you to Auberge du Soleil, one of the region's most romantic and luxurious places to rest, with a French-inspired restaurant. This adults-only hotel also boasts one of the most sublime views of the sun-kissed Napa Valley.

ON TO NAPA

As you edge ever closer to Napa, make Stags' Leap winery your next stop, a farther 9 miles (15 km) along the trail. First planted in 1893, this was one of the first wine estates established in the region—a heritage recalled by its 19th-century stone manor house. Today, it runs 90-minute tours and tastings, finishing at the gift shop. Souvenirs secured, make a quick detour across the Napa River to nearby Yountville, a quaint picture-perfect town peppered with luxury hotels, boutiques, and Michelin-starred restaurants.

From here, it's just a 15-minute drive on to Napa, though there's more to explore when you reach the city. Napa is known for its arts scene—including galleries and live music—and of course its tasting rooms. Take your pick, and don't forget to clink glasses with your designated driver for charting your course through, in wine terms at least, America's best.

Treat yourself to the locally leaning menu at five-star Meadowood Hotel's upscale restaurant, with ingredients sourced from Meadowood's own farm.

ABOVE A hot-air balloon rising from Yountville's vineyards

OPPOSITE TOP The towering turrets of Castello di Amorosa

OPPOSITE BELOW Tree-lined streets of downtown St. Helena

YOSEMITE NATIONAL PARK

Oakhurst ▸ Lee Vining

START/FINISH
Oakhurst, California/ Lee Vining, California

DISTANCE
125 miles (200 km)

DURATION
2–3 days

ROAD CONDITIONS
Well-maintained paved roads

THE BEST TIME TO GO
Early summer, for peak waterfall flow and to avoid road closures

OPPOSITE Driving toward El Capitan, a gargantuan granite monolith in Yosemite

Carve your way through Yosemite National Park's granite heart on this unforgettable road trip. Witness the power of cascading waterfalls, marvel at the beauty of the Eastern Sierra, and hike through ancient sequoia groves.

Unfurl the map and let the anticipation build. This is more than a road trip; it's a pilgrimage to one of nature's finest cathedrals. Showcasing some of Yosemite's grandest landscapes, the route winds past towering peaks and thundering waterfalls, offering an iconic image of the U.S.'s natural majesty.

THE WILDERNESS AWAITS

Your journey begins in the small gateway town of Oakhurst, 15 miles (25 km) from Yosemite National Park's southern entrance. As you begin your ascent up Highway 41, watch wildflower meadows give way to lofty ponderosa pines and sun-dappled roads. Pass through the peaceful hamlet of Fish Camp, and within minutes you'll reach the official park entrance and the turnoff to Mariposa Grove, a haven for towering sequoia trees, some estimated to be up to 3,000 years old. Explore at your own pace on one of the trails—the paved Grizzly Giant Loop takes you past the California Tunnel Tree, which you can walk through, while the Mariposa Grove Trail offers a longer hike to Wawona Point, a scenic overlook with epic views.

Leaving Mariposa Grove behind, continue north on Wawona Road to South Fork of the Merced River, passing the Victorian-era Wawona Hotel. Keep an eye out for grazing mule deer or golden-mantled ground squirrels. The forest here—rolling hills cloaked in black cottonwood and incense cedar—is a stark contrast to the cliffs ahead, so wind down the windows and enjoy the fragrant woody scents. Soon you'll

OAKHURST

START

OAKHURST
This quaint resort town is home to a life-size bear statue that welcomes visitors.
0 MILES

MARIPOSA GROVE
Towering sequoia trees rise into the sky here, with some nearly 3,000 years old.
16 MILES

WAWONA HOTEL
Step back in time at one of California's original mountain resorts.
20 MILES

A GRIZZLY END

Despite the grizzly bear being depicted on the California state flag, it's been 100 years since a sighting. In Yosemite, there are an estimated 300–500 black bears, each able to run up to an impressive 30 mph (50 km/h).

approach the historic Wawona Tunnel, a masterpiece of engineering blasted through solid granite bedrock in the late 19th century. Emerging on the other side, the Yosemite "Tunnel View" unfolds before you—an epic, cinematic vista of Yosemite Valley, with the vertical face of El Capitan dominating the foreground and Half Dome in the distance. Lush meadows, cascading Bridalveil Falls, and the meandering Merced River complete the picture-perfect scene.

The descent into the valley continues along Southside Drive. On the banks of the Merced River, Cathedral Beach is a great spot for a picnic and an energizing dip in the river. If you're eagle-eyed, you might even spot climbers scaling the dizzying rock face of El Capitan.

After a few miles you'll arrive at Curry Village. Here, and in neighboring Yosemite Village, you'll find a variety of lodging options from campgrounds to upscale hotel rooms, as well as easy access to some of Yosemite's greatest sights and activities. Choose from rock climbing and white-water rafting, or opt for a rewarding hike to Yosemite Falls.

CLIMBING TOWARD TIOGA PASS

When it's time to move on, motor along Northside Drive and up onto the Tioga Pass through the Sierra Nevada. Watch the valley floor disappear in the rearview mirror as you ascend and keep your eyes peeled for wildlife—there's an ever-present chance of spotting a golden eagle circling overhead.

Completed in 1914, Tioga Pass is the highest drivable pass in California at 9,945 ft (3,032 m). It winds past subalpine grassland and glacial lakes, and as you climb to higher altitudes, the air thins and the temperature dips. After 30 miles (50 km), pull over at Olmsted Point. Named after landscape architects Frederick Law Olmsted and Frederick Law Olmsted, Jr., who were instrumental in the protection and planning of the park, the viewpoint is popular with visitors and marmots alike. Expect to

YOSEMITE FALLS

Snap incredible photos of these thundering falls, which are the highest in the park.

49 MILES

OLMSTED POINT

Soak up views of the Sierra Nevada, Mount Dana, and the northern face of Half Dome.

93 MILES

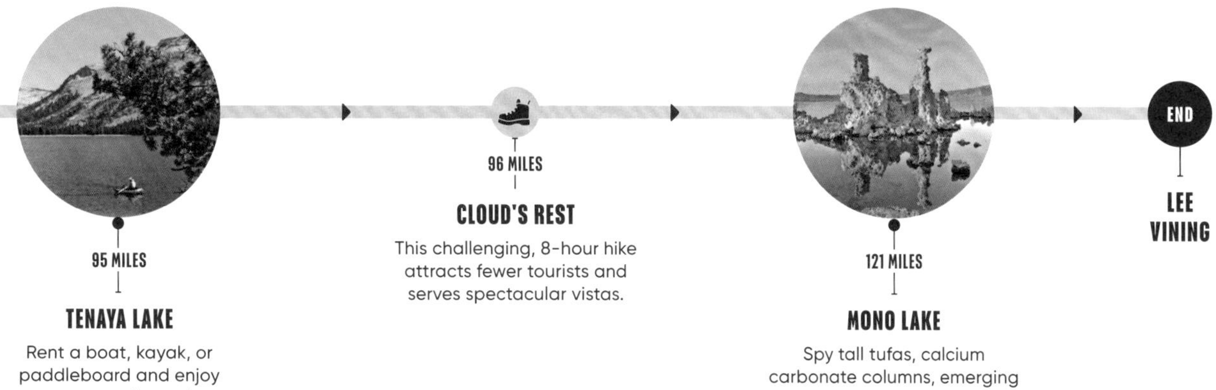

see the gray peaks of Yosemite to the west, while the Sierra Nevada continues its striking sweep toward Death Valley to the east.

INTO THE CLOUDS

It's a mile or so from here to tranquil Tenaya Lake. Created by the Tenaya Glacier, it is one of the highest lakes in Yosemite and a popular recreation spot for swimming, kayaking, and stand-up paddleboarding. You can also hike from here to the summit of Cloud's Rest, a challenging feat rewarded with mind-blowing views, including the top of Half Dome over 1,000 ft (305 m) below.

Exiting the park, and descending the eastern slope of Tioga Pass, the scenery changes once again. Barren, volcanic landscapes yield to sagebrush flats, and Mono Lake, a unique and diverse ecosystem, comes into view. Dotting its surface are otherworldly tufa towers, formed by the interaction of freshwater springs and the lake's highly alkaline and saline water. These unusual formations, combined with their stark surroundings, create an almost lunar-like scene.

Your journey draws to a close in Lee Vining, a small town at the base of the Sierra. A haven for weary travelers, and seasonal skiers, this former mining town is the perfect place to exchange stories, reflect on your Yosemite highlights, and plot your next National Park adventure.

LEFT A campground in Curry Village, near Yosemite Village

BELOW Taking a break at the summit of Cloud's Rest

OPPOSITE The Yosemite "Tunnel View," featuring El Capitan

PACIFIC COAST HIGHWAY

San Francisco

Los Angeles

START/FINISH
Los Angeles, California/
San Francisco, California

DISTANCE
485 miles (780 km)

DURATION
5–7 days

ROAD CONDITIONS
Well-maintained paved roads

THE BEST TIME TO GO
Late spring, for great weather and thinner crowds

OPPOSITE The soaring Bixby Bridge at sunset, on the scenic Big Sur coast of California

California 1 gives you all that glitters in the Golden State: Hollywood glamour, quirky artist colonies, fine dining, and epic ocean vistas. So put your shades on, pull the top down, and spark up the engine. It's all golden, baby.

This just might be America's most mythologized stretch of tarmac. The Pacific Coast Highway knits together L.A.'s silver-screen dreams and San Francisco's utopian ideals with some of the most awe-inspiring scenery in the country: noble redwood forests, beaches backed by skyscraping palms, and mountains that drop straight into the sea. Driving the highway means chasing the ghosts of Jack Kerouac and the Beats, indulging in some of the world's best wine and farm-to-table dining, and inevitably falling under the same Pacific spell that's lured surfers, celebrities, and artists to the region for over a century.

Before you hit the open road, though, you might find yourself stuck in Los Angeles. The culprit could be the city's notoriously gridlocked traffic, but it's just as likely to be the many things there are to do here. The stretch of California 1 that goes through L.A. and its suburbs is the drive's least picturesque, so there's absolutely no shame in detouring to chase Tinseltown's shiny diversions. A web of freeways leads to signature sights like the Hollywood sign and the Walk of Fame. These freeways are also the arteries that link together supremely cool neighborhoods like Silver Lake and Los Feliz, as well as Koreatown, Little Armenia, Tehrangeles, Thai Town, and more, allowing Angelenos the chance to eat their way around the world.

LIFE'S A BEACH

As the road starts to exit the city, it puts L.A.'s singular beach culture on display. Venice Boardwalk is an unusual mix of

LOS ANGELES

LOS ANGELES
L.A. isn't just about movies; the City of Angels also has incredible art, food, and music.

0 MILES

VENICE BEACH
The iconic boardwalk in this buzzing beach town is everything you'd expect.

13 MILES

113 MILES

SANTA BARBARA

Mountains and beaches make the city a paradise for outdoorsy types.

148 MILES

LAS CRUCES

Decide here if you'll stick to California 1 or opt for wine and Danish pastries.

TOP Palm trees swaying in front of Santa Monica pier

ABOVE The 19th-century Santa Barbara Mission

bodybuilders, skateboarders, magicians, and free spirits, and Santa Monica Pier attracts thrill-seekers to the rides of Pacific Park, where iconic sunsets behind the Ferris wheel are a given.

From L.A.'s edge, the highway begins to hug the coast, penned in between the chaparral-covered Santa Monica Mountains and the shimmering Pacific. The road cuts through stylish Malibu before turning northwest and arriving in Santa Barbara, a bewitching mix of beach vibes and Spanish Colonial Revival architecture, with an envy-inducing natural setting. Behind the city, the Santa Ynez Mountains provide playgrounds for hiking and picnicking, while the city's beaches offer space to surf, kayak, and paraglide. Dolphins are regular offshore visitors, and from February to September, the Santa Barbara Channel is a major migration route for humpback, blue, and other whales. In town, the early 19th-century Old Mission preserves Indigenous Chumash culture, while right by the highway, Funk Zone's converted warehouses are home to restaurants, wine bars, boutiques, and graffiti murals.

TURNING INLAND

About 30 miles (50 km) west of Santa Barbara, the highway waves goodbye to the ocean and cuts inland. When you reach Las Cruces, you have a decision to make. Staying on California 1 will take you through Vandenberg Space Force Base (did you remember to add missile coverage to your rental car's insurance?), but the junction also offers a tempting route through the Santa Ynez Valley. To take it, veer onto Highway 101, and then head east on California 246. (You'll know you're on the right track when you spot the ostrich ranch on your right.) That'll bring you into Solvang, which was founded by Danish immigrants in 1911. The town plays up its heritage with Danish-style windmills, souvenir shops selling wooden shoes and cuckoo clocks, and bakeries that offer Danish treats like spherical *æbleskiver* pastries. The only tell you're still in Southern California is the weather.

WINE COUNTRY

Continue east on 246 to the junction with California 154, then drive north to Los Olivos. Founded as a stagecoach stop back in the 1860s, it now has a population of just over 1,000 people, yet is home to more than two dozen wineries. The region is especially known for its rosés, which are best sampled in spring at vineyards like Demetria, a 20-minute drive north of town.

California 1 keeps its distance from the ocean as it heads north. For much of this stretch, it's flanked by fields of strawberries, lettuce, and other crops that thrive in the mild Mediterranean climate. Farmers' markets and tiny produce stands with hand-painted signs offer ample opportunity to sample the local bounty.

Founded as a stagecoach stop back in the 1860s, Los Olivos now has a population of just over 1,000 people, yet is home to more than two dozen wineries.

Wine regains prominence in San Luis Obispo, which gave birth to the state's vaunted wine industry when Father Junipero Serra and his fellow friars began growing grapes to make Communion wine during the late 18th century. While they don't have Napa's name-recognition, San Luis Obispo and the Edna Valley produce grapes with flavors of remarkable balance and complexity, thanks to their proximity to the coast and exceptionally long growing season. Chardonnay and Pinot Noir are the headliners here, but this part of the state is also home to excellent Zinfandels and Rieslings, plus lesser-known varietals like Albariño and Grüner Veltliner.

TOP A tasting room overlooking lush Edna Valley vineyards

ABOVE Panoramic views of San Luis Obispo

SOLVANG

Windmills, wooden shoes, and cuckoo clocks put the town's Danish heritage on display.

160 MILES

LOS OLIVOS

Sample some rosés at the vineyards surrounding this charming wine town.

170 MILES

SAN LUIS OBISPO

The birthplace of California's wine industry is known for its Pinot Noirs and Chardonnays.

227 MILES

MORRO BAY

Local denizens include peregrine falcons, sea lions, and sea otters.

239 MILES

CAMBRIA

Take in Pacific views from the Fiscalini Ranch Preserve, which offers miles of walking trails.

261 MILES

BIG SUR

Redwood forests and dramatic vistas provide some of the most unforgettable scenery.

337 MILES

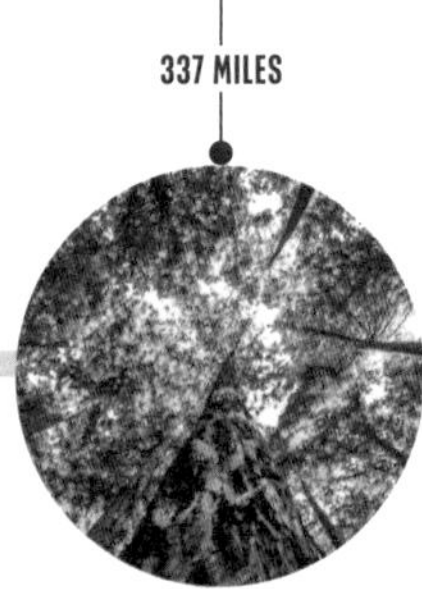

HITTING THE COAST

Trunk now full of bottles, you'll motor back to the coast at Morro Bay, a town of astonishing natural blessings. At the tip of a headland on the north side of town is the unmissable Morro Rock, a 576-ft (176-m) volcanic plug that's a nesting site for peregrine falcons. The area is fabulous for birding, with blue herons, hummingbirds, and grebes filling the skies and wetlands of Morro Bay State Park and Morro Bay Estuary. Sea lions and sea otters also favor the park, Morro Bay State Marine Reserve, and even off the Embarcadero pier.

From Morro Bay, the highway runs through a stretch of gently undulating hills, soon bringing you to Fiscalini Ranch Preserve, a huge swath of coastal land where trails lead to epiphanic Pacific views. You might even spy migrating whales. Surrounding the preserve, the town of Cambria is a true California charmer, serving up galleries, boutiques, and warm slices of olallieberry pie.

Just a few miles up the coast, neighboring San Simeon is home to elephant seal rookeries that see some 15,000 of the big guys haul out on the beach every year. Pupping season in January is an especially good time to visit, and observation points along the highway provide opportunities to pull over and observe the blubbery masses.

Big Sur is unquestionably the star of the Pacific Coast Highway. Redwood forests that challenge your sense of perspective, cliffs that rise straight out of the ocean, fog that turns the coastline into a dream—it's no wonder the region has enchanted American artists from Walt Whitman to Jack Kerouac. Numerous scenic viewpoints provide places to stop, none more famous than the one overlooking Bixby Bridge. At Big Sur's northern edge is Carmel-by-the-Sea, a swanky beach town that's home to Michelin-star restaurants, dozens of art galleries, the 18th-century Mission San Carlos Borromeo de Carmelo, and Pebble Beach, the country's best public

HEARST CASTLE

The media tycoon William Randolph Hearst spent nearly three decades building this 165-room mansion on his vast ranch in the hills above San Simeon. Among its extravagant highlights are a swimming pool with a faux Roman temple, lounges filled with Baroque tapestries, and the world's largest private zoo. It's sited off the highway at mile 270.

408 MILES

SANTA CRUZ

The boardwalk's Giant Dipper rollercoaster has thrilled riders since 1924.

485 MILES

SAN FRANCISCO

The drive ends—fog-bound or not—at San Francisco's legendary Golden Gate Bridge.

END

SAN FRANCISCO

golf course. Next door is Monterey and its lauded Monterey Bay Aquarium, occupying a former sardine cannery.

The highway loops around Monterey Bay before pulling into Santa Cruz. And here it is: *Californus mythicus*, the Golden State of legend. Surfers paddle out to catch the city's many excellent breaks, students tread the idyllic University of California, Santa Cruz campus (go Banana Slugs!), and seekers of good old-fashioned American fun ride a century-old wooden roller coaster, and stuff their faces with cotton candy at the Santa Cruz Beach Boardwalk.

INTO THE GOLDEN GATE CITY

Ninety minutes on, the highway arrives in San Francisco. Despite sitting on the very edge of the country, the city is often at the center of the U.S.'s cultural shifts—from hippies and the counterculture through the blossoming of the gay rights movement to the tech entrepreneurs of today. San Francisco's always game to try something new, so before you cut the engine, embrace the spirit by going for a drag brunch, attending a hacker-friendly workshop in Noisebridge, or sampling the Ferry Building Marketplace's gourmet offerings. Then end your road trip in appropriately dramatic fashion by following California 1 across the iconic Golden Gate Bridge.

ABOVE Snapping jellyfish at Monterey Bay Aquarium

RIGHT San Francisco's skyline, fronted by the Ferry Building

OPPOSITE Waves lapping the coast below Morro Rock

SOUTHERN PACIFIC

START/FINISH
San Diego, California/ Savannah, Georgia

DISTANCE
2,500 miles (4,025 km)

DURATION
12–14 days

ROAD CONDITIONS
Well-maintained paved roads

THE BEST TIME TO GO
Spring and the fall, for mild temperatures and smaller crowds

OPPOSITE Drifting through cypress trees and swampland on the Texas-Louisiana border

A fantastically diverse path across America's southern quarter, this route sweeps through desert plains, poignant Civil Rights sites, and moss-cloaked towns. It's the nostalgic side of the southern states that's often overlooked.

The mighty U.S. 80 once wiggled all the way across the south, joining up the sun-washed shores of San Diego, California in the west with the alluring city of Savannah, Georgia in the east. Now, after decades' worth of shifting infrastructure, the route is altogether more elusive, unfolding in tantalizingly bucolic segments before reconnecting with the Interstate.

SANDY BEACHES AND DESERT PLAINS

Your journey begins in San Diego, two hours south of blockbuster L.A. Ignore the call of the road for at least a day to roam rugged beaches and the sprawling Balboa Park, where Casa de Balboa is a vision of Spanish Renaissance-style architecture. The city's rich Chicano culture is revealed in Barrio Logan, where kaleidoscopic murals call for social justice and local neighborhood joints serve some of the best Mexican food in the U.S.

The road pushes east, flirting with the Mexican border as it wends its way to Jacumba. This is the place to look upward: the border town's star-splashed skies are some of the darkest in the U.S., while the Desert View Tower rewards travelers with sweeping vistas of the stark plains all around.

Pancake-flat desert plains continue to unfold as you motor across the Arizona border, and the eventual emergence of towering Saguaro cacti announces your approach to Tucson. Spend ample time in charming Barrio Viejo, replete with colorful Sonoran row houses dating to the 19th century. They're now filled with hip coffeehouses, Mexican restaurants,

SAN DIEGO

START

SAN DIEGO
Get lost in Balboa Park, with its snaking trails and Spanish-inspired architecture.

0 MILES

JACUMBA
Drink in the dazzling night skies in Jacumba, a southern California community.

77 MILES

ABOVE The colorful theater in Barrio Viejo, Tuscon

LEFT Murphy Saloon, in Shakespeare Ghost Town

OPPOSITE The sun setting on Mississippi's river bridges

and independent art galleries. The route catapults you farther into the Wild West as it swoops out of Tucson and inches toward Tombstone. Nicknamed the "Town Too Tough To Die," this old mining town hosts regular reenactments of Old West shootouts.

Watch the rust-red Chiricahua and Peloncillo mountains dance on the horizon after you push northeast and cross the New Mexico border. On your way to Las Cruces—known for its green chili dishes and early Spanish architecture—you'll cross the snaking Rio Grande and pass by Shakespeare Ghost Town. The Gold Rush town went from boom to bust in the 1920s, and today its bones remain moldering in the desert.

CHASING DOWN TEXAS

You'll slip beneath the Texas border as you cruise toward Carlsbad Caverns National Park, one of the most underrated sites in the entire park system. This mesmerizing world of stalactites and stalagmites plays out beneath the desert floor, while hiking trails beat out into the backcountry.

Continuing east, a mighty stretch of the road marches across Texas—the largest state in the contiguous U.S. You'll pass by sweeping meadows and great swaths of farmland, before curling into Fort Worth. Here the historic Stockyards

CARLSBAD CAVERNS NATIONAL PARK

Marvel at subterranean stalagmites and stalactites.

871 MILES

FORT WORTH

This historic Texan city has cowboy charm, and a twice-daily cattle drive.

1,317 MILES

1,687 MILES

POVERTY POINT WORLD HERITAGE SITE

View a series of protected earthworks on foot.

1,741 MILES

VICKSBURG

This quaint Mississippi town has poignant Civil War sites and 1800s-era architecture.

1,742 MILES

VICKSBURG CIVIL WAR MUSEUM

Learn about rare artefacts, hidden relics, and Black history in the Civil War era.

BUS BOYCOTTS

Rosa Parks became an icon of the U.S. Civil Rights Movement after she refused to give up her bus seat for a white man in Montgomery, Alabama. Her arrest in 1955 triggered the Montgomery Bus Boycott, a powerful protest that ultimately led to the desegregation of public buses in 1956.

offer further whispers of the Old West and there's still a twice-daily cattle drive at 11:30am and 4pm.

The route becomes progressively greener as you head eastward still. Cross the Louisiana border and you've entered the true Deep South, where tangled swamps and pine forests reveal themselves. The standout site along this stretch of road is Poverty Point World Heritage Site, a fascinating series of mounds and earthworks linked to an Indigenous culture that thrived here over 3,000 years ago. Take a guided tour or stretch your legs on the 2.5-mile (4-km) hiking trail before returning to the car.

ACROSS THE BIG MUDDY

The Vicksburg Bridge (adjacent to the Old Mississippi River Bridge) carries you across the Louisiana/Mississippi state line into the riverside city of Vicksburg. Ditch the car and explore the quaint downtown area and historic attractions such as the Vicksburg Civil War Museum and the Vicksburg National Military Park, where a major conflict was fought. Much of the onward road is hugged by pine trees as you slice through the belly of Mississippi, pausing for respite in delicate Southern cities like Clinton or Meridian. Wherever you stop, you're guaranteed to find a spot serving plates of fried chicken and refreshing iced tea.

The road arrows east, passing into Alabama, where you'll soon be immersed in somber and poignant history. This region was a cradle for the U.S. Civil Rights Movement, during which time African Americans fought for the right to vote and live free from discrimination. Freedom fighters marched along U.S. 80, from Selma to Montgomery, to demand their civil liberties before the Alabama State Capitol. If time allows, spend time in Selma by the Edmund Pettus Bridge, site of the infamous "Bloody Sunday," when peaceful protesters were brutally beaten back by state troopers during their first march attempt. Brown Chapel A.M.E. Church, where the marches began, is another important stop.

BELOW Savannah trees draped in Spanish moss

Onward to Montgomery and more significant Civil Rights sites await, including the Equal Justice Initiative Legacy Museum, which tells stories of the African American experience from slavery to modern-day fights for justice. Other poignant stops include the Rosa Parks Library and Museum, and the Dexter Avenue Baptist Church, where Dr. Martin Luther King, Jr. served as a pastor. Farther east, Tuskegee Airmen National Historic Site in Tuskegee shares Civil Rights stories about a group of Black military servicemen who fought in World War II but faced notable discrimination in their home country.

ROLLING INTO THE PEACH STATE

The enigmatic state of Georgia is your final prize. Macon, your first stop, is an underrated music-filled college town known as the birthplace of Southern rock and the historic Capricorn Studios. This is the best place to immerse yourself in this musical history. Venture outside of downtown to visit Ocmulgee Mounds National Historical Park, too: this series of mounds, built by Indigenous cultures during the Mississippian period, reveals stories about the land's original inhabitants—ancestors of the modern-day Muscogee people.

The road finally sinks into Savannah, the "Hostess City of the South," where you'll be welcomed with a warm embrace. Expect squares filled with oak trees wrapped in Spanish moss, and cobbled streets opening out by the Savannah River. Highlights include Forsyth Park—the city's emerald heart and a perfect place to stroll—and the Cathedral of St. John the Baptist, designed in the French Gothic style. If you can tear yourself away from Savannah proper, drive on to Tybee Island, nicknamed "Savannah's Beach," to enjoy beachside food joints and sand the color of sugar. There are few more perfect endings to this Southern odyssey than sinking your toes into the sand and gazing out across the Atlantic.

EXTEND YOUR TRIP

From Savannah, strike south and travel down Georgia's gloriously unspoiled coastline. Learn about Gullah Geechee culture on sand-trimmed and lighthouse-studded Sapelo Island, which is home to the descendants of enslaved Africans. Then motor on to Jekyll Island, boasting the sumptuous Jekyll Island Club Resort and the Georgia Sea Turtle Center.

MACON

Big names such as Percy Sledge recorded here at Capricorn Studios.

2,211 MILES

OCMULGEE MOUNDS NATIONAL HISTORICAL PARK

Explore Indigenous heritage and vast earthen mounds.

2,215 MILES

TYBEE ISLAND

Located near downtown Savannah, this barrier island has pristine beaches.

2,425 MILES

SAVANNAH

THE AMERICAN DINER AND MOTEL

On the ladder of American needs, food and shelter may be the only things that outrank the open road. Little wonder, then, that a pair of institutions, the motel and the diner, grew up on the highway.

When it came time to call it a day, the earliest motorists had two options: drive into a city to find a downtown hotel, or pitch a tent. As car ownership grew, however, entrepreneurs began setting up auto camps on the outskirts of towns. The Ritz they were not. Most offered well water and a safe place to camp, but little else. Eventually, these were replaced by cottage courts: groupings of cottages, often with a gas station and restaurant on site.

The first motel, at least in name, was the Milestone Mo-Tel, which opened in San Luis Obispo, California, in 1925, but the iconic American motel—neon "No Vacancy" sign buzzing in the night; rooms filled with forbidden lovers, fleeing fugitives, and families on vacation—was a product of the post-World War II years.

Diners started to appear around the same time auto camps did, when the Worcester Lunch Car Company began shipping eateries on wheels across the East Coast from its Massachusetts factory in 1906. A decade and a half later, J.G. Kirby and Reuben W. Jackson opened Kirby's Pig Stand in Dallas, the country's first drive-in, with waiters delivering barbecue pork and Coca-Cola straight to customers' cars.

Because they first catered to factory workers and late-night crowds, diners acquired an unsavory reputation early on; Atlantic City, New Jersey, and Buffalo, New York, even banned them for a time. But like motels, diners won their places in American hearts because they were accessible to everyone. Anybody could pull up a seat at the Formica counter, order meatloaf, and have change left over for the jukebox. They're ideal for long drives, too. When you've been on the road for hours, that flashing diner sign can feel like a revelation.

Today, motels and diners exist as much in the realm of nostalgia as they do in the real world, with many squeezed out by national chains. But drive the country's smaller highways and byways and you can still find these beloved icons of the American road trip.

Diners started to appear around the same time auto camps did, when the Worcester Lunch Car Company began shipping eateries on wheels across the East Coast.

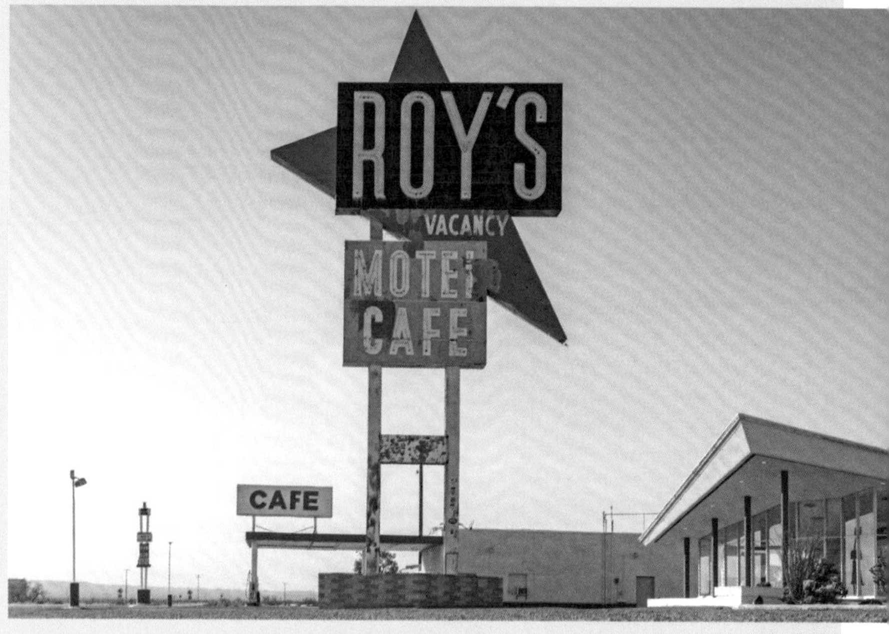

ABOVE The iconic sign for Roy's Motel, in Amboy, California

EXTRATERRESTRIAL HIGHWAY

Tonopah ▸ Hiko

START/FINISH
Tonopah, Nevada/ Hiko, Nevada

DISTANCE
150 miles (240 km)

DURATION
2–3 days

ROAD CONDITIONS
Well-maintained paved roads

THE BEST TIME TO GO
Spring and fall; expect extreme temperatures in summer and winter

OPPOSITE The decorated Extraterrestrial Highway road sign, near Warm Springs

Wonderful weirdness awaits along Nevada's Extraterrestrial Highway. This peculiar road trip takes you deep into the beating heart of America's Alien Country, an otherworldly orbit that skirts the top-secret Area 51.

High-rolling casinos and epic canyons are to be expected in Nevada. Perhaps, too, a jumpsuited Elvis impersonator shaking his bejeweled legs outside a drive-through wedding chapel. But unless you've taken the road less traveled, you may not be aware that the state is also a hotspot with visitors from another planet entirely.

Nevada State Route 375, better known as the Extraterrestrial Highway, has more reported U.F.O. sightings than any other road in the country. Which makes sense when you consider its unique location, tucked into the remote reaches of south-central Nevada. This far-out highway skirts Area 51, a hush-hush military test site that some believe to be a top-secret laboratory for captured alien spacecraft. What happens behind security fences remains a mystery, but quirky businesses and attractions have sprung up at the curbside of this eerily desolate highway, appealing to the alien-curious road tripper.

GALAXIES AND GRAVESTONES

Begin your drive in Tonopah, one of the finest places in the country to gaze up at the Milky Way. On the edge of the town take the dirt road to Clair Blackburn Memorial Stargazing Park to marvel at a blanket of 7,000 twinkling stars lighting up the night's sky. During the summer, coincide your visit with Tonopah's monthly star parties, where budding astrophiles congregate to focus their telescopes on awe-inspiring meteor showers. Alternatively, explore the Old Tonopah Cemetery and its crumbling

TONOPAH

START

TONOPAH
Get ringside seats to some of the best stargazing in the country as night falls.

0 MILES

OLD TONOPAH CEMETERY
A spooky self-guided ghost walk around this cemetery's gravestones is a must.

1 MILE

EXTRATERRESTRIAL
STEVIE
REALITY COFFEE CO.
A51
NASA
JAE 54
STRUG
NASCAR Sprint CUP SERIES
TEAM SCAR
got milk?
FORD MAYOR
BRC

RIGHT The Lunar Crater landmark, a volcanic caldera

OPPOSITE TOP Posing by the U.F.O. mural at E.T. Fresh Jerky

OPPOSITE BELOW Caribbean blue waters in Crystal Springs

U.F.O. WORLD CAPITAL

The minuscule town of Rachel, home to just 54 people, became the official U.F.O. capital of the world in 1996, after Nevada State Route 375 was officially designated the Extraterrestrial Highway by the state. The town was named Rachel in 1978 after the first baby born in this valley, Rachel Jones.

headstones at night, many of which belonged to those who worked in the Nevada mines during the Gold Rush era.

ALIEN ENCOUNTERS

At daybreak, hit the open road southwest toward Rachel, passing Lunar Crater volcanic fields along the way. Two asphalt lanes cut a path through the apocalyptic desert landscape, past rocky peaks, wide dusty plains, and bone-dry lakes. Keep a look out for the tiny ghost town of Warm Springs at the roadside, a blink-and-you'll-miss-it cluster of two rickety abandoned buildings that stands as a reminder of a once-thriving mining community.

The Extraterrestrial Highway is one of Nevada's loneliest roads, seeing a mere 200 cars per day. While the solitude can certainly be blissful, just be sure to pack the trunk with supplies and top up the tank beforehand, as gas stations are spotted with less frequency than little green Martians around here. Approaching Rachel, as spiky Joshua trees sprout at the roadside, don't let the occasional sonic booms coming from nearby Area 51 distract you—it's just test planes blasting, nothing to be alarmed about.

A broken-down spaceship at the front of Little A'Le'Inn (pronounced Little Alien) in Rachel means that you can't miss your next pit stop. "Earthlings welcome" reads the handwritten sign at the doorway of the dining room, where alien burgers fly out of the kitchen's atomic hatch. Keen to prove that you've been to the mythical Area 51 site? Purchase a vial of

WARM SPRINGS

This small roadside ghost town is now home to just two abandoned buildings.

51 MILES

EXTRATERRESTRIAL HIGHWAY

Take a photo with the Extraterrestrial Highway sign to show the folks back home.

51 MILES

RACHEL

Scoff an alien burger at Little A'Le'Inn before perusing the gift store for otherworldly souvenirs.

110 MILES

131 MILES

BLACK MAILBOX

This iconic mailbox near Crystal Springs is used to connect with extraterrestrial beings (maybe).

149 MILES

ALIEN RESEARCH CENTER

This shiny building sells some of the best alien tequila—a drinks cabinet staple—on this planet.

END

HIKO

dirt from Little A'Le'Inn's gift store. Collected from the patrolled borders of this highly classified United States Air Force facility within the Nevada Test and Training Range, this unusual souvenir will only set you back $5.99.

Before blasting off from Rachel, take the highway to the outskirts of the town to visit the area's famous black mailbox. For decades this rusting old container on a stick has become a slightly bizarre meeting point for those hoping to communicate with life on other planets, or just connect with fellow alien appreciators traveling through.

SHIMMERING HORIZONS

After snapping a quick photo, continue toward Crystal Springs, watching the landscape outside the window transform from barren wasteland to lush marshes, thanks to a system of geothermal springs buried deep underground. Up ahead, the silver dome of the Alien Research Center hovers on the horizon, much like a shiny spaceship. Ease into the car park and pass the soaring scrap-metal Martian greeting guests at the entrance. Inside this giant tin can of a store, shelves are crammed with trippy curiosities and out-of-this-world merch. There's just enough time to pick up a bottle of alien tequila before you are beamed to your final destination.

Round off your visit to the final frontier with a stop at the E.T. Fresh Jerky in nearby Hiko, a wacky spot serving up cured meat snacks in space-invader packaging. Stock up on a handful of lean beef jerky strips for the road, grab one last "I-come-in-peace" selfie before the green man mural, then head off into the mysteries of the pitch-black night, eyes scanning for saucers flying overhead. Because on Nevada's Extraterrestrial Highway, the truth is out there, somewhere.

SPEED
LIMIT
25

HIGHWAY 50: THE LONELIEST ROAD

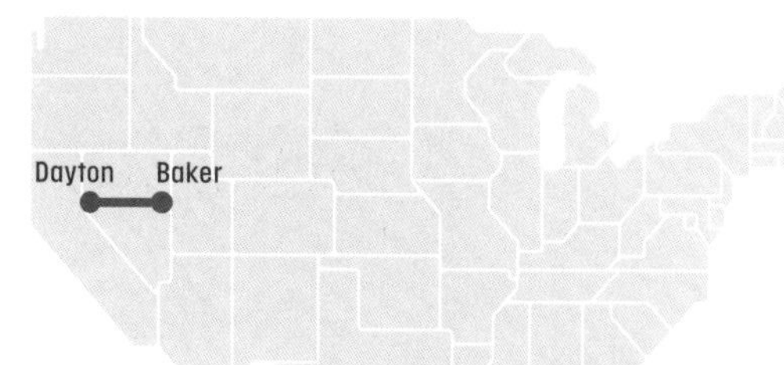

START/FINISH
Dayton, Nevada/ Baker, Nevada

DISTANCE
440 miles (710 km)

DURATION
5–7 days

ROAD CONDITIONS
Well-maintained paved roads; be prepared for snowy conditions

THE BEST TIME TO GO
Fall, for fiery foliage and more moderate temperatures

OPPOSITE The sloping Sand Mountain, fronted by a lonely stretch of Highway 50

Striking across the middle of the Silver State, this remote road promises total escape, and total solitude. Buckle up for epic desert and mountain vistas, atmospheric ghost towns, and classic Old West saloons.

It was *Life* magazine that first called Nevada's share of Highway 50 "The Loneliest Road in America" due to its sheer remoteness and its reported lack of amenities—you'll likely travel miles without seeing another soul. And while this might seem a condemnatory description, the highway's seclusion is its ultimate appeal.

FROM DUST TO RICHES

The little town of Dayton will prime you for this epic trip through the West. This was the first place gold was discovered in Nevada, a historic event that would shape both the state's story and its physical landscape, as mining boomtowns sprang up across the desert. Spend a little time drinking in the old-school Western architecture downtown: a highlight is the Odeon Saloon, which opened back in 1863.

Ease yourself from Dayton out onto the open road, and it won't be long before classic Highway 50 panoramas reveal themselves. The road marches on, cinching into a neat point on the horizon, with pancake-flat plains. You'll see the snow-crested peaks of the Sierra Nevada mountain range in a haze in the distance.

Though you've barely started, it's well worth taking a quick detour on Nevada State Route 116 to the Stillwater National Wildlife Refuge. Some 200 species of migratory birds descend on these desert wetlands each year, from American white pelicans to swans. You'll also see something that's rather scarce along this dusty desert road trip—water, and lots of it. Enjoy sweeping views of the landscape

DAYTON

START

DAYTON
Get a taste of the Old West in this small town filled with saloons and 1800s architecture.

0 MILES

STILLWATER NATIONAL WILDLIFE REFUGE
The wetlands are the perfect place to see migratory birds.

67 MILES

122 MILES

MIDDLEGATE STATION

Fill up on nostalgia and burgers at this long-serving roadhouse and saloon.

186 MILES

AUSTIN

Explore Main Street, with its Western false fronts, churches, and saloons.

from the Stillwater Point Reservoir observation platform, easily reached via a mellow interpretive trail.

A JOURNEY BACK THROUGH TIME

Make your way back to Highway 50 and settle back into the wide expanses that stretch as far as the eye can see. The desert plains whip by like an old Western movie on fast forward, only occasionally interrupted by a herd of cattle or a huddle of farm buildings. Eventually, they're also broken up by Middlegate Station, an old-school saloon and roadhouse that's stood the test of time. It was originally a station along the Pony Express (a historic mail trail that saw riders travel from the Midwest to California) and it still rises like a mirage from the desert, promising refreshing cold drinks and hearty burgers to weary travelers. It's best known for the mighty triple-decker "Monster Burger." Be sure to fill up on fuel while you're here: the gas station pumps might look old, but they work just fine (in fact, it pays to plan all pit stops ahead.)

Once sated, return to the road and push on east. Those unfettered desertscapes will be familiar to you now—but their sheer size and emptiness should be no less awe-inspiring. The small town of Austin will eventually emerge and it's a sure bet for a comfy place to overnight. Stretch your legs on

The desert plains whip by like an old Western movie on fast forward, occasionally interrupted by a herd of cattle or a huddle of farm buildings.

Main Street, which could have been pulled straight from an old Western movie: it unfolds in a string of charming false fronts, churches, and nostalgic saloons. Just outside of Austin proper, the Lucky Spur Saloon is a classic—pull up a stool and enjoy a cold one with impressive views of the Kingston Canyon, or head to the nearby Spencer Hot Springs to soothe travel-tired limbs.

The mountains become more mighty, and inch closer to the road, as you continue eastward across the heart of

BELOW A hazy sunrise over Highway 50, west of Eureka

LEFT An illuminated hotel and casino in remote Ely

NEVADA NATURE

Nevada packs a natural punch. The Silver State is home to the largest desert situated entirely within the U.S.—the Great Basin Desert—and the most mountain ranges of any contiguous state. The name Nevada derives from the Spanish word *nevada*, meaning snowfall or snow-clad.

Nevada, through the former mining town of Eureka. Allegedly the "friendliest town on the loneliest road of America," Eureka is a gateway to major bluffs including Prospect Peak, ideal for experienced hikers. The dramatic views from the very top are worth the considerable effort. It's also just a short 20-minute drive on White Pine County Road 9 to Belmont Mill, a ghost of the state's fabled mining history. Dating back to the 1900s, the cracked and deserted mining buildings make for eerie viewing. The four-story mill, the office, and the boarding house are among the structures that remain semi-intact today.

Leave Nevada's mining history in the dust, and drive on through yet more brush-trimmed desert, before eventually returning to civilization in Ely. This remote, mountain-fringed town is known for its murals and the Renaissance Village: a collection of artefact-filled buildings that tell stories about the region's earliest settlers, from the Italians to the Chinese. If you're feeling as parched as the terrain around you, swing by Economy Drug and Old Fashioned Soda Fountain. Open since 1946, this quintessentially American pharmacy and diner is the perfect place to reflect on your journey over a glass of fizzy pop. You can also duck inside the East Ely Railroad Depot Museum for a hit of mining and locomotive history—learn about the key railroad milestones and explore various employee offices, including that of the traffic manager, complete with original typewriter.

HIGH UP ON THE HIGHWAY

The final stretches of Highway 50 ripple out from here and the elevation continues to rise, too. Depending on the season, it's not unlikely that the surrounding mountains and high desert

PROSPECT PEAK

Drink in epic views from the summit, reached via a steep and rugged hike.

266 MILES

BELMONT MILL

Discover remnants of Nevada's industrial history, with its deserted mining buildings.

315 MILES

ELY

Immerse yourself in the region's locomotive history at East Ely Railroad Depot Museum.

373 MILES

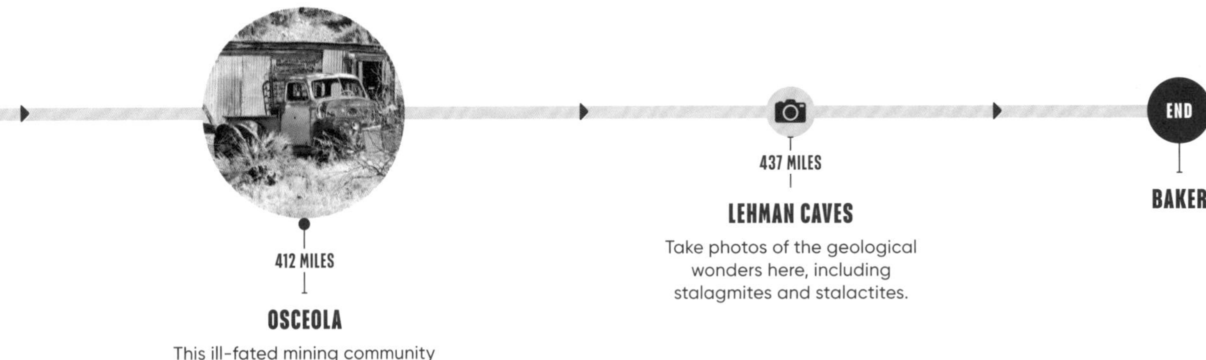

EXTEND YOUR TRIP

National Parks are just around the corner—it's just two and a half hours to Zion, home to the epic Angels Landing Trail. Arches, Capitol Reef, Canyonlands, and Bryce are all within kissing distance too.

ABOVE Bristlecone pine in the sparse Great Basin Desert

will be blanketed in snow. Trundle past the creaking remains of Osceola, another of Nevada's ubiquitous ghost towns. Prospectors struck gold in 1872 and Osceola mushroomed—but a fire damaged the settlement in the 1940s. The ruinous remains and rusted out vehicles are now an unnerving sight in Nevada's juniper-scattered backcountry.

NATIONAL PARK ADVENTURES

From here, you'll wend your way toward the last stop on the Loneliest Road: the quirky town of Baker. But before you park up, get one last adventure under your belt at the underrated Great Basin National Park. It's a playground of soaring peaks, underground caverns, and breathtaking hiking trails and just a stone's throw away from the little-visited Baker.

Spend a little longer behind the wheel to take advantage of the Wheeler Peak Scenic Drive. Named for the park's most gargantuan mountain, the road weaves its way through the South Snake Range for 12 miles (20 km), climbing 4,000 ft (1,220 m) in elevation and offering epic vistas of the Great Basin Desert as it goes. Plenty of hiking trails arrow off this scenic driving route, including the Alpine Lakes Loop, which peels into the wilderness, with postcard-perfect views of lakes, streams, and wildflower-flecked meadows (depending on the season). The strenuous 9-mile (15-km) trek to the summit of Wheeler Peak is also popular and it affords the hardy hiker some of the finest views in the state.

There are treasures below the ground here too. Spoiler: it's not gold. No, it's the Lehman Caves. This fascinating world of caverns sprawls out in a riot of intricate stalagmites and stalactites. Take a tour to uncover their formation and history. For the final part of this road trip, head above ground and look to the skies. The park is known for its dark, star-filled heavens—a product of its remoteness. Visit the Astronomy Amphitheater for a ranger-led "star party"—the cosmos make for a dazzling finale.

GHOST TOWNS

The American landscape is haunted by ghost towns, settlements that grew in dreams of prosperity only to wither in disappointment. Many were once mining communities, established after a vein was discovered and forsaken once the supply was exhausted. Elsewhere, especially in Texas, the same pattern played out with oil. Other ghost towns took root where founders believed railroads would be built as the nation expanded west, but when tracks didn't materialize, folks packed up and left.

In an uncomfortable preview of what may be to come, numerous towns were also abandoned for environmental reasons. In the 1930s, drought and dust storms brought an end to agricultural communities across the Great Plains. Steins, New Mexico, was a desert mining town whose only source of water was whatever the railroad carried in. When the trains stopped, residents had no choice but to leave. Another angel of civic death, and an ironic one for road-trippers, has been highways. As the national web of roads grew, some towns built around railroads disappeared.

Not all towns were small. Bodie was a California Gold Rush boomtown of 8,000, with its own newspaper, while some 10,000 people lived in Bannack in the mid-1800s—the city was briefly the capital of the Montana Territory. By the 1940s, both were gone.

Ghost towns can be found in every state—even Rhode Island—but most are in the Great Plains and the West. Several of these are accessible from Highway 50. Near Silver Springs, Fort Churchill was built to safeguard pioneers and pony express riders, but it was deserted in 1869. Meanwhile, a detour from Middlegate or Austin takes you to Berlin, a company mining town whose 250 souls included charcoal makers, woodcutters, and a doctor. The settlement lasted barely a decade before its demise in 1911.

Another angel of civic death, and an ironic one for road-trippers, has been highways. As the national web of roads grew, some towns built around railroads disappeared.

In the same region was the silver boomtown of Belmont, which at one point had 15,000 residents. The aerial tramway that carried ore from mine to mill is still intact, and you can also explore a bank, and a 100-ft (30-m) chimney pocked with bullet holes from when U.S. pilots used it for target practice during World War II.

ABOVE Clouds looming over the ghost town of Bannack

HELLS CANYON SCENIC BYWAY

La Grande ▸ Baker City

START/FINISH
La Grande, Oregon/ Baker City, Oregon

DISTANCE
205 miles (330 km)

DURATION
2–3 days

ROAD CONDITIONS
Well-maintained paved roads, with some narrow, steep sections

THE BEST TIME TO GO
Summer (after May), to avoid road closures

OPPOSITE Rafts and kayaks traveling down the Snake River in Hells Canyon

With its cowboy towns and mountain railoads, driving the Hells Canyon Scenic Byway into the rugged Wallowa Mountains can feel like a journey back in time. But this twisty road is the ideal option for a modern-day adventure.

Looping around the Wallowas from La Grande to Baker City, Hells Canyon Scenic Byway offers a window into one of America's most remote regions, a landscape daubed with white-water rivers and craggy peaks. It's easy to see why the scenery takes center stage here.

Begin your journey at the laid-back college community of La Grande, home of Eastern Oregon University and a charming downtown of small shops, cafés, and bars. From here the route follows U.S. 82 northeast across the broad, flat plain of the Grande Ronde Valley, a patchwork of wheat farms and apple orchards, with the Blue Mountains far to the west. At Elgin, 20 miles (32 km) north of La Grande, concerts are still performed at the stately Opera House, built in 1911. The town is also the terminus of the Eagle Cap Excursion Train, which runs along the Grande Ronde and Wallowa rivers in summer, when the banks are smothered in wildflowers.

WINDING ALONG THE WALLOWA RIVER

East of Elgin, the route leaves the Grande Ronde to cut across a high plateau of barren grassland to the village of Minam on the Wallowa River. The Wallowa is a deep blue torrent; you can join white-water rafting trips at Minam Store, or stretch your legs at Minam State Recreation Area, where steelhead fishers cast off, and bald eagles glide high above in winter.

Keep your eyes peeled for more wildlife as the road hugs the winding Wallowa River and rises through the pinewoods—mule deer and elk often

LA GRANDE

LA GRANDE
Begin your journey in this small but lively college town, home to Eastern Oregon University.

0 MILES

MINAM
Go white-water rafting down the broiling Wallowa River.

33 MILES

graze along the verge. Before long, the highway passes through the small town of Wallowa, where the Nez Perce Wallowa Homeland Visitor Center introduces the culture of the namesake Indigenous people. It also acts as a hub for Tamkaliks, the annual powwow (get-together) held each July. This is the heartland of the wal'wá•ma band of Nez Perce, the people led by iconic Chief Joseph during the Nez Perce War (1877).

INTO THE VALLEYS

The byway continues southeast up the turbulent Wallowa and Lostine rivers, with the towering peaks of the Wallowa Mountains now looming to the south. Stop at Z's BBQ Lostine Tavern for sumptuous ribs and pulled pork, or continue to Enterprise, which sits at the top of the Wallowa Valley and serves up award-winning beers at Terminal Gravity Brewery. Here, a plateau of ranchland spreads out to the south, backed by the giant snowcapped Wallowas, with rolling prairies to the north.

Just ten minutes on, the town of Joseph has a completely different feel. An old logging community, it is almost exclusively dedicated to the arts, with bronze sculptures and galleries galore. In September, the town hosts the popular Wallowa Valley Festival of the Arts.

Ready to get back into nature? Take a short detour south to Wallowa Lake, a beautiful blue-black stretch of icy water enveloped by dense forest and jagged mountains. From the lakeshore, the

CHIEF JOSEPH

In 1877, with his people facing resettlement, Chief Joseph attempted to lead his 800 followers to safety in Canada. They were pursued by the U.S. Army, and after a trek of around 1,700 miles (2,735 km), Joseph was finally forced to surrender, just 40 miles (65 km) short of the border.

Z'S BBQ LOSTINE TAVERN

Dine on smoked brisket ribs, pulled pork, and key lime pie.

55 MILES

JOSEPH

This artsy mountain town has an eclectic mix of galleries, chocolatiers, and distilleries.

71 MILES

WALLOWA LAKE

Take a short detour to this gorgeous body of water, backed by towering peaks.

Wallowa Lake Tramway soars straight up to the 8,150-ft (2,485-m) summit of Mount Howard, where there are jaw-dropping views of the Eagle Cap Wilderness and the Wallowa range.

Back on the main route, follow Highway 350 east for 8 miles (13 km) from Joseph to the junction with Forest Road 39, also known as the Wallowa Mountain Loop Road. This narrow but well-paved minor byway winds through the most rugged section of the Wallowa-Whitman National Forest: expect stunning views of the Wallowas and the Seven Devils mountains on the Idaho side of the Snake River. The adjacent Salt Creek Summit Recreation Park is a good place to stretch your legs, but if you're looking for a stellar photo, take the 3-mile (5-km) side-trip on Forest Road 490 to Hells Canyon Overlook, a loft perch far above the Snake River.

The Wallowa Loop Road eventually spills out onto wider U.S. 86 in the arid Pine Creek Valley, not far from Halfway, a popular outdoor sports destination in winter. For a caffeine boost, swing by Cornucopia Coffee House, one of the state's best coffee roasters, before motoring south across rolling grasslands and descending into the Powder River Valley at Richland. As its name suggests, this fertile portion of the valley supports several farms and ranches.

TOAST THE JOURNEY IN BAKER CITY

Continue to follow the narrowing Powder River west from Richland, up through rolling sagebrush-covered plateaus and past the site of the Hole in the Wall Landslide, which covered the highway and dammed the river back in 1984.

The byway officially ends in Baker City, in the flat, baking high desert between the Blue and Wallowa mountains. Once known as the "Queen City of the Mines," this former gold-mining hub features some grand examples of 19th-century architecture along its Main Street, testimony to the city's former prosperity. End your journey at Barley Brown's Taphouse, on Main Street, a pilgrimage site for beer geeks everywhere—and arguably for road-trippers now, too.

ABOVE Green hills rolling away to Seven Devils mountains

OPPOSITE TOP Tamkaliks Powwow, the Wallowa Valley

OPPOSITE BELOW Wallowa Lake, glistening in the sun

116 MILES

HELLS CANYON OVERLOOK

An overlook with mesmerizing panoramic views of the canyonlands far below.

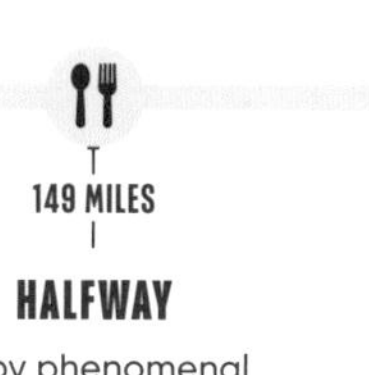

149 MILES

HALFWAY

Enjoy phenomenal coffee at the atmospheric Cornucopia Coffee House.

205 MILES

BAKER CITY

Wonderfully preserved 19th-century architecture—and a fine craft brewery to boot.

BAKER CITY

GOING-TO-THE-SUN ROAD

West Glacier ▸ St. Mary

START/FINISH
West Glacier, Montana/ St. Mary, Montana

DISTANCE
50 miles (80 km)

DURATION
2–5 hours

ROAD CONDITIONS
Paved; inclement weather can cause unexpected hazards; blind curves

THE BEST TIME TO GO
Summer, as the alpine portion of the road closes from mid-October to late June (exact dates vary), but expect congestion

OPPOSITE The imposing Glacier National Park, with roads carved into mountains

All hail, Helios! Going-to-the-Sun Road carries you over the Rocky Mountains and the Continental Divide, delivering transcendent views of pristine glaciers, hulking mountain peaks, and wildflower-bedecked alpine meadows.

The main route through Glacier National Park, Going-to-the-Sun Road is an engineering marvel. Building it required men to clear 60-ft (18-m) snowdrifts, dangle by ropes from sheer cliffs, and haul excavated rock out by hand—an endeavor equalled only by the resulting road's majesty. Since opening in 1933, this spectacular drive has brought motorists seemingly within touching distance of the heavens.

UP INTO THE WILDERNESS

You'll start your ascent from the hamlet of West Glacier, where Going-to-the-Sun Road departs from U.S. Route 2. Just a couple of miles up the road is the welcoming village of Apgar, the jumping-off point for the national park. The park visitor center here has the latest on road conditions—always a good thing to check—and Eddie's Cafe & Mercantile offers hearty breakfasts and burgers. If you have a 4WD, you could strike out along Camas Road to explore untouched wilderness, homesteading sites, and Glacier National Park's remotest reaches.

From Apgar, Going-to-the-Sun Road begins to trace the eastern shore of Lake McDonald, a beguiling blue reminder of glaciers' earth-sculpting power. It's the national park's largest lake, with water so clear you can look out your window and count the stones on the lakebed from the driver's seat. Reflected on the lake's surface are mountain peaks, hanging valleys, and stands of hemlocks and western red cedars. It's a view that's been drawing

WEST GLACIER

START

APGAR

The pretty lakeside village of Apgar is a hub of activity and home to a park visitor center.

2 MILES

LAKE MCDONALD

This pristine lake is the perfect location to rent a kayak and spend some time on the water.

4 MILES

LAKE MCDONALD LODGE

This century-old, Swiss-style lodge is a great base for an extended visit.

11 MILES

THE LOOP

Named after the only hairpin turn on the mountain, the Loop offers views of Heavens Peak.

24 MILES

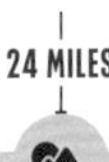

BIRD WOMAN FALLS OVERLOOK

Pull over to gaze at a 492-ft (150-m) waterfall pouring out of a hanging valley.

27 MILES

RIGHT Driving past the Weeping Wall's rainbow spray

BELOW Water gushing over the rocks at Logan Pass

OPPOSITE Wild Goose Island, surrounded by still waters

travelers to the shoreside Lake McDonald Lodge for more than a century. Built in 1913, the inn was modeled on Swiss hunting chalets.

When Going-to-the-Sun's route was first planned in the 1910s, one proposal incorporated 15 switchbacks to traverse the steep terrain. The final design was considerably more elegant. It incorporated just one, which you reach about 15 minutes after passing Avalanche Creek, a popular spot for camping and hiking. For a few miles, the road seems determined to climb straight northwest, but then it suddenly changes its mind, hairpinning and heading back southeast at a spot known as the Loop.

The road is still on its way up when it reaches the overlook for Bird Woman Falls, a 492-ft (150-m) waterfall that pours out of a hanging valley suspended between Mount Cannon and Mount Oberlin. More watery wonders await at the Weeping Wall, where rivulets of spring water and snowmelt pour down rock abutting the road. In August, after the snows are gone, the wall does weep, but in spring, the fresh melt means it bawls, and if you're driving west you'll pass right through its spray.

ON TOP OF THE WORLD

About 3 miles (5 km) from the Weeping Wall, you reach the highest point on the drive. At 6,646 ft (2,026 m), Logan Pass marks the Continental Divide, what the Indigenous Blackfoot people called the "backbone of the world." Pause here to savor being on top of the continent and to soak in the surrounding mountain peaks. Going-to-the-Sun Mountain, the road's namesake, is directly to the east. If you need a break, hike the Highline Trail for some of the drive's best views. Keep your eye out for mountain goats. The park's most famous residents, these white bundles of muscle have no trouble navigating slopes of up to 60 degrees.

DESCENT TO ST. MARY

It's all downhill from Logan Pass. As you descend, you'll go through the 408-ft (124-m) East Side Tunnel. To build it, workers had to construct a 3.5-mile (5.5-km) trail from the pass and then carry equipment on their backs 200 ft (60 m) down a series of ladders and switchbacks. Power equipment couldn't reach the tunnel, so all the rock that was blasted from the side of Piegan Mountain had to be carried out by hand.

Not long after you exit the tunnel, pull over at the Jackson Glacier Overlook to view one of the park's largest ice sheets, while you still can. The Indigenous Kootenai people called the area the park now occupies Ya·qawiswit̓xuki, "the place of much ice," but climate change is all too rapidly making the name obsolete. In the past six decades, Jackson Glacier has shrunk by around 40 percent, and since 1850 the total number of glaciers in the park that are at least 25 acres (10 hectares) in size has fallen from 80 to just 26.

Your drive ends much as it began, along the shore of a 10-mile (15-km) glacial lake. By now the road has descended far enough that subalpine vegetation has given way to forests and hillsides graced with lupine, Indian paintbrush, and other wildflowers. As you motor along, keep an eye out the passenger side for the diminutive Wild Goose Island, an almost comically tiny speck amid the surrounding mountain behemoths. Then, with one last turn, you leave the heavens behind and come back down to earth, finishing your drive in the tiny community of St. Mary.

SOUR SPIRIT

The road's name comes from Going-to-the-Sun Mountain, but where did the mountain's unique name originate? One explanation suggests it comes from a Blackfoot legend telling of the deity Sour Spirit, who descended from the sun to teach men to hunt. On his return to the sun, the god left his image on the mountain to serve as inspiration to the Blackfoot peoples.

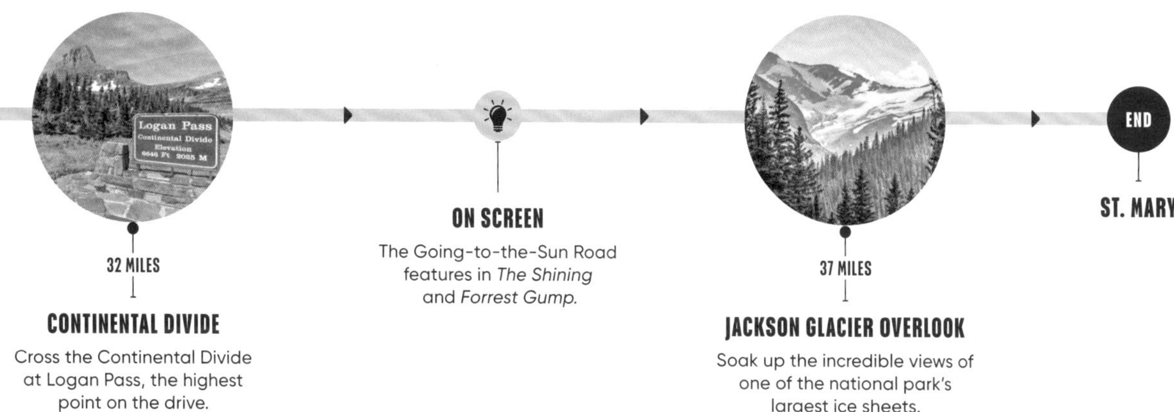

AMERICA'S NATIONAL PARK HIGHWAY

Babb-Piegan

Flagstaff

START/FINISH
Babb-Piegan, Montana/ Flagstaff, Arizona

DISTANCE
1,400 miles (2,255 km)

DURATION
2–3 weeks

ROAD CONDITIONS
Well-maintained paved roads

THE BEST TIME TO GO
Spring or fall for wildlife-watching

OPPOSITE Gazing at the jagged peaks of Grand Teton National Park

U.S. 89, snaking between the Rockies and the Arizona desert, connects various national parks and takes in the best of the West: bison and grizzly bears, ghost towns, cowboy saloons, snowy peaks, and bubbling hot springs.

America's National Park Highway cuts across the U.S.'s most awe-inspiring landscapes, knitting together the wide-open spaces of Montana and Arizona with some of the country's greatest national parks: the geysers of Yellowstone, the jagged peaks of Grand Teton, and the soaring canyons of Zion.

Beginning at the Canadian border, U.S. 89 runs south across the pancake-flat Montana prairies, skirting Glacier National Park. The Going-to-the-Sun Road (p83) offers a tempting detour into the park, but stay on course and you'll cut through the heart of the Blackfeet Indian Reservation. The plains appear to stretch to the horizon, offering an endless ocean of scrub and grass.

THROUGH THE ROCKIES

South of the city of Great Falls, the Kings Hill Scenic Byway is a 70-mile (115-km) stretch of U.S. 89 that winds through the Little Belt Mountains, a quiet, densely wooded sector of the Lewis and Clark National Forest. At Livingston, the road begins to follow the Yellowstone River back into the Rockies. This was the original route to Yellowstone National Park, and at Gardiner you'll see the Roosevelt Arch, marking the northern gateway to America's greatest slice of preserved wilderness.

U.S. 89 is the backbone for two national parks in Wyoming; in Yellowstone, it runs from Mammoth Hot Springs south to the steaming Norris Geyser Basin and Old Faithful geyser before cutting through pine and spruce forest to neighboring Grand Teton National Park. On the way, look

BABB-PIEGAN

START

BORDER TO BORDER
Until 1992, U.S. 89 ran all the way south to the Mexican border at Nogales.

LITTLE BELT MOUNTAINS
Stretch your legs on a short hike to Memorial Falls in the heart of the mountains.

233 MILES

JENNY LAKE

A turnoff at Moose leads to the lake, with mesmerizing views of the Teton range.

587 MILES

SALT RIVER PASS OVERLOOK

Enjoy one last startling view of the Wyoming Rockies.

694 MILES

SALT LAKE CITY

The best place to learn about the Mormons and the city's founder, Brigham Young.

882 MILES

out for deer, moose, and bears. In Grand Teton, the scenery takes center stage, with a great ridge of sawtooth pinnacles, some 12,000 ft (3,660 m) high. The towering peaks are reflected in a series of clear blue mountain lakes—the hiking trails around Jenny Lake are especially stunning. The highway exits the park at the friendly cowboy town of Jackson, where in summer actors stage Western gunfights in the town square.

When the smoke clears, hop back behind the wheel and continue south along the Grand Canyon of the Snake River, famed for fishing, white-water rafting, and kayaking, before crossing the Salt River Range into Star Valley.

The route twists and turns over a series of passes and forest-smothered canyons, many with stunning viewpoints such as Salt River Pass Scenic Overlook.

After passing through Idaho, there are two more ranges to cross before the halfway point in the journey. The Logan Canyon Scenic Byway cuts through the Bear River Range to Logan, home of Utah State University, before the highway makes a final swerve across the Wellsville Mountains down to Brigham City and the heart of Mormon country.

The Mormons settled in Utah in the 19th century, their neat, prosperous towns marked by wide streets and distinctive spire-topped churches and temples. The biggest settlement is Salt Lake City itself, its skyline dominated by the fairytale Salt Lake Utah Temple and the elegant State Capitol.

INTO THE COLORADO PLATEAU

Just beyond Provo, the highway rises once again, this time into the dry hills of the Colorado Plateau and the scattered remains of Thistle, a ghost town abandoned in the 1980s. From here U.S. 89 slices through the center of Utah via the Sanpete and Sevier valleys, both peppered by Mormon farms and ranches. The landscape is much drier now, the hills parched and brown, especially in summer.

THE LATTER-DAY SAINTS

U.S. 89 slices through the heartlands of the Church of Jesus Christ of Latter-day Saints, better known as the Mormons. Based in Salt Lake City, the church was actually established in New York State by Joseph Smith in 1830. Conflict with other settlers pushed the movement westward, and Brigham Young led Mormon pioneers to modern-day Utah in 1847.

1,093 MILES

CIRCLEVILLE

Visit the humble wood cabin in which outlaw Butch Cassidy grew up in the late 1860s.

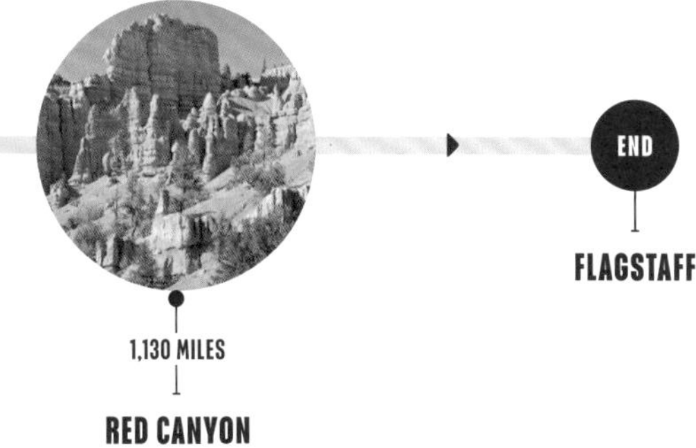

1,130 MILES

RED CANYON

A short detour leads to the red sandstone spires of Utah's most photogenic natural wonder.

END

FLAGSTAFF

In Circleville, you'll spot Butch Cassidy's humble childhood home, and at the southern end of the Sevier Valley a series of roads branch off the highway for some of the West's greatest wonders: the sandstone spires of Red Canyon; Zion and Bryce Canyon national parks; and the twisted rock formations at Cedar Breaks National Monument.

THE OLD WEST

South of Mount Carmel, the landscape changes dramatically again, with orangey sands pockmarked by scrub and sagebrush. At Kanab, there's a choice of routes into Arizona, each offering mesmerizing desert scenery. Either stay on the U.S. 89 through the southern Utah desert or take the 89A via the Kaibab Plateau and the spectacular Vermilion Cliffs. The routes merge south of Page for the final run, through the candy-colored rock formations of the Painted Desert and the lands of the Navajo Nation. This is the Old West of popular imagination, with red rock outcrops and hoodoos, sagebrush and cactus, and Navajo trading posts hemmed in by crumbling cliffs. Slowly, the highway begins to rise for a final time through more temperate, wooded country before arriving at Flagstaff—the gateway to the Grand Canyon, 75 miles (120 km) to the north.

LEFT Bizarrely eroded pinnacles at Cedar Breaks National Monument

BELOW Exploring the Vermilion Cliffs in southern Utah

OPPOSITE Rafting on Grand Canyon of the Snake River

This is the Old West of popular imagination, with red rock outcrops and hoodoos, and Navajo trading posts hemmed in by crumbling cliffs.

BEARTOOTH HIGHWAY

Red Lodge ▸ Cooke City

START/FINISH
Red Lodge, Montana/ Cooke City, Montana

DISTANCE
65 miles (110 km)

DURATION
2–4 hours

ROAD CONDITIONS
Paved roads, with plenty of switchbacks

THE BEST TIME TO GO
Mid-May to mid-October, weather conditions permitting

OPPOSITE The highway winding across the barren plateau up to Beartooth Pass

Rising to nearly 11,000 ft (3,355 m) above sea level, this short but stunning drive takes in everything from lodgepole pine forests to Arctic-like tundra. At the summit await alpine lakes, wildflowers, and even snow in summer.

Connecting central Montana with Yellowstone National Park, the Beartooth Highway (also known as U.S. 212), has been dubbed America's most beautiful road. It certainly delivers plenty of thrills, climbing 5,000 ft (1,525 m) up from the plains, via jaw-dropping switchbacks and overlooks, with snow and ice at the highest pass, even in midsummer.

The highway officially begins in Red Lodge, a former coal-mining town at the foot of the mountains. Tourism drives the economy today, with nearby Red Lodge Mountain a popular ski resort and the Beartooth Highway pulling in road-trippers. The main drag, Broadway Avenue, is lined with Old West-style saloons, restaurants, and art galleries.

UP TO THE PLATEAU

Leaving civilization far behind, the highway runs southwest from Red Lodge, along Rock Creek Valley and cutting into the dense Custer Gallatin National Forest. After around 15 miles (25 km), it begins to rise, with craggy outcrops visible on the far side of the valley.

Your first major switchback zigzags up in an amazing feat of engineering, as the road—lined with steel guardrails, thankfully—covers several thousand feet in just a few miles. At the top, stretch your legs at Vista Point Observation Site, a heady 9,190 ft (2,800 m) above sea level. The rocky promontory provides 360-degree views of the Rock Creek Canyon far below and of Hellroaring Plateau on the other side, a spellbinding panorama of steep slopes and cliffs scarred by landslides and rockfalls and pitted with dark green forest. Look out

RED LODGE

START

RED LODGE
Fuel up at Red Box Car, a Red Lodge diner known for its "box car burgers" and shakes.

0 MILES

VISTA POINT OBSERVATION SITE
Take in the mesmerizing views from Vista Point Observation Site.

20 MILES

LEFT Mountain goats on the Beartooth Plateau

BELOW Alpine Gardner Lake

OPPOSITE The granite crag of Bears Tooth peak, rising distinct from the rest of the Beartooth Mountains

for wildlife: marmots and chipmunks scurry between the rocks, and bighorn sheep, mountain goats, and deer are sometimes spied grazing in the distance.

ON TOP OF THE WORLD

Beyond the Quad Creek overlook, the highway snakes across the bleak Beartooth Plateau. Above the tree line, it's barren tundra—cold and windswept—the landscape lightened by patches of snow and wildflowers in high summer. All around you loom the peaks of the Absaroka and Beartooth mountains—20 reaching over 12,000 ft (3,650 m) high.

The road crosses into Wyoming at the 45th Parallel, passing high above the navy blue Twin Lakes and on to the Beartooth Basin Summer Ski Area. Just around the next bend lies Gardner Lake Pullout, the best place to view its namesake lake far below, a blue sliver hemmed in by scree-lined slopes.

As the highway approaches the highest pass, look out for a small sign on the right: the two posts here frame a distant view of the Bears Tooth, the pyramidal spire of rock that gives the range its name. A little farther and you'll reach the top: Beartooth Pass. Stop at the viewpoint here and soak up the scenery, embrace the icy winds, and inhale the scent of pine wafting up from the valleys below. At 10,947 ft (3,337 m) up, the vast expanse of the Absaroka-

BEARTOOTH PLATEAU

Wildflowers and patches of snow dot the landscape on the Beartooth Plateau.

23 MILES

BEARTOOTH PASS VISTA

You're on top of the world: take in the panorama, at almost 11,000 ft (3,350 m).

31 MILES

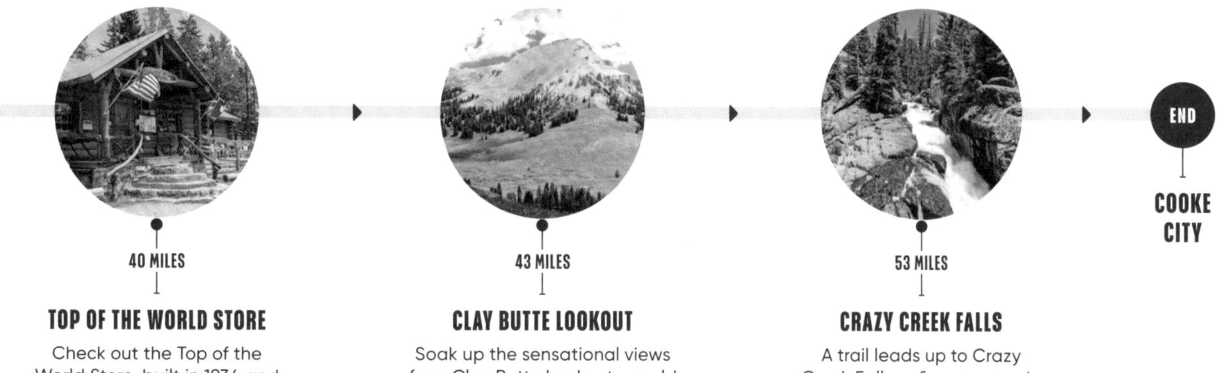

40 MILES

TOP OF THE WORLD STORE

Check out the Top of the World Store, built in 1934 and moved here in the 1960s.

43 MILES

CLAY BUTTE LOOKOUT

Soak up the sensational views from Clay Butte Lookout, an old fire tower built in 1942.

53 MILES

CRAZY CREEK FALLS

A trail leads up to Crazy Creek Falls, a fierce cascade peppered with fallen trees.

END

COOKE CITY

Beartooth Wilderness is laid out before you: tiny lakes, deep gorges, and snowy summits—including Granite Peak, the highest in Montana. On a clear day, the clouds seem close enough to touch, the dark blue skies contrasting with gem-like corries, deeply gouged granite walls, and huge blocks of roadside ice. The halfway point on your journey, the pass is a stunning place for a picnic if you've packed your thermals—even in high summer, much of the tundra is blanketed in snow. Thanks to the local algae, the snow turns pink when crushed.

DESCENT TO COOKE CITY

Another series of switchbacks brings you down below the tree line again, to a plateau sprinkled with enchanting alpine lakes. After the Island Lake Campground, you reach the incongruous Top of the World Store, a log cabin crammed with souvenirs at 9,396 ft (2,864 m). The store, moved here in 1964, was originally built on nearby Beartooth Lake, a popular spot for kayaking and hiking against the backdrop of Beartooth Butte.

A little farther on, a 3-mile (5-km) detour along a gravel road takes you to the Clay Butte Lookout. The 1940s fire tower offers closer views of Granite Peak and houses displays about the wildfires that devastated this region in 1988. Back on the main road, Yellowstone Overlook provides your first glimpse of the distinctive pointed summits of Pilot and Index peaks.

The route continues west, down into the Clark's Fork River Valley, where it begins its final run up through thick forests back into Montana. On the way, you'll get good views at the Clark's Fork Overlook, and can stop at the frothy Lake Falls and Crazy Creek Falls. In late summer, patches of yellow aspen trees contrast with the background of dark mountains in the distance.

Civilization re-emerges at Cooke City, a one-street town surrounded by the steep slopes of Soda Butte Creek Valley. This ex-mining camp mainly serves tourists to Yellowstone these days, but its timber motels and cafés still have heaps of Western charm. Celebrate a successful drive with a juicy buffalo burger, bowl of chili, or plate of smoked trout at the Beartooth Café, toasting the trip with a local huckleberry hard cider.

THE BEARS TOOTH

The inspiration for the name of the Beartooth Mountains (and the highway) allegedly comes from a striking peak to the west of the road. Known to the Indigenous Apsáalooke (Crow) people as "Na Piet Say," or "Bears Tooth," the distant spike—visible from the highway—does indeed resemble a sharp bear canine.

GRAND TETON TO YELLOWSTONE

Moose ▸ Mammoth Springs

START/FINISH
Moose, Wyoming/ Mammoth Springs, Wyoming

DISTANCE
135 miles (215 km)

DURATION
2–3 days

ROAD CONDITIONS
Well-maintained paved roads, with winter closures

THE BEST TIME TO GO
Spring or fall to avoid snow and congestion

OPPOSITE The incredible colors of Yellowstone National Park's Grand Prismatic Spring

This south-to-north route slices through two of the U.S.'s most spectacular national parks. Grand Teton and Yellowstone have it all: famous geysers, snowy peaks, alpine lakes, bison, and grizzlies. Come and enjoy the show.

Connecting the soaring peaks and mountain lakes of Grand Teton National Park with the geothermal wonders of Yellowstone, this scenic route begins in Moose, the southern entrance to Grand Teton. Teton Park Road breaks off U.S. 191 to cross the wide, deep blue Snake River here—and if it's warm, you'd be forgiven for temporarily ditching the wheels for a float downriver in a kayak or canoe.

EXPLORING GRAND TETON

Leaving Moose, you cross the wide, sagebrush plains of Jackson Hole, Snake River's broad "valley," which dominates the southern half of the park. Far to the east lie the Gros Ventre Mountains, while the Grand Tetons themselves command the horizon to the northwest. Teton Glacier Turnout offers your first iconic photo opportunity, with the main Teton peaks rising from the massif like jagged fangs—the tiny, glistening patch of white in the center is all that remains of the Teton Glacier.

A few minutes north, you reach brilliantly clear Jenny Lake—this is the closest you'll get to the main Teton range without hiking. If time allows, take a scenic cruise or catch the shuttle across for hikes deep into the mountains. On the lake's southern side, the two tiny Moose Ponds really do attract moose, while local patches of thimbleberries are popular with black bears in the summer.

Keep the camera handy as you continue north on Teton Park Road—more iconic views await at the Mountain View and Mount Moran turnouts—before slicing into the thick pine woods that

MOOSE

START

MOOSE
An ideal spot for floating or kayaking down the Snake River.

0 MILES

TETON GLACIER TURNOUT
Soak up your first view of the jagged, snowcapped Grand Teton range.

5 MILES

MOUNTAIN VIEW TURNOUT
Get an iconic view of the whole Grand Teton Range at Mountain View Turnout.

10 MILES

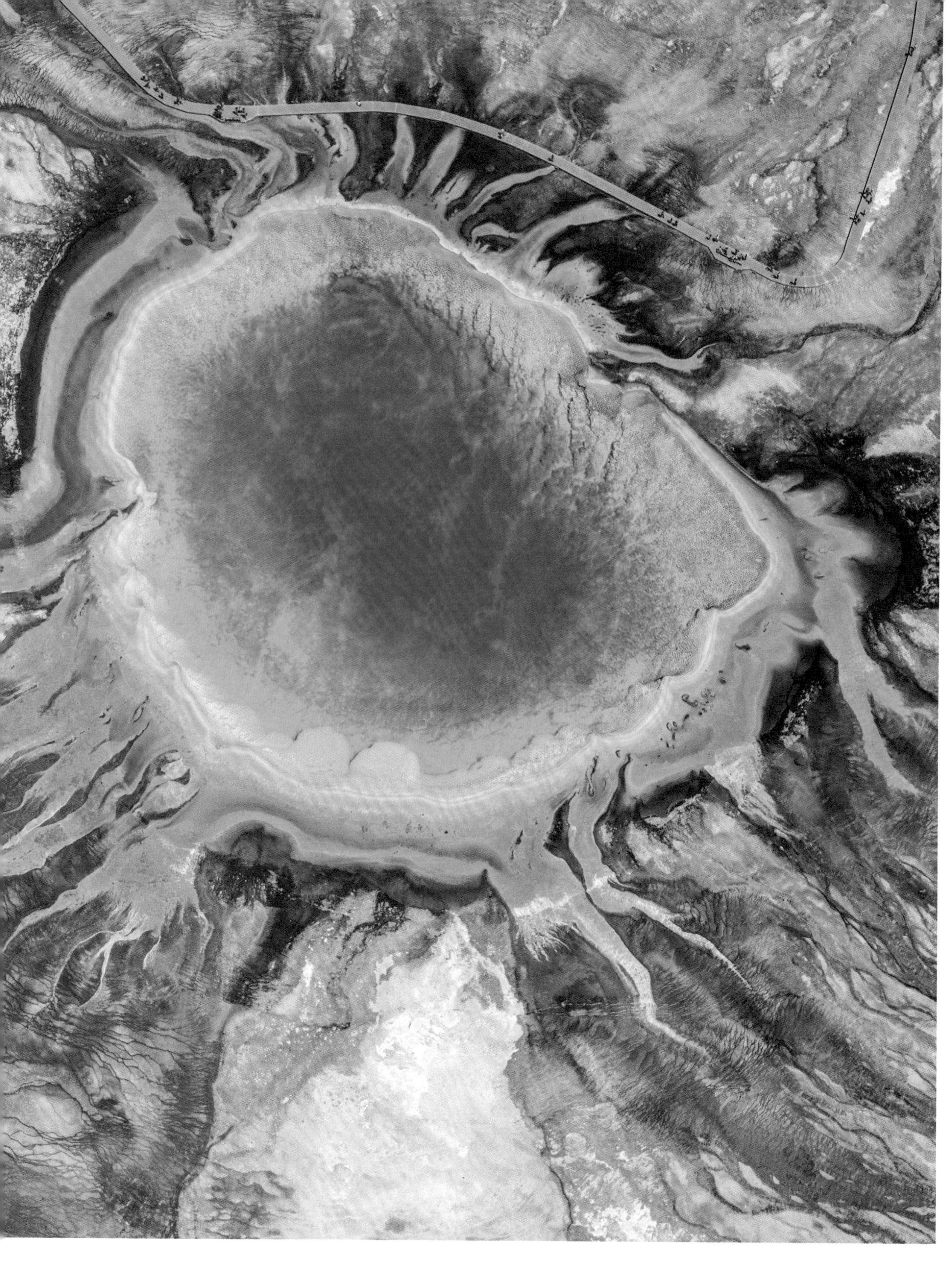

JACKSON LAKE LODGE

A 1950s gem, this lodge has fantastic panoramic views from its back terrace.

18 MILES

COLTER BAY VILLAGE

Enjoy barbecue delights at the family-friendly John Colter's Ranch House.

24 MILES

WEST THUMB

See hot springs fizzing into Yellowstone Lake at West Thumb Geyser Basin.

65 MILES

surround Jackson Lake, the park's biggest body of water. The main route crosses the Snake River again at Jackson Lake Dam, where the forest falls away and wide, open lake views across to the Tetons reappear.

Just after you rejoin U.S. 191, you'll pass Jackson Lake Lodge, a gorgeous 1950s hotel with grand panoramas, before reaching Colter Bay Village, a stop for supplies or cruises on Jackson Lake.

INTO YELLOWSTONE

Soon, you leave the lake—and Grand Teton National Park—behind, as the highway winds through the forests of the upper Snake Valley. After passing the Flagg Ranch Information Station, it slips into Yellowstone National Park at the South Entrance. The road rises gently through dense pine forest, passing Lewis Falls and tranquil Lewis Lake before crossing the Continental Divide at 7,988 ft (2,435 m). Follow the road as it drops slightly into the main Yellowstone crater, a massive geothermal caldera, some 45 miles (70 km) wide. Thankfully, it hasn't exploded for 640,000 years.

A few miles ahead, you get your first real glimpse of the deceptively calm Yellowstone Lake—North America's largest alpine lake—at Grant Village Visitor Center. A vast expanse of blue, it sits at 7,733 ft (2,357 m) above sea level.

THE GRAND LOOP

It's a short drive up the shoreline to West Thumb, where you take the left-hand fork for the more scenic west side of the "Grand" loop. This leads you high above the lake before descending through forest to the Upper Geyser Basin where Old Faithful awaits. On average, this iconic geyser blows every 65 to 92 minutes. Here, you can also eat at the historic Old Faithful Inn, and explore the trails along the steaming Firehole River, where the massive Grand Geyser explodes just twice daily.

The Grand Loop Road continues down the river to the Midway Geyser

BIG BEASTS

More than 1,000 grizzly bears are thought to live in Yellowstone. Over 100 gray wolves and just under 5,000 bison also inhabit the park.

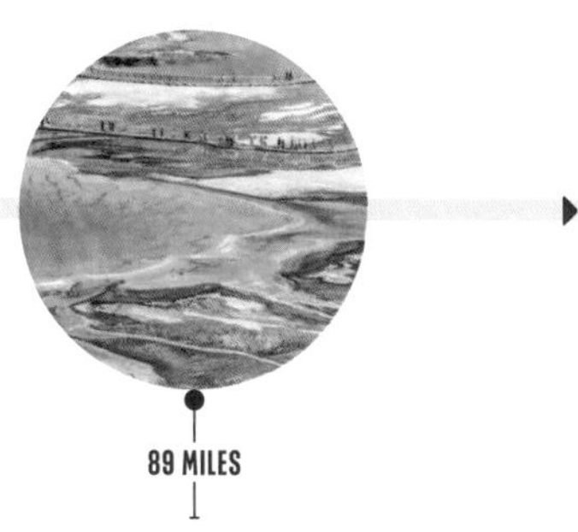

89 MILES

GRAND PRISMATIC SPRING

Stop at the Midway Geyser Basin to view the pool surrounded by colored bands.

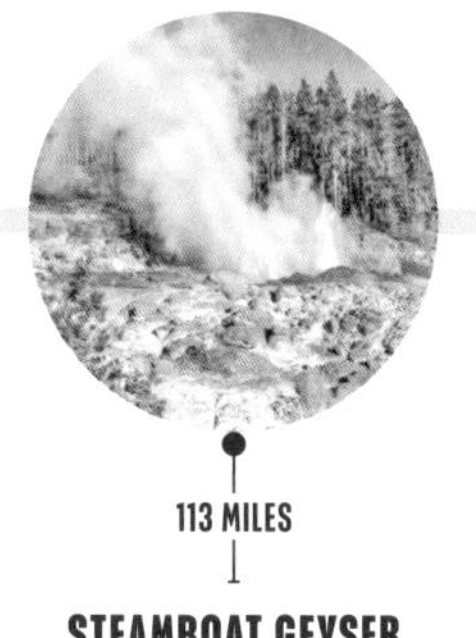

113 MILES

STEAMBOAT GEYSER

The Norris Geyser Basin is pitted with fumaroles, including the tallest geyser in the world.

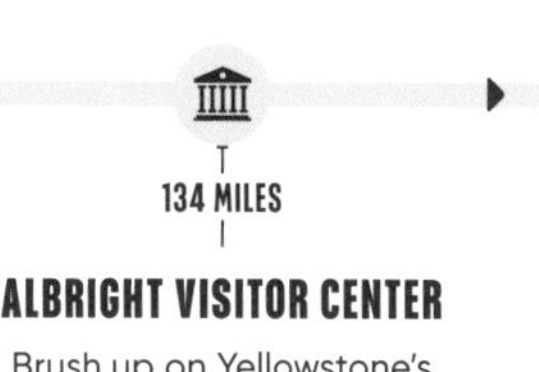

134 MILES

ALBRIGHT VISITOR CENTER

Brush up on Yellowstone's human past at this museum, housed in a historic building.

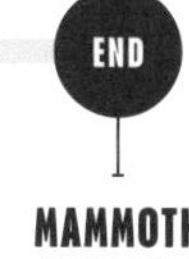

MAMMOTH SPRINGS

Basin, another sulfur-scented geothermal area. It's best known for the Grand Prismatic Spring, a steaming pool surrounded by bands of turquoise, yellow, orange, and brown, in an otherwise blasted volcanic landscape of mud and white ash. From high up, it looks like a giant blue eye, with tangerine tendrils stretching out on all sides. It's a farther 25 miles (40 km) of winding road to the Norris Geyser Basin, another ashy white landscape of steaming fumaroles, whistling vents, and geysers: highlights include Steamboat, the world's tallest geyser (sometimes blowing up to 300 ft/90 m), and Echinus, which produces vinegary eruptions of acid-water every 35 to 75 minutes.

ON TO MAMMOTH HOT SPRINGS

From here, the highway cuts due north to the park village of Mammoth Hot Springs, where elk are often seen grazing nonchalantly on the grass in the colder months. Visit the Albright Visitor Center and Museum to learn about the park's human history, but the main attraction is the namesake hot springs. End your Yellowstone odyssey by admiring the travertine terraces of barnacle-like deposits they create. Stained green, gold, brown, and orange by algae, the springs are the last in a long line of geothermal wonders on this epic trip.

ABOVE Treading the boardwalk at Norris Geyser Basin

RIGHT Travertine terraces at Mammoth Hot Springs

OPPOSITE The Teton Range, towering above Jackson Lake

THE MIGHTY 5

Zion National Park
Moab

START/FINISH
Moab, Utah/Zion National Park, Utah

DISTANCE
410 miles (660 km)

DURATION
5–7 days

ROAD CONDITIONS
Paved state and federal highways; National Parks contain a mix of pavement and off-road terrain

THE BEST TIME TO GO
Spring, to see the desert in full bloom, or fall for perfect temperatures

OPPOSITE The Moab desert, glowing red beneath the evening sun

Check off some of the United States' most beautiful national parks on an enchanting desert odyssey through Southern Utah, taking in red-rock canyons, dusty mesas, and otherworldly sandstone formations.

Stringing together the five national parks of Utah's canyon country—Arches, Canyonlands, Capitol Reef, Bryce Canyon, and Zion—the Mighty 5 is an epic roam through the American West. But this isn't about collecting stamps in your national parks passport. It's a road trip of cinematic character, with open desert highways, mysterious landscapes, and a sense of unbridled freedom. Its siren call has lured explorers, artists, outlaws, and outcasts for centuries.

MOAB OR MARS?

Your journey starts in Moab, an oasis with a Mars-like setting of towering rock spires, dominating buttes, and gravity-defying arches. Set in a narrow valley, this former uranium-mining hub is now a basecamp for all things outdoors, with superb mountain biking, rock climbing, and white-water rafting on its doorstep. It's also the gateway to the first two National Parks on your journey: Arches and Canyonlands.

Start with a stroll along Moab's Main Street, populated by art galleries, organic co-ops, and tourists donning newly minted Patagonia jackets and hiking boots. Once you're ready to hit the road, head out of town on U.S. 191 for the 5-mile (8-km) drive to the entrance for Arches. You'll likely need to wait in line to enter the park, but don't let this kill your momentum. Once through the gates, the road immediately begins switchbacking up a cliff face in dramatic fashion. At the top, you're greeted with looming columns, balanced rocks that seem to defy the laws of physics, and

MOAB

MOAB
Shop authentic Indigenous artwork and jewelry at Lema's Kokopelli Gallery.

0 MILES

ARCHES NATIONAL PARK
Landscape Arch, the longest in the park, is a natural arch spanning 306 ft (93 m).

5 MILES

EXTEND YOUR TRIP

Make a loop by completing the Grand Circle, an extension of The Mighty 5 that takes you through four more Southwestern states, with stops at the Grand Canyon, Four Corners, Monument Valley, Mesa Verde, and other noteworthy sites along the way.

more than 2,000 of the rock arches that give the park its name.

In spring, blooms of prickly pear cactus, globemallow, and Indian paintbrush coat the desert with bright oranges, deep reds, and cheerful pinks. Lizards scurry through sandy washes, and Hopi chipmunks seek out pools of rain. Make time to explore on foot, whether trekking to Delicate Arch or navigating the maze-like Fiery Furnace.

You could easily spend days in Arches, but Canyonlands is calling your name. On the half-hour drive, you'll be treated to sweeping views of striated sandstone and the Monitor and Merrimac buttes. The road narrows and climbs until it flattens out at the top of Island in the Sky, a peninsula-shaped mesa sitting high above the Green and Colorado rivers. In the park, 1,000-ft (305-m) sandstone cliffs tower over the network of canyons below, which hold treasures for those who venture into them, from ghostlike rock art to the ruins of ancient Indigenous dwellings.

THE HIGHWAY TO HANKSVILLE

It might feel like you're on another planet, but the truth is you've barely left the county, so it's time to hit the road once more. Leave the park the way you came and take 191 north to the I-70 intersection (a 20 minute detour east to Sego Canyon offers easy-to-spot petroglyphs). Heading west, after a brief stint on a four-lane, you'll soon return to the quieter backroads. The rock cliffs and mesas soften, giving way to loosely defined dirt hills. State Route 24 takes you through miles of immensely beautiful yet barren gray-brown hills. This is cowboy country, the land of The Eagles and The Highwaymen, where you catch yourself praying you don't run out of gas.

The little town of Hanksville provides an answer to your prayers. Fill up your car and stomach at Hollow Mountain,

CANYONLANDS NATIONAL PARK

In a park that's all about the vistas, there's none better than the one from Grand View Point.

31 MILES

SEGO CANYON

This preserved ghost town is the perfect detour to view petroglyphs.

81 MILES

HANKSVILLE

It took 2.5 tons (2.2 tonnes) of dynamite to carve store space for Hollow Mountain.

196 MILES

CAPITOL REEF

Snack on homemade pies at Gifford Homestead, an old Mormon settlement in the park.

216 MILES

TORREY

Utah's first International Dark Sky Community, Torrey is an ideal spot for stargazing.

254 MILES

BOULDER

Hell's Backbone Grill and Farm offers fine dining in one of the U.S.'s most remote towns.

a convenience store carved into the face of a rock, with a gas station positioned out front. You're not the only one who has stocked up here over the years; it was known as a supply post for outlaw Butch Cassidy, who used to hide out in the canyons of nearby Robbers Roost in the late 1800s.

OPPOSITE Posing under the freestanding Delicate Arch

BELOW A roadside barn in Fruita, a Mormon settlement

BELOW RIGHT The rugged Grand Staircase-Escalante National Monument

CAPITOL REEF AND BEYOND

Thirty minutes west, the road enters Capitol Reef National Park and is transformed into a scenic byway through the Waterpocket Fold, a "wrinkle" in the earth's crust birthing more red rock formations. The park offers interesting insights into pioneer life in the region, particularly at Fruita, an 1880s Mormon settlement with orchards, barns, a schoolhouse, and an old homestead that still serves freshly baked pies and ice cream (enjoyed best in the desert).

As you leave Capitol Reef, pass through Torrey, a high-altitude outpost that conjures up images of the Old West with its general stores, trading posts, and Western-themed glamping resorts, where you can sleep and unwind in luxury replicas of tepees and covered wagons. The town's higher elevation means cooler temperatures, tree-lined streets, and the occasional meadow—a welcome respite from the heat and harsh landscape.

In the West, a change in altitude can whisk you from wasteland to pine trees in a matter of miles—which is exactly what scenic byway U.T. 12 does, as it carries you up to 9,000 ft (2,745 m). Travel through Boulder, one of the nation's most remote towns—and the unexpected location of a farm-to-table James Beard nominee, Hell's Backbone Grill. The Hogback, a narrow spine of road, delivers you back into red rock country in the town of Escalante, home to the Grand Staircase-Escalante National Monument, petrified forests, and dozens of slot canyons.

THROUGH BRYCE CANYON TO ZION

With three parks already under your belt, your next stop is Bryce Canyon, famous for having the highest concentration of hoodoos on earth. As if formed by a child drizzling wet sand by the sea, these naturally carved rock columns take on

383 MILES

MOUNT CARMEL JUNCTION

Chow down on burritos at the Thunderbird Restaurant, a classic American diner.

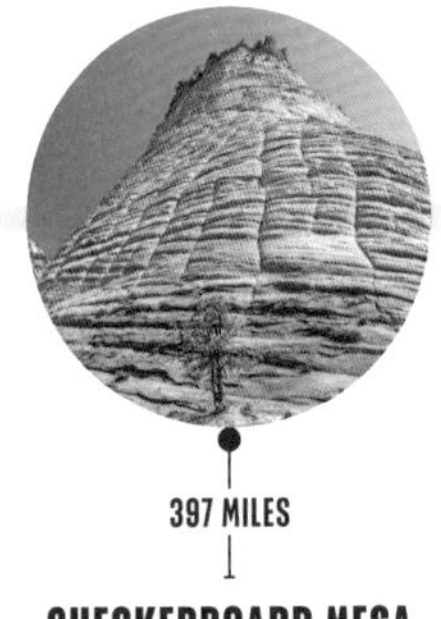

397 MILES

CHECKERBOARD MESA

This 6,520-ft (1,985-m) sandstone peak is a popular spot with bighorn sheep.

409 MILES

ZION NATIONAL PARK LODGE

Catch up on some R&R at Zion's in-park lodge with epic views of the surrounding canyon.

ZION NATIONAL PARK

mythical shapes, giving them an almost spiritual air that's underscored by names like "Thor's Hammer" and "The Hunter."

Make your way to Sunrise Point for stunning vistas of Bryce's amphitheater, a bowl-shaped collection of pink-tinted pillars. The sun's rays act like a paintbrush on the canyon walls, turning them fiery orange in midday light or deep shades of purple in the diffused beams of sunset. On clear days, you can see all the way to Arizona and New Mexico, and on clear nights, you can watch the Milky Way cut across the sky. Several hikes depart from Sunrise Point, ranging in difficulty and length, making for an opportunity to stretch your legs before beginning the final—and shortest—leg of your drive to Zion National Park.

Blood pumping, exit Bryce on U.T. 12 to U.S. 89 and travel south through arid grasslands populated by ranches and RV parks until you get to Mount Carmel Junction, a no-stoplight, unincorporated town with limited amenities. From here, the crossroads direct you onto the U.T. 9, a National Scenic Byway, into Zion.

Landmarks herald your arrival, including Checkerboard Mesa, a frozen sand dune with a net-like pattern of lines carved into the stone, and the mile-long Zion-Mount Carmel Tunnel (don't try to hold your breath for this one). Once out the other side, you're at the top of Zion Canyon, the final destination on this desert pilgrimage. Switchbacks take you down through the red rock walls to the canyon's floor, the sparkling Virgin River, and the main visitor center by the town of Springdale.

THE MIGHTY FINALE

Once in Zion, it's time to let someone else take the wheel. The park uses shuttles to transport you through the canyon, allowing you to sit back and enjoy the ride. There will be plenty of time to wade in the waters of The Narrows, live on the edge at Angels Landing, or look for bighorn sheep; for now, unwind in the shade with a much-deserved brew from Zion Brewery, or an earthy cocktail made with herbs grown at the Zion Lodge.

LEGEND PEOPLE

Paiute folklore states Bryce Canyon's hoodoos were once living members of the Legend People—humanoid birds, lizards, and other animals that were turned into rock as punishment for their evil deeds. This earned the area an Indigenous name meaning "red painted faces."

BELOW Wading through the shallow waters of The Narrows

RV LIFE

For lots of folks, the urge to hit the road is matched by an equal and opposite impulse to just stay home. Out there, freedom and adventure. In here, a comfy bed and all your stuff.

Almost as soon as Americans had highways, they were looking for ways to take home with them. Travelers and garage tinkerers began creating what would later be known as recreational vehicles (RVs) even before the first Model T rolled off the assembly line. The RV was a 1904 hand-built contraption with four bunks and space for an icebox. The concept took a major leap forward in 1915, when Roland and Mary Conklin set off on a cross-country trip with their family in a custom-built 25-ft (7.5-m), 8-ton vehicle that had sleeping berths, a kitchen, a generator, and several small appliances. Media coverage of their journey made the concept of a home on wheels an object of national fascination.

More than a century later, that fascination hasn't abated. Social media feeds are filled with #vanlife or #rvlife, and numerous publications cover topics such as models and decor. RV sales have climbed steadily since 1980, and they boomed during the COVID-19 pandemic, when nothing could provide the combination of isolation and escapism quite like an RV.

Today, some 40 million Americans travel with an RV each year. For many, RVs are a ready-made vacation, offering all the pleasures of camping with none of the inconveniences. For the hopelessly footloose, they're a way to work remotely. And as Chloé Zhao's film *Nomadland* depicted, RV life is also an option for people who reject more "traditional" ways of living, or a refuge for those with tricky economic circumstances.

RVs have come a long way from their home-garage origins. Contemporary options range from tent trailers and camper vans to multi-bedroom motor coaches. If you've got the money, you're really only limited by what the highway can handle. Case in point, movie star Vin Diesel used to roll in a 1,200-sq-ft (110-sq-m) trailer that included a full kitchen, two lounges, and a bathroom with marble countertops. That's enough to make even the Conklins jealous.

Today, some 40 million Americans travel with an RV each year. For many, RVs are a ready-made vacation, offering all the pleasures of camping with none of the inconveniences.

ABOVE An RV driving through tall redwood forests

TRAIL OF THE ANCIENTS

Albuquerque ▸ Albuquerque

START/FINISH
Albuquerque, New Mexico/Albuquerque, New Mexico

DISTANCE
950 miles (1,530 km)

DURATION
5–7 days

ROAD CONDITIONS
Most roads are paved, but a 4WD vehicle is recommended

THE BEST TIME TO GO
Fall, when the heat subsides and Albuquerque hosts its famous balloon fiesta

OPPOSITE Taking in the sweeping spires of Monument Valley

Ruins of ancient pueblo villages are a feature of this route through Monument Valley, but much of the drive is also through modern Indigenous reservation land. Slip behind the wheel and get ready to take in the past and present.

The Trail of the Ancients begins in the metropolis of Albuquerque, New Mexico. Founded by European settlers in 1706, the city's Spanish roots can be found in Old Town Albuquerque, which preserves many of the historic adobe buildings that originally made up the settlement.

Indigenous peoples existed here long before Europeans, of course, and their history is best explored on the outskirts of town. Hop in the car from Old Town, and drive around 5 miles (8 km) to Petroglyphs National Monument, crossing over the Rio Grande as you go. Surrounded by suburban Albuquerque, this sacred park preserves some 25,000 examples of ancient rock art, several of which are believed to have been drawn by the ancient Puebloan people as far back as 2000 BCE. With multiple trails to choose from, ditch the car and don the hiking boots, keeping your eyes peeled for engravings (and rattlesnakes).

INTO THE HIGH DESERT

The spectacular high desert west of Albuquerque is mostly reservation land. Set against a red-rock butte, Casamero Pueblo, your next stop, was built between 1000 and 1125 CE and serves as a preview for nearby Chaco Canyon, just 90 minutes north along a roughly paved road. A massive site, spanning about 35,000 acres (14,000 hectares), Chaco Culture National Historical Park was once the center of the area's ancient world. Consisting of 13 major structures and hundreds of smaller ones, it is thought to have been inhabited between 850 and 1250 CE.

ALBUQUERQUE

OLD TOWN ALBUQUERQUE
Stroll past shops and historic buildings in Old Town Albuquerque.
0 MILES

PETROGLYPHS NATIONAL MONUMENT
Marvel at countless examples of ancient rock art.
5 MILES

RIGHT Mesa Verde's incredible Cliff Palace

BELOW Reconstructed houses at Salmon Ruins Museum

BOTTOM Ruins at Hovenweep National Monument

OPPOSITE Hiking in the rugged Canyon de Chelly

As you continue north on U.S. 550, the stark white-and-red rock landscapes morph into something akin to grassland. The grounds surrounding Salmon Ruins Museum in Bloomfield are particularly verdant. This educational site features an excavated village and reconstructed dwellings, while the city itself is a great place to stock up on snacks and gas before hitting the road again.

Motor north for 20 minutes on U.S. 550 to the Aztec Ruins National Monument. The "Great House" at this site became the main cultural center in the area after the decline of the community at Chaco.

INTO COLORADO AND UTAH

Drive across the state border and exchange the blooms of New Mexico for the mountains of Colorado. Pass through the Ute reservation toward Mesa Verde National Park, which has some of the best preserved examples of cliff dwellings in the country. The most impressive, Cliff Palace, is a 150-room complex set back in a cavern, under an overhang of red rocks. Want to discover more about the people who built these cities? Visit the Canyons of the Ancients Visitor Center and Museum, located just an hour from the site at Mesa Verde. It's one of the premier museums in the state covering Indigenous history.

Mind sufficiently boggled, head west on County Road 10 to Utah, where the dusty desert landscape returns, punctuated by dramatically towering buttes. Swing by the Hovenweep National Monument, a must-visit in spring, when the seemingly barren landscape comes alive with beautiful wildflowers. Natural Bridges National Monument, 75 miles (120 km) farther east, also showcases beauty that is not human made. Although its three

237 MILES

AZTEC RUINS NATIONAL MONUMENT

Learn more about Indigenous crops on the Native Plant Trail.

368 MILES

HOVENWEEP NATIONAL MONUMENT

The wildflowers here form a spectacular backdrop in spring.

443 MILES

NATURAL BRIDGES NATIONAL MONUMENT

The first International Dark Sky Park in the world.

enormous rock formations look like they have been carved, they're actually formed by water erosion. They're not the only thing worth seeing here—the area is the world's first International Dark Sky Park. On a clear night, the sheer number of stars visible is astonishing.

MONUMENT VALLEY

Your final stop in Utah is the Valley of the Gods, where dramatic red-rock buttes jut from the desert floor, before you're off into Arizona and the equally jaw-dropping Monument Valley. Scientists reckon these majestic sandstone towers, some of which reach 1,000 ft (305 m) in height, were created millions of years ago when a shallow sea deposited massive formations of ancient sandstones and shale. The local Navajo people, however, believe that the spires contain the souls of warriors and consider them sacred.

Continue farther south into Arizona and the heart of the Navajo Nation along the desolate Navajo Service Route 59, with its impressive mountain views. The road eventually brings you to the small town of Many Farms, where you can stretch your legs and refill your tank before stopping at Canyon de Chelly National Monument to snap Spider Rock, a sandstone spire that rises more than 800 ft (245 m) above the canyon floor.

The local Navajo people believe that Monument Valley's spires contain the souls of warriors and consider them sacred.

As you take the hour-and-a-half drive back into New Mexico, make one final stop to view the layers of history engraved into El Morro National Monument, where Indigenous peoples, Spanish conquistadors, and even early American military men all quite literally made their mark on the rocks here.

The small city of Grants, where you link up with I-40 to complete the drive back to Albuquerque, is the first sign that you're back in modern-day America, with a chunk of time-traveling under your belt and a deeper understanding of the Southwest's Indigenous peoples and their rich history.

EXTEND YOUR TRIP

You can lengthen your journey by checking out more of the smaller sites along the route, such as Yucca House National Monument, Bears Ears, or Edge of the Cedars State Park.

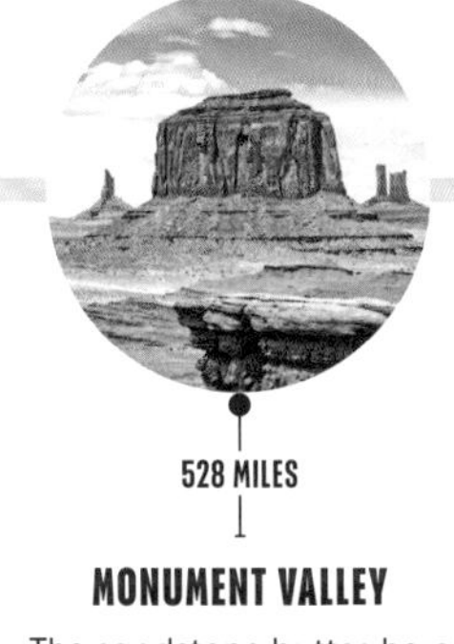

528 MILES

MONUMENT VALLEY

The sandstone buttes here range from 400 to 1,000 ft (120 to 305 m) high.

773 MILES

EL MORRO NATIONAL MONUMENT

Hike up to the carvings at Inscription Rock.

ALBUQUERQUE

HIGH ROAD TO TAOS

Santa Fe ▸ Taos

START/FINISH
Santa Fe, New Mexico/ Taos, New Mexico

DISTANCE
100 miles (160 km)

DURATION
1–2 days

ROAD CONDITIONS
Winding, two-lane highway

THE BEST TIME TO GO
The landscapes of north New Mexico are never more beautiful than fall

OPPOSITE The road wending up toward Taos and the Sangre de Cristo Mountains

The high road to Taos takes visitors through one of the most stunning and unique landscapes in the U.S. High desert gives way to juniper and pinyon forest, in an area known for its thriving Indigenous cultures.

Santa Fe, your journey's starting point, can sometimes feel like a whole different country to the rest of the U.S. The combination of Spanish colonial and Indigenous adobe architecture that makes up much of the city is something you'll only find in the Southwest. Here, this marriage is also reflected in the city's culture, as well as the many art galleries, museums, and markets that draw visitors from around the world.

Stroll through the Historic District, making sure to stop at the Palace of the Governors, where you'll find Indigenous artisans selling handmade pottery, woodwork, and jewelry. Though many places in Santa Fe sell Indigenous "inspired" work, the pieces here are undeniably authentic, as vendors are only allowed to sell their own work or that of a close relative.

NORTH TO TRUCHAS

It would be easy to spend an entire week exploring all that the city has to offer. Give yourself a day or two, but then it's time for Taos. Head north, with the scrub brush and white hills lining the roadside, to your first stop, outside of Española: the Iglesia de la Santa Cruz de la Canada, an adobe-style Catholic church built in 1748.

Along the way here, you'll pass through several pueblos, Indigenous American reservation communities, including the Tewa pueblo of Santa Clara, which lies just a mile (1.5 km) from Santa Cruz de la Canada. Although pueblos are open to visitors, particularly for festivals and community

SANTA FE
START

SANTA FE
Buy authentic Indigenous crafts at the Palace of the Governors, in Santa Fe's Historic District.

0 MILES

ESPAÑOLA
Marvel at the architecture of the Iglesia de la Santa Cruz de la Canada.

25 MILES

Truchas sits on a mesa at the base of Truchas Peak, at over 13,000 ft (3,960 m) high, the second highest in the state.

ABOVE Santuario de Chimayo, a popular pilgrimage spot

LEFT The mesa-top town of Truchas, dusted with snow

OPPOSITE Ancient dwelling in Taos Pueblo

celebrations, it's important to call ahead to confirm and abide by some simple rules of etiquette: don't take photos without permission; don't enter sacred areas such as ceremonial kivas or graveyards; and don't talk or applaud during or after dances or ceremonies.

Heading east out of Española toward Chimayo, you'll notice the hills start to take on a distinctive red cast and that only one side of the road seems to be inhabited. The little town of Chimayo itself is best known for the Santuario de Chimayo, a popular pilgrimage spot. Long before Catholicism arrived with the Spanish, the Indigenous Tewa people came here to visit a (now dried up) hot spring, said to have healing properties. When the church was built in 1813, several priests also experienced miraculous events at this site. Today, people come to gather soil, which is believed to have retained those curative powers. Join them, then make your way to Plaza del Cerro, thought to be the only fortified colonial plaza of its kind remaining in the state of New Mexico.

As you continue northeast out of Chimayo along I-76, you climb in altitude and the valley below becomes a sea of green outside Truchas. This little town sits on a mesa at the base of Truchas Peak, at over 13,000 ft (3,960 m) high, the second highest in the state. Although the town itself isn't much to look at,

CHIMAYO

Join the pilgrims collecting holy dirt at the Santuario de Chimayo, an old hot spring.

33 MILES

PLAZA DEL CERRO

Chimayo's main square is one of the last fortified plazas in the U.S.

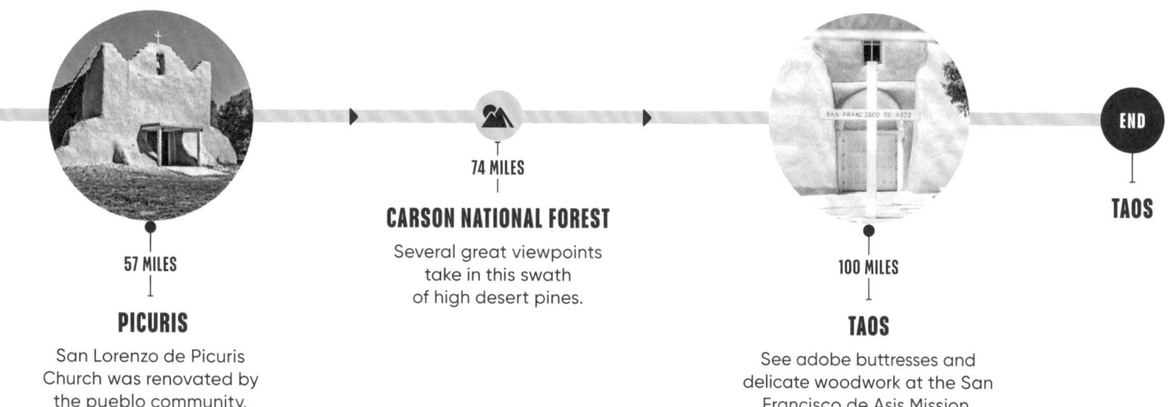

the views both up the mountain and down into the wooded valley below are spectacular. Truchas is also the location of another historic church, the Nuestra Señora del Rosario Church, built in 1805 and featuring some of the oldest *santero* artwork (paintings of saints) in the state.

TO TAOS

Twenty minutes up the road from Truchas, you'll enter the community of Picuris Pueblo. Originally one of the largest pueblos inhabited by the Tewa people, it's now one of the smallest, with a population of a little less than 2,000 people. Even so, the community hosts many annual events that are open to visitors, including the High Country Arts and Crafts Fair and the San Lorenzo Feast Day. They're also responsible for restoring the historic San Lorenzo de Picuris Church, an adobe mission.

To learn more about the history of the local Indigenous peoples, visit Pot Creek Cultural Site, just a 30-minute drive from Picuris, through the lush green pines of Carson National Forest. Built some time in the 13th century, it's believed to be the largest adobe pueblo of its kind north of Santa Fe. The site that's accessible to the public consists of several room blocks, each of which surround their own small plaza and kiva, a round room that is set into the ground and used for spiritual ceremonies. The trail that leads visitors through the site is dotted with placards explaining both the structures you're seeing and the history and culture of the people who built them.

You're less than 10 miles (15 km) from Taos now, but there are still several scenic viewpoints to distract you on your way to your final destination. Once finally in town, take in Taos Plaza, in the center of the Taos Historic District, and the San Francisco de Asis Mission, perhaps the most famous site in Taos. This stunning adobe structure was built in the early 17th century and has been immortalized in paintings by artists such as Georgia O'Keeffe, who called the town home. Historic Taos Pueblo, north of the modern town, is the perfect finale: inhabited for around 1,000 years, its adobe buildings have been designated a UNESCO World Heritage Site.

EXTEND YOUR TRIP

Continue an hour south of Santa Fe to Albuquerque, the largest city in New Mexico. This is a great place to try New Mexican cuisine, featuring the state's numerous chili varieties–a good spot to start is Barelas Coffee Shop, known for its green chili stew.

TRAIL RIDGE ROAD

Estes Park ▸ Grand Lake

START/FINISH
Estes Park, Colorado/ Grand Lake, Colorado

DISTANCE
50 miles (80 km)

DURATION
4–5 hours

ROAD CONDITIONS
Paved two-lane roads; rapidly changing weather is possible

THE BEST TIME TO GO
Summer; the road is closed between mid-October and late May

Drive through the clouds on the highest continuous paved road in the United States, a breathtaking journey into Rocky Mountain National Park's rugged alpine tundra, mesmerizing landscapes, and sky-high summits.

Taking you high into Colorado's Rocky Mountains at an elevation of 12,183 ft (3,713 m), the Trail Ridge Road unlocks a land of extreme terrain and extreme beauty. When it opened in 1932, this route revealed landscapes that were once accessible only to mountaineers. Today, anyone with a vehicle can travel to the park's highest elevations but don't let its relatively easy driving fool you—the weather can turn on a dime, nature is still the boss here; we're just lucky to be her guest.

To get started, pick up U.S. 34 in Estes Park, a quaint village with a lively downtown area, and follow it to the entrance of Rocky Mountain National Park, where it soon becomes Trail Ridge Road. Golden meadows of cottonwoods greet you as you meander along the valley floor, while peaks in the distance tease what's to come. After 15 minutes, you'll spy Sheep Lakes, a popular spot for bighorn sheep and elk, before continuing your ascent 4,600 ft (1,400 m) to the junction of U.S. 36 and U.S. 34.

UP, UP, AND AWAY

The challenge of this drive, with its jaw-dropping views, is keeping your eyes on the road. Stay strong for 4 miles (7 km) before pulling into Many Parks Curve. Follow trails from the parking lot to admire vistas of Moraine Park, a green valley formed by glaciers, and Longs Peak, the highest mountain in the park at 14,259 ft (4,346 m).

Back on the road, a horseshoe bend propels you upward, and in a matter of miles, you climb through three climate

OPPOSITE The curving Trail Ridge Road, climbing toward the peaks and clouds

ESTES PARK

ESTES PARK
Satisfy your sweet tooth at one of Estes Park's taffy, fudge, or ice-cream shops.

0 MILES

MANY PARKS CURVE
Pause to notice how far you've climbed at one of the drive's first dramatic viewpoints.

13 MILES

RAINBOW CURVE OVERLOOK

Sitting on the edge of the treeline, this is the ultimate gateway to the tundra.

17 MILES

TUNDRA COMMUNITIES TRAIL

This accessible alpine hike is especially scenic in spring when the trail's wildflowers bloom.

23 MILES

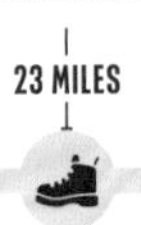

ALPINE VISITOR CENTER

The highest visitor center in the U.S. (11,796 ft/3,595 m) is at the halfway point of your drive.

26 MILES

ABOVE Walking the Tundra Communities Trail

OPPOSITE ABOVE A moose cooling off at Beaver Ponds

OPPOSITE BELOW Blue skies above Grand Lake's shores

zones. In the evergreen montane zone, golden-hour sun filters through the leaves, and breaks in the trees reveal summits growing ever closer. As you enter the subalpine zone, the trees get shorter and thinner, as if they are aging before your eyes.

At Rainbow Curve Overlook, the treeline breaks, and you're transported into a different world: an alpine tundra marked by a dramatic landscape and extreme conditions. Short, tan grass coats the bald hills, and small shrubs poke through rock outcroppings. Its own ecosystem, the tundra is home to rare wildlife: mule deer, marmot, and the camouflaged feathered ptarmigan. Above the trees, you're treated to wonderfully unobstructed views of some of the country's highest peaks. The Rocky Mountains sprawl before you, and snow-covered summits feel close enough to touch.

ALPINE TRAILS

If you decide to stop at Forest Canyon Overlook, around 8 miles (13 km) beyond Rainbow Curve, you'll notice the way the wind roars—unbroken by trees or land—as well as the chill in the air, and the feeling of the oxygen being siphoned out of the atmosphere. A few minutes beyond Forest Canyon Overlook, the Tundra Communities Trail offers walkers of all abilities the chance to experience a hike through the alpine environment. A paved trail leads up a sloping meadow that ascends only 190 ft (60 m) but leaves you huffing and puffing thanks to the altitude. Keep an eye out for miniature wildflowers and the American pika, a small member of the rabbit family that can only be found at high elevations.

Back on the road, you'll know you're nearing the summit when you see a strange break in the tundra: steep, black cliffs formed by prehistoric lava flows. Near the road's peak, the Alpine Visitor Center, the highest visitor center in the U.S., welcomes you with an inviting cup

SERIOUS SNOW

It takes around 40 days to successfully plow Trail Ridge Road before it opens to the public each May. Winds can reach up to 150 mph (240 km/h) and snowdrifts can be 25 ft (8 m) tall, burying the Alpine Visitor Center. Sometimes only its roof can be spotted.

of coffee or soup. Though the building's design is cozy, it's also practical, able to withstand 100-mph (170-km/h) winds. Savor your final moments in the tundra as you approach Medicine Bow Curve, a tight turn that steers you back into the trees where the air is rich and fills your lungs. Four miles (6 km) later, the road crosses the Continental Divide, an invisible line that cuts across North and South America and determines which ocean the rainwater ends up in.

CRUISING INTO WETLANDS

The grade never exceeds 7 percent on Trail Ridge Road, but you will still find yourself thankful for working brakes as you zigzag down several narrow hairpin turns. As the road levels out, you can ease into the drive and pause to explore peaceful Lake Irene or take a longer break to tackle the challenging hike to Timber Lake, a picturesque lagoon surrounded by green meadows and rocky cliffs. Alternatively, picnic at Beaver Ponds and stroll the short boardwalk through wildlife-rich wetland.

Your drive comes to an end in a flat, open valley, where the sun feels warm on your skin. Exit the park and follow the U.S. 34 into Grand Lake, a waterfront town on two connected lakes. Though you've just traveled through snowy mountain ranges, it doesn't mean you have to say goodbye to the peaks just yet. Commandeer a different kind of vehicle—a kayak or paddleboard—and enjoy a new view from the middle of the water, all while reflecting on your epic drive in the heavens.

TEXAS HILL COUNTRY

START/FINISH
San Antonio, Texas/
San Antonio, Texas

DISTANCE
375 miles (605 km)

DURATION
3–5 days

ROAD CONDITIONS
Road conditions vary drastically; 4WD advised

THE BEST TIME TO GO
Spring, for temperate climes and blooming wildflowers

OPPOSITE Swaying fields of tall grass and colorful wildflowers in Texas Hill Country

Many people picture Texas as a never-ending desert, but those people have clearly never seen the Hill Country in eastern Texas, where lush landscapes are filled with rivers, waterfalls, and rolling fields of blooming wildflowers.

Begin your journey in San Antonio, one of the most beautiful cities in Texas. It's well worth hanging up the car keys for a few hours to appreciate its splendor on foot, (or by boat). The downtown area is filled with green spaces and historic buildings, including the Alamo, a historic Spanish mission involved in the 1836 Battle of the Alamo, located near the winding San Antonio river. The Riverwalk area is a major draw here too, with over a mile of colorful lights, busy restaurants, and river cruises taking locals and tourists up and down the river. It makes an excellent spot for people-watching.

Once you've explored the city, hit the road and escape to the countryside. Though the I-10 will get you to Kerrville much faster, a ride along state highway 16 is a bit more scenic. More importantly, it will take you through the town of Bandera, home of the Bandera Brewery, a charming artisanal craft brewery with a beer garden, and a resident cat.

Just a 30-minute drive from the brewery is Kerrville, a quaint town that is often referred to as the "Capital of the Hill Country." Located on the Guadalupe River, it is the perfect backdrop for a a riverside amble before driving 25 miles (40 km) west to the city of Fredericksburg.

WINE COUNTRY

Once named the prettiest town in Texas, Fredericksburg still retains a lot of "Wild West" charm in the downtown area, with historical brick buildings and wooden balconies. It also makes a great stop for wine lovers, with around 60 wineries located in and around town,

SAN ANTONIO

SAN ANTONIO
Stroll along the San Antonio Riverwalk, watching the neon lights bounce off the river.

0 MILES

BANDERA
Have a cold one at Bandera Brewery, a community-focused artisanal brewery.

45 MILES

115 MILES

ENCHANTED ROCK STATE NATURAL AREA

Choose from eight trails, all varying in length and difficulty.

206 MILES

LONGHORN CAVERN STATE PARK

Take a tour through the park's limestone caves and look out for tricolored bats.

228 MILES

KRAUSE SPRINGS

Take the edge off the Texan heat with a dip at this popular swimming hole.

ABOVE Hiking in the Enchanted Rock State Natural Area

RIGHT Natural waterfalls in the Pedernales Falls State Park

OPPOSITE Bats flying over spectators in Austin

forming part of the Urban Wine Trail. While in the city, you can explore the area's German heritage, with local establishments like Altstadt Brewery serving a variety of beers and German-inspired pub food. It's just a short drive away from Enchanted Rock State Natural Area, home to around 10 miles (15 km) of hiking trails, punctuated by a spectacular pink granite rock dome.

WATERFALLS AND NATURAL WONDERS

Leave Fredericksburg and motor an hour northwest along Highway 290, passing several local wineries until you reach Marble Falls, named after waterfalls that have since submerged under Lake Marble Falls. Stop for a spot of shopping or join the locals on the Colorado River, frequented by anglers and wakeboarders.

Natural wonders are all within 20 minutes' drive of Marble Falls, including Longhorn Cavern State Park. Carved out by an underground river, this limestone cave formation is one of the most impressive in Texas. Look out for crystals and tiny tricolored bats on a walking tour, or opt for the "Wild Cave" tour through less accessible parts of the caves. The tranquil Pedernales Falls in nearby Pedernales Falls State Park also won't disappoint. Enjoy gentle hikes and swing by Krause Springs, a popular swimming hole, to cool off.

The hill country is particularly beautiful in spring when the wildflowers bloom, and the journey between Marble Falls and Austin is the perfect place to spot the bluebonnet, the Texas state flower. Though the flowers may seem to grow spontaneously, many bluebonnets are the result of a concentrated effort by the First Lady Claudia Alta Taylor "Lady Bird" Johnson to beautify the highways.

SWOOPING INTO THE CITY

As you emerge from the hills and near the city of Austin, the swaying foliage thins and the noise levels increase. You'll still be able to spot nature in the city, though. At sunset, thousands of Mexican free-tailed bats swarm out into the night from under Congress Avenue Bridge. If you're feeling nocturnal, make the pilgrimage to 6th Street in downtown Austin. Don't let the crowds dissuade you—follow them to catch some of the city's excellent live music.

You can keep the vibes going as you head out of Austin: take the 30-minute drive south along I-35 to San Marcos and you'll be rewarded with art galleries, farmers' markets, and a quirky downtown square that comes alive as the sun goes down. There's opportunity to get on the water here, too, with kayaking and glass-bottom boat tours on the crystal clear waters of Spring Lake available; look out for fish and turtles.

Hit the I-35 once more for 20 miles (30 km) and you'll soon arrive at New Braunfels, a popular small city with strong German heritage. Explore this further at the Sophienburg Museum and Archives, which is dedicated to the area's German history, before swinging by Gruene Hall. Built in 1878, it's Texas's oldest and still functioning dance hall.

Return once more to the trusty I-35 to complete the final stretch of the drive, exchanging German influences for Spanish flavors as you get ever closer to San Antonio. After a journey through such diverse and enchanting country-side, it'll be easy to see why the Lone Star State's Texas Hill Country is worthy of five stars.

AUSTIN'S BAT CAVE

From late March through to early fall, much of Austin gathers to watch the nightly migration of Mexican free-tailed bats swoop out from under the Congress Avenue Bridge. These nocturnal mammals, which arrived in 1980 following the renovation of the bridge, are popular residents today due to their excellent insect-hunting skills.

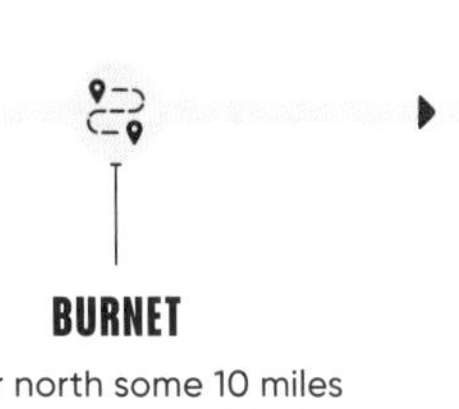

BURNET

Detour north some 10 miles (15 km) to see some of the best bluebonnet flowers Texas.

264 MILES

AUSTIN

Experience Austin's famous nightlife firsthand on the famous 6th Street.

294 MILES

SPRING LAKE

Take a glass-bottom boat tour in San Marcos to see underwater flora and fauna.

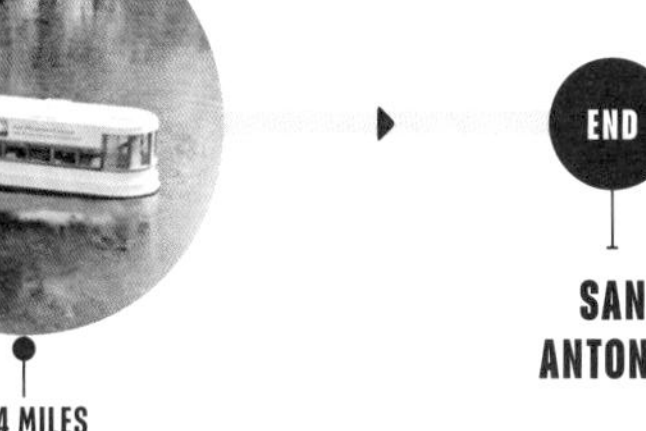

END

SAN ANTONIO

NEBRASKA HIGHWAY 2

Alliance

Grand Island

START/FINISH
Grand Island, Nebraska/ Alliance, Nebraska

DISTANCE
270 miles (435 km)

DURATION
1-3 days

ROAD CONDITIONS
Paved; rural stretches where travel and cell services are limited

THE BEST TIME TO GO
Mid-February through mid-April, to witness the sandhill crane migration

OPPOSITE The Middle Loup River, meandering its way through Nebraska's Sandhills

Nebraska Highway 2 runs through the state's Sandhills, grassy dunes that rise and fall across millions of hypnotic acres. It's a long, lonesome road, except in spring, when vast flocks of sandhill cranes visit on their annual migration.

For a few weeks each spring, more than half a million sandhill cranes, roughly 80 percent of the species, descend on Nebraska's Platte River valley to rest as they migrate to Alaska and northern Canada. The red-masked birds' trilling is audible up and down the valley, and their dancing—jumping, flapping, and bowing—turns a 75-mile (120-km) stretch of American heartland into the Bolshoi-on-the-Plains.

To witness this natural spectacle, make for the city of Grand Island, the starting point of the Sandhills Journey National Scenic Byway, more prosaically known as Nebraska Highway 2. The road will take you to more natural wonders —the Sandhills, notably—but the cranes stick close to the river south of town, so don't drive away too fast. A good place to observe them is the Crane Trust Nature and Visitor Center. Just off Interstate 80, 15 miles (25 km) southwest of Grand Island, it offers guided tours to riverfront blinds.

PRAIRIES AND FARMLAND
Leaving Grand Island, you quickly find yourself in farm country. The towns here revolve around agriculture, even if the names suggest otherwise. Pioneers dubbed the first town you come to Cairo, on account of the area's sand; the second is called Ravenna, after the Italian city. As you drive, mostly what you see are fields: orderly rows of corn and cylindrical bales of hay like so many soup cans on their sides. Freight trains run on tracks alongside the highway. It's therapeutic in its straightforwardness.

GRAND ISLAND

GRAND ISLAND

The city is a good base for witnessing the spring sandhill crane migration.

0 MILES

CAIRO

Street names in this sleepy farm town—Suez, Nile, Nubia—follow a Middle Eastern theme.

16 MILES

ABOVE Tanking along Nebraska's waterways

BELOW The Byway Visitor Center, housed in a red barn

Eighty-one miles (130 km) from Grand Island, you'll pull into Broken Bow. If you're spending more than a day on the byway, this is a good place to stay overnight, with several lodging and food options. On the edge of town is the Sandhills Journey Scenic Byway Visitor Center, where you can get the basics on the drive and local culture.

INTO THE SANDHILLS

Driving northwest from Broken Bow, you enter the Sandhills. These arid hills were created when a prehistoric inland sea disappeared and winds deposited the exposed sediment here. They are, essentially, sand dunes held in place by grasses such as Indiangrass and bluestem. This vast, undulating expanse has been called the "Great American Desert," and driving through it can feel like crossing the Gobi. Yet you'll also probably notice that this so-called desert is suspiciously wet. The Sandhills lie atop the Ogallala Aquifer, one of the largest in the world. It births spring-fed rivers like the Middle Loup, and spawns more than a million acres of wetlands. Just before Hyannis, stop by Beem Lake to experience Highway 2's soggy side, and spy migrating pelicans.

Above all, though, the Sandhills is cattle ranching country. You can still get a dose of cowboy life at Morgan's Cowpoke Haven in Ellsworth, at mile 241

TANKING

One of Nebraska's great pastimes—maybe the greatest—is tanking, floating down a river in a livestock water tank, basically a big ol' metal tub that has enough room for a few lawn chairs, a cooler full of beer, and a radio. On Highway 2, Glidden Canoe Rentals, in Mullen, and Sandhill River Trips, in Thedford, rent tanks for trips down the Middle Loup River.

BROKEN BOW

Sip a beer while gazing out over cornfields at Kinkaider Brewing Co.

81 MILES

HYANNIS

In warm months, pelicans gather in Beem Lake, just outside of town.

213 MILES

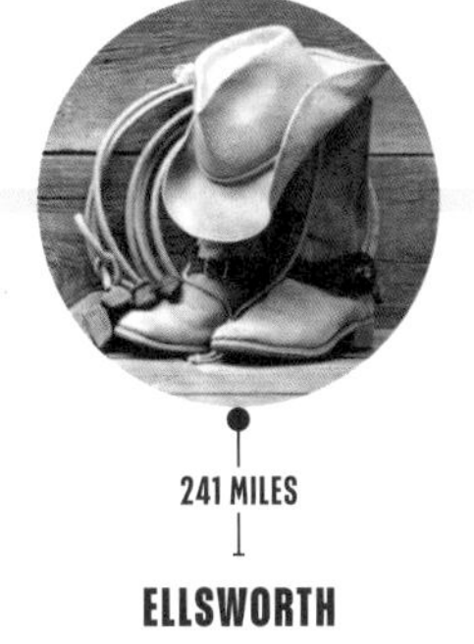

241 MILES

ELLSWORTH

Open since 1898, Morgan's Cowpoke Haven sells cowboy essentials.

248 MILES

LAKESIDE

Take a side trip from this village to Crescent Lake National Wildlife Refuge.

ALLIANCE

of the drive. Opened in 1898 as the supply store for the huge Spade Ranch, it still sells cowpuncher essentials like Western clothing, spurs, and guns.

Spade Ranch is just one of several sprawling ranches in the area. The hills' sandy soil is no good for farming (something the pioneers learned the hard way), a fact that has left the land relatively undisturbed—a vestige of the time when the Indigenous Lakota people crossed the prairie in search of bison. Nowadays, as you head along the highway, you'll likely see cowboys driving herds of cattle over the hills, and if your timing is lucky, you may even roll into one of the small towns at the same time as the local rodeo.

From Lakeside, a detour south on 296th Trail leads to Crescent Lake National Wildlife Refuge, a spattering of lakes, marshes, and wet meadows that supports bald eagles, trumpeter swans, and other birds. Also dependent on the Ogallala Aquifer is the Nebraska National Forest, Bessey Ranger District, where male prairie chickens perform mating dances in spring, inflating their neck sacks until they look like tangerines.

HIGHWAY TO HENGE

As you approach Alliance and the end of the drive, the Sandhills diminish and then disappear. Alliance is a railroad town, and those freight trains that have been shadowing you the entire drive pull in here, too. It's an attractive place to end up, filled with brick buildings from the early 1900s that often have the names of the original owners carved into their facades. The town's highlight is the Carnegie Arts Center, which displays the work of regional artists.

Though you've reached the end of Highway 2, you can't come all the way to Alliance and not also make the 3-mile (5-km) drive up Highway 87 to one of the U.S.'s truly great roadside attractions. In 1987, to honor his dead father, Jim Reinders created Carhenge, a reproduction of England's Stonehenge made from 39 full-size automobiles, complete with a 1962 Cadillac as the heel stone. Are their mysteries as deep as those of the ancient stones? Do they hum with the same primitive magic? Will they, too, speak to the ages after all around them is dust?

ABOVE Snaking coal trains at the rail yard, Alliance

BELOW The carefully balanced Carhenge, glowing at dusk

SPEED
LIMIT
35

BADLANDS LOOP SCENIC BYWAY

START/FINISH
Wall, South Dakota/ Cactus Flat, South Dakota

DISTANCE
40 miles (65 km)

DURATION
4–5 hours

ROAD CONDITIONS
Well-maintained paved roads

THE BEST TIME TO GO
In the spring, when the Badlands erupt in bloom

OPPOSITE Highway 240, curving through a wildly eroded stretch of Badlands National Park

Driving the Badlands Loop Scenic Byway feels a little like exploring the surface of another planet. Take this ancient landscape of rocky canyons and soaring buttes at a leisurely pace to soak up the surreal sights on show.

It would be easy to put your foot on the gas and drive the Badlands Loop Scenic Byway in around an hour. But that would be missing the point. Driving this breathtaking curve of backcountry is a masterclass in the fine art of patience, rewarding those who take their time with an abundance of staggering landscapes and rugged wilderness.

Start at Wall, a dainty town named after the natural rock formations in the nearby Badlands National Park. Its quirky claim to fame is the Wall Drug Store, a cowboy-themed shopping outlet that first opened in 1931. These days, a staggering two million people visit annually to browse the cluster of Western-leaning stores, stocked with rows of cowboy boots and free bumper stickers asking, "Have You Dug Wall Drug?" Stop at the rustic wood-paneled dining room, where steaming-hot beef sandwiches are washed down with fizzy pop from the antique soda fountain. Before you leave, snap a selfie sitting astride the 40-ft (12-m) giant jackalope statue in the courtyard.

INTO THE BADLANDS

Sugar levels restored, it's time to join the Badlands Loop Scenic Byway, known locally as Highway 240. Wind down the window to inhale the earthy aroma of sage growing by the roadside, as you drive through the pancake-flat grassy prairies toward the entrance to Badlands National Park.

As one of the highest elevation spots in the park, Pinnacles Overlook offers your first taste of the rugged

WALL

WALL
Wall Drug Store, a local landmark, offers an extensive collection of cowboy hats.

0 MILES

PINNACLES OVERLOOK
Spot sage grouse, white-tailed deer, bighorn sheep, and bison out in the wilds.

9 MILES

The winding road twists and turns to reach the Yellow Mounds Overlook. It's the perfect perch to soak up blockbuster views of the formations, eroded by harsh sun and powerful winds.

Badlands, with a bird's-eye view of the sculpted landform waves, striped in astonishing purple, red, and burnt orange layers. Keep an eye out for bighorn sheep and roaming bison, spotted with thrilling frequency in this patch. On a clear day, you may even be able to make out the Black Hills mountain range, home to Mount Rushmore, jutting on the horizon.

The winding road twists and turns to reach the Yellow Mounds Overlook. It's the perfect perch to soak up blockbuster views of the formations, eroded by harsh sun and powerful winds. A marker points out that South Dakota's Badlands were named by the Lakota, who lived and hunted here for 11,000 years. They called the area "Mako Sica"—"Bad Lands"—because it's such difficult terrain to cross.

UNDERGROUND TREASURES

Moving on, there are more endless vistas from the Panorama Point Overlook, 9 miles (15 km) along the road, before you reach the Fossil Exhibit Trail—an essential stop for a stroll along the creaky paved boardwalk. Some 75 million years ago, this area was hidden deep underwater, before the sea gradually drained and exposed the ocean floor to the elements. The gentle hike snakes for just under half a mile (1 km) through the resulting fossil-rich bluffs. Along the way, get hands-on with replica exhibits of the creatures that once called this region home. Recent digs in the area have unearthed treasures including the bones of three-toed horses and a hornless rhinoceros, so budding paleontologists are in for a treat.

TOP LEFT Yellow Mounds, an area of distinctly colored sculpted humps

ABOVE A prairie dog, in alert mode, near Cedar Pass Lodge

YELLOW MOUNDS OVERLOOK

Marvel at the Badlands from one of the best vantage points in the national park.

12 MILES

PANORAMA POINT OVERLOOK

Pull over at Panorama Point for widescreen views that lead toward the White River Valley.

21 MILES

FOSSIL EXHIBIT TRAIL

Step back 75 million years in time as you stroll the trail's boardwalk.

25 MILES

FAR LEFT The sun rising over Badlands National Park

LEFT Jagged rock formations, seen from Pinnacles Overlook

THE BADLANDS BANSHEE

Many believe South Dakota's Badlands to be haunted by the Badlands Banshee, a female ghost that alarms visitors to the park with chilling shrieks, especially around the Watch Dog Butte area. Legend has it that she's the ghost of a woman who died at this very spot. The Badlands Banshee has since been immortalized in posters and postcards in the area.

FURRY FAUNA

Back behind the wheel, be prepared for animal crossings and go extra slow as you approach Cedar Pass Lodge. This section is a popular hangout for prairie dogs—jaunty and adorable-looking rodents, similar in appearance to chipmunks. These sociable animals live in underground homes, some of which line the highway, and can be found standing alert on their hind legs, watching the traffic pass in wide-eyed wonder. If luck is on your side, you may also catch a glimpse of the black-footed ferret, a rare mammal that has been successfully reintroduced in the park.

THE FINAL STRETCH

No visit to South Dakota would be complete without trying the Native American dish of Indian taco. This large fluffy fry bread is smothered with refried beans, buffalo meat, shredded vegetables, and a dollop of tangy salsa. The restaurant at Cedar Park Lodge—the only place to stay in the park—is famed for its version, made with local ingredients. Tuck into this meaty feast from the comfort of a time-worn leather booth, taking in the views of pinnacles and spires.

Next door, the shelves of the gift store jostle with handcrafted beaded jewelry and feathered dreamcatchers. Swing by to purchase a road-trip memento before making one last stop at nearby Cactus Flat, a small town frequented by prairie dogs that offers a delicious sense of remoteness. Sunset is an arresting time to visit: the buttery light turns the nearby canyons a rich shade of gold, offering a particularly scenic send-off.

30 MILES

CEDAR PASS LODGE

Tuck into an Indian taco at the restaurant and pick up regional crafts at the gift store.

40 MILES

CACTUS FLAT

The town and its surroundings are home to a colony of prairie dogs.

CACTUS FLAT

BLACK HILLS LOOP

START/FINISH
Rapid City, South Dakota/ Rapid City, South Dakota

DISTANCE
235 miles (380 km)

DURATION
2–5 days

ROAD CONDITIONS
Single-lane tunnels, narrow switchbacks

THE BEST TIME TO GO
Early summer and fall; Needles Highway closes in winter

OPPOSITE The Needles Highway, threading through Custer State Park

Dramatic landscapes, thundering herds of bison, legendary Lakota warriors, notorious gunslingers, and gold prospectors: the Black Hills have all the ingredients for a real Wild West adventure.

In Indigenous Lakota myth, the first people to walk the earth did so in the Black Hills. Set foot here yourself, and it's easy to see why. Surrounded by badlands and arid plains, it's a beautiful, life-giving region of pine forests, rivers, and rocky outcrops. It turned out those hills had gold, too, and its discovery in 1874 created boomtowns that lured in prospectors, gamblers, and outlaws.

TO RUSHMORE AND BEYOND

Black Hills trips typically start in Rapid City, South Dakota's second-biggest city. It's the gateway to Mount Rushmore, but visitors can get their presidential fix before they leave town, as life-size statues of every president up to Barack Obama line Main and St. Joseph streets. Mount Rushmore National Memorial, half an hour to the southwest, was the brainchild of Doane Robinson, a South Dakota historian who envisioned it as a way to attract tourists. It worked. Each year, more than two million people stare up at the 60-ft- (18-m-) high faces of George Washington, Thomas Jefferson, Theodore Roosevelt, and Abraham Lincoln.

Heading south from Mount Rushmore on U.S. Highway 16A leads along a stretch known as Iron Mountain Road. Built in the 1930s, it winds through pine forests and three rock tunnels, and around three "pigtails," 180-degree turns that deal with sudden changes in elevation. It's basically a go-kart track for grown-ups. Eventually, you'll reach Wildlife Loop Road, which arcs across gently rolling prairie in the heart

RAPID CITY

RAPID CITY
The Skyline Wilderness Area provides lofty views of the city and Black Hills.

0 MILES

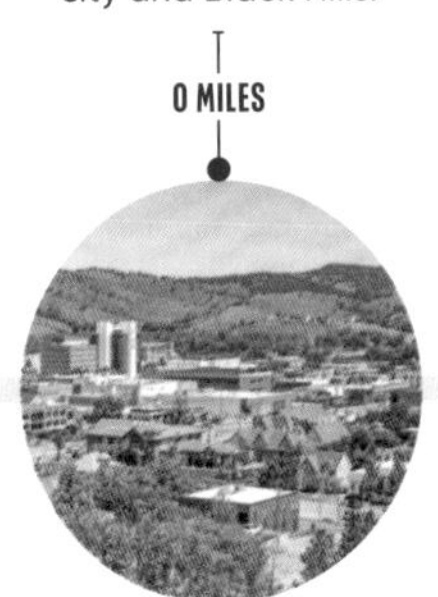

IRON MOUNTAIN ROAD
Looking north, the road's three stone tunnels all frame Mount Rushmore in the distance.

25 MILES

WIND CAVE NATIONAL PARK

The park offers several cave tours, including one that's wheelchair accessible.

74 MILES

CRAZY HORSE MEMORIAL

The memorial grounds are also home to the Indian Museum of North America.

97 MILES

NEEDLES HIGHWAY

Just 9 ft 9 inches (3 m) high and 8 ft (2.7 m) wide, the road's smallest tunnel is a squeeze.

103 MILES

of Custer State Park. Drive slowly, as you'll likely find yourself sharing the road with some of the park's 1,400 bison. Before they were hunted to near extinction in the late 1800s, bison (also called buffalo) roamed across the continent. Today, they exist only in pockets, and this is one of the best places in the country to spot them.

At the end of the loop, follow the road south to Wind Cave National Park. It was from this cave the Lakota Sioux believe the first humans emerged. Inside, the idea that it leads to the spirit realm doesn't seem so implausible; more than 160 miles (260 km) have been explored, but no one's ever reached its end.

MEMORIALS AND MINES

Head north on U.S. 385 through Custer to the Crazy Horse Memorial, another monumental mountain carving, begun as a response to Mount Rushmore. A member of the Oglala Lakota, Crazy Horse is most famous for leading a group of warriors against the 7th Cavalry at the Battle of the Little Bighorn, where General George Custer was killed. To honor him, the Sioux chief Henry Standing Bear initiated the memorial project in 1939, hiring the sculptor Korczak Ziolkowski. Nearly 90 years into the project, only Crazy Horse's face and hand are discernable, but when completed, the monument will stand 563 ft (172 m) high and 641 ft (195 m) long, dwarfing Mount Rushmore.

After viewing Crazy Horse, continue north for 6 miles (10 km) to Highway 87. Called Needles Highway for the thin stone formations that poke into the sky along the route, it's the journey's other great drive, switchbacking through forests of spruce and ponderosa pine and passing through narrow tunnels carved into the rock.

Needles Highway ends at U.S. Highway 16A. Take 16A west back to Custer, and then rejoin 385 north, driving for about an hour until you reach Lead, a well-preserved gold-mining

RUSHMORE'S TARNISHED LEGACY

Despite its majesty, Mount Rushmore bears a tarnished legacy. In the 1868 Treaty of Fort Laramie, the U.S. promised the Lakota the Black Hills, but when General George Custer discovered gold here six years later, the government tore up the agreement, and white prospectors flooded the land. The mountain, Tunkasila Sakpe Paha (Six Grandfathers Mountain) to the Lakota, was renamed for a New York attorney. Furthermore, Gutzon Borglum, the monument's sculptor, was a white supremacist and associate of the Ku Klux Klan.

LEFT Buffalo round-up in Custer State Park

OPPOSITE ABOVE Deadwood, once home to Calamity Jane and Wild Bill Hickok

OPPOSITE BELOW Riders in the Sturgis Motorcycle Rally

town where you can see the remnants of a gigantic open-pit mine right off the main drag. Active from 1876 to 2001, the Homestake Mine was the deepest and most productive gold mine in the Western Hemisphere, producing more than 2.5 million lbs (1 million kg) of ore. Following its retirement, the mine was turned into the Sanford Underground Research Facility, where scientists now study neutrinos and dark matter.

ROUND TO RAPID CITY

Up the road from Lead is Deadwood, the boomiest of Black Hills Gold Rush boomtowns. In the 1870s, it pulled in sharpshooters like Calamity Jane and gunslingers like Wild Bill Hickok, who was shot to death in Nuttal & Mann's Saloon, mid-poker game. Realizing that 21st-century gold is found not in creekbeds but in tourists' pockets, Deadwood shamelessly capitalizes on its notorious past with attractions like ghost tours, brothel museums, gunfight reenactments, and plenty of casinos. You'll either love it or hate it.

U.S. Highway 14A runs northeast to Sturgis, which fills each August when up to half a million people show up to ride in the town's motorcycle rally. Get your bike fix at the Sturgis Motorcycle Museum and Hall of Fame before motoring on for half an hour back into Rapid City.

LEWIS AND CLARK TRAIL

Cape Disappointment State Park

Pittsburgh

START/FINISH
Pittsburgh, Pennsylvania/ Cape Disappointment State Park, Washington

DISTANCE
3,765 miles (7,885 km)

DURATION
3–4 weeks

ROAD CONDITIONS
Well-maintained paved roads, with optional off-road trails in some sections

THE BEST TIME TO GO
Spring, when the riverbanks bloom

OPPOSITE Whitman Mission National Historic Site, one of many historic sites toward the trail's end in Washington State

Snaking from Pittsburgh to the Pacific, the Lewis and Clark Trail is an epic journey through remote wilderness and bustling cities, taking in snowy peaks, canyons, grasslands, and the urban centers of the Midwest.

The Lewis and Clark Trail is a true American adventure. It traces the route taken by the Lewis and Clark Expedition of 1803–1806, a groundbreaking journey across the west of the U.S. led by Meriwether Lewis and William Clark. The route features a plethora of historic sites, each testifying to the early adventures of the country's pioneers, and related visitor centers. It follows the Ohio, Mississippi, and Missouri rivers across prairies, over mountain passes in Idaho and Montana, and along the gorge carved out by the Columbia River.

Your trip begins in Pittsburgh, once a smoky steel city, today a diverse cultural hotbed. From Point State Park, where the Monongahela and Allegheny rivers join to form the Ohio, the trail shadows the river west through the Appalachians, making a giant loop along the West Virginia then Kentucky border with Ohio. The route meanders on through the Ohio River Valley, running between gentle wooded slopes and historic river towns.

INTO THE MISSISSIPPI BASIN

The Ohio River eventually flows into Cincinnati, with its pretty riverfront and a smattering of attractions that includes the National Underground Railroad Freedom Center, which shines a light on the network that helped people escape slavery in the South in the 1800s. Ahead of Cincinnati lies the increasingly flat, humid Mississippi Basin, mostly rich farmland on both sides of the Ohio River. Louisville, Kentucky, around

PITTSBURGH

START

PITTSBURGH
Begin your journey at Point State Park, the start of the mighty Ohio River.

0 MILES

NATIONAL UNDERGROUND RAILROAD FREEDOM CENTER
Cincinnatti was a key stop on the route north to freedom.

100 miles (160 km) south of Cincinnati, is another riverine city that has reinvented itself in recent decades. Stop by Frazier History Museum, where the Lewis and Clark Experience is an immersive, family-friendly exhibit detailing the history of the expedition.

A series of minor roads continue to shadow the Ohio, now wide, brown, and sluggish, as it oozes along the Kentucky border with Indiana and then Illinois before finally pouring into the sludgy main channel of the great Mississippi at Cairo, on the Illinois-Missouri border. Not much is left of the nearby Wickliffe Mounds State Historic Site, a thriving Indigenous settlement between 1100 and 1350, but it's brought to life at the site museum.

The Mississippi is notoriously prone to flooding between here and St. Louis, so the trail follows a series of roads that track inland, through low-lying woods and farmland enriched by alluvial soil. Small port towns like Fort de Chartres reveal their French colonial origins, as does the city of St. Louis itself, founded in 1764 by French fur trader Pierre Laclède. It was to here that the Lewis and Clark Expedition returned in 1806 after their journey west, a portentous event now commemorated by Eero Saarinen's Gateway Arch downtown.

The Missouri joins the Mississippi just north of St. Louis: the point is marked by

It was to St. Louis that the Lewis and Clark Expedition returned in 1806 after their journey west, a portentous event now commemorated by Gateway Arch.

ABOVE Eero Saarinen's Gateway Arch, St. Louis

LOUISVILLE

Visit the Lewis and Clark Experience at the city's Frazier History Museum.

565 MILES

ST. LOUIS

The 630-ft- (190-m-) high stainless-steel Gateway Arch commands views of the Mississippi.

1,045 MILES

1,395 MILES

KANSAS CITY

Kansas City is known for serving some of America's best smoked barbecue and "burnt ends."

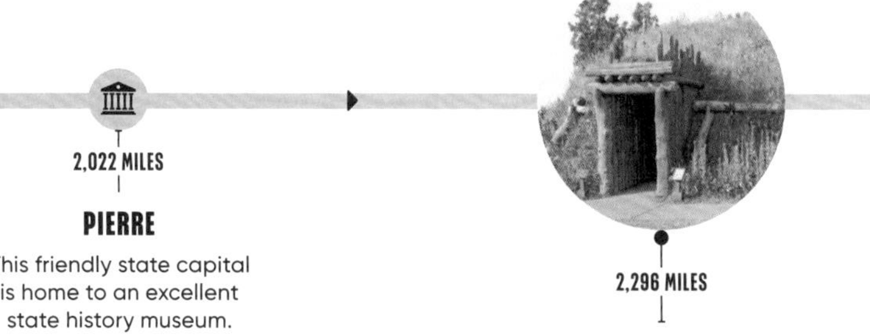

2,022 MILES

PIERRE

This friendly state capital is home to an excellent state history museum.

2,296 MILES

KNIFE RIVER INDIAN VILLAGES

See the evocative reconstruction of Hidatsa earthlodges at this historic site.

the Lewis and Clark Confluence Tower and a reproduction of the expedition's Camp River Dubois on the Illinois side. From here, you'll be shadowing the Missouri well into the Rockies, beginning by cutting across the pancake-flat cornfields of Kansas. The river winds its way past Kansas City itself.

ACROSS THE GREAT PLAINS

The road continues northwest along the Missouri, through the seemingly endless plains of corn and wheat in Iowa and Nebraska. There are a couple of enticing rest stops along the way: Omaha, Nebraska, with its boho-chic downtown, indie music scene, and Lewis and Clark Historic Trail Visitor Center; and Sioux City in Iowa, whose Lewis and Clark Interpretive Center is one of the best museums in the Midwest – the poignant Sergeant Floyd Monument here is dedicated to the only member of the expedition to die on route.

Rolling farmland continues to hug the Missouri as it cuts across the heart of South Dakota. Six dams built for hydropower between 1933 and 1964 have radically transformed the river in the Dakotas since the days of Lewis and Clark; it's now a series of long reservoirs and lakes, with the route running across the plains some way from the shoreline. You'll get a closer look at the river at charming, tree-lined Pierre, the tiny state capital of South Dakota. A few hours' drive away in North Dakota, the farmland falls away and wild grassland takes up the baton, as far as the eye can see. In Bismarck, the equally small capital of North Dakota, you'll find a statue of Sacagawea, the expedition's indefatigable Shoshone guide, outside the capitol building, and On-A-Slant Village, an atmospheric replica of six Mandan earthlodges from the 18th century. On-A-Slant was already abandoned when Lewis and Clark passed through, but they encountered the Mandan some 40 miles (65 km) upriver, near three older Hidatsa villages, commemorated today at the Knife River

TOP Lewis and Clark Interpretive Center, Sioux City

ABOVE Re-creation of a Mandan earthlodge at On-A-Slant Village

2,915 MILES

GREAT FALLS

See the remnants of the once great Missouri waterfalls.

3,765 MILES

CAPE DISAPPOINTMENT

Visit your final monument to the expedition at the Lewis and Clark Interpretive Center.

CAPE DISAPPOINTMENT STATE PARK

SACAGAWEA

Sacagawea was a Shoshone woman kidnapped by the Hidatsa people as a young girl and later sold as a wife to French-Canadian trapper Toussaint Charbonneau. The couple met Lewis and Clark in what is now North Dakota in the winter of 1804; Charbonneau was hired as a guide and interpreter, but it was his 16-year-old wife's ability to reassure suspicious Indigenous peoples that was more helpful, particularly when the expedition reached her own people in Montana.

Indian Villages National Historic Site. This is where the team hired Sacagawea and her husband, Toussaint Charbonneau; you can learn more at the Lewis and Clark Interpretive Center nearby.

WEST OF THE ROCKIES

At Fort Union, take the fork through northern Montana to Great Falls, beyond which you'll finally spy the Rockies. West of the Continental Divide, the road follows U.S. 12 deep into the Bitterroot Mountains, the wildest, most rugged part of the journey, broadly following the old Nez Perce Lolo Trail used by the expedition. You'll skirt the hot mineral pools at Lolo Hot Springs and cross into Idaho at the Lolo Pass. Vast, snow-dusted peaks fill the skyline, with nothing but pine trees all around. The road wriggles its way down the narrow Lochsa River gorge until you finally emerge from the mountains at Clearwater River and the more temperate high plains of the Nez Perce Indian Reservation.

From Sacajawea Historical State Park in Pasco, Washington, it's a relatively straightforward run along the spectacular Columbia River Gorge (the border between Oregon and Washington) on I-84, all the way to the Pacific. Dry, desert-like terrain becomes vast forests and peaks from the Columbia Gorge Discovery Center onward. Stretch your legs on a hike to spectacular Multnomah Falls; at 620 ft (189 m), it's Oregon's tallest cascade.

The route passes through Portland, Oregon, before splitting at the Columbia River estuary. Turn north and end your journey at Cape Disappointment: this beautiful, moody spot towering above pounding waves is a letdown in name only. Your final Lewis and Clark Interpretive Center chronicles the grim winter the party spent here in 1805, aided by the local Chinook and Clatsop peoples. Take in the ocean views and be glad that, unlike Lewis and Clark, you don't have to turn around and go all the way back to the start on foot.

ABOVE The Bitterroot Mountains, the most rugged part of the trail

AMERICAN TRAILBLAZERS

Unlike trains, planes, or even buses, with their Point A to Point B routes, cars have a special way of making anyone feel like a trailblazer. While we're all our own expedition leaders, some people have revolutionized the road trip in more profound ways. The first trailblazers were Indigenous Americans who carved out trails for trade, hunting, and migration. Their footpaths, some hundreds of miles long, were later used by European settlers, including Lewis and Clark. In one of their expedition's most dramatic passages, the company followed a Shoshone guide across Montana's Bitterroot Mountains via the Lolo Trail, known to the local Salish people as *Naptnišaqs*. Eventually, some Indigenous trails became bridle paths, then wagon roads, and, later, city streets or highways. Today, roads as varied as downtown Chicago's Clark Street, West Virginia's Midland Trail Scenic Byway, and Massachusetts Route 2 can trace their origins to Indigenous pathways.

Once roads began to crisscross the continent, there was the question of who should drive them. Alice Huyler Ramsey, for one, said, "Give me the keys." An avid motorist, the 22-year-old set out to become the first woman to drive coast to coast in 1909, departing from New York City in a dark green, 30-horsepower Maxwell DA touring car. On her 3,800-mile (6,116-km) adventure, she navigated by telegraph lines, was heckled with shouts of "Get a horse!" and reached a top speed of 42 mph (68 km/h). Fifty-nine days after she set out, she arrived in San Francisco.

An avid motorist, Alice Huyler Ramsey became the first woman to drive coast to coast in 1909, departing from New York City in a dark green, 30-horsepower Maxwell DA touring car.

Ramsey would later become the first woman in the Automotive Hall of Fame.

While every road-tripper has to deal with inconveniences, African American motorists have also had to cope with the perils of "driving while Black." To aid Black travelers, the postal worker and writer Victor Hugo Green began publishing a guidebook to Black-owned hotels, restaurants, service stations, and other establishments. The first edition of *The Negro Motorist Green Book*, published in 1936, was limited to Green's native New York City, but within a few years it had expanded to cover the entire U.S., instilling a new generation of Black motorists to hit the open road.

ABOVE Motorist Alice Huyler Ramsey, with her touring car

GREAT RIVER ROAD

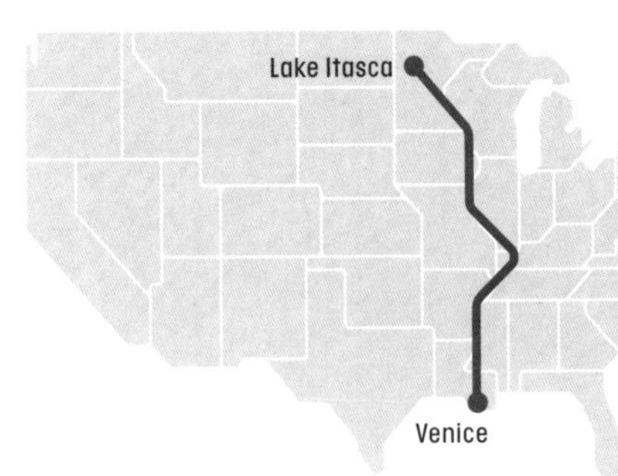

START/FINISH
Lake Itasca, Minnesota/ Venice, Louisiana

DISTANCE
2,160 miles (3,475 km)

DURATION
1–2 weeks

ROAD CONDITIONS
Paved; possibly icy conditions in northern states in winter

THE BEST TIME TO GO
Spring to fall, for the most reliable weather

OPPOSITE Lowry Bridge, Minneapolis, arching over the tranquil Mississippi River

The Mississippi River was America's original highway, carrying people between north and south long before there were roads. Roll along the river today to absorb the country's tale, from religious visions to Civil Rights struggles.

The word Mississippi comes from the Ojibwe name Misi-ziibi, meaning "big river." It's an appropriately straight-forward moniker. This is the country's largest and most important river, the river where so many of North America's other great rivers end up. It's the big one, especially in the American imagination, so it's strange to arrive at its source and find something so puny you can just about jump across it.

BIG RIVER, LITTLE RIVER

The Mississippi begins at the tip of Lake Itasca, in northern Minnesota, and that's where the Great River Road begins, too. This National Scenic Byway and All-American Road then follows the river through 10 states and countless towns, along U.S. highways and county roads, all the way to the Gulf of Mexico. If Huckleberry Finn were around today, this is the route he'd likely ramble down, swapping his wooden raft for a rusty pickup. Follow the road from source to sea, and by the end you'll have found your own novel's worth of adventures.

For the first miles of the drive, you'll see the river only fleetingly. It's still a small backwoods stream at this point, making occasional appearances as it crosses county roads or swells temporarily into one of Minnesota's more than 10,000 lakes. The pleasures here come from driving through welcoming Northwoods towns like Bemidji, which claims to be the home of folk hero Paul Bunyan, and untamed natural areas, like Chippewa National Forest, one of the country's largest bald eagle breeding sites.

LAKE ITASCA

LAKE ITASCA
Walk across the mini Mississippi at its source in Lake Itasca State Park.
0 MILES

BEMIDJI
Sample Minnesota's lake life in Bemidji, reputed hometown of folk hero Paul Bunyan.
33 MILES

326 MILES

MINNEAPOLIS AND ST. PAUL

These stylish and diverse cities have innovative art and dining scenes.

396 MILES

STOCKHOLM

Order a slice (or two) of freshly made pie at this quaint riverside village.

548 MILES

EFFIGY MOUNDS

Effigy Mounds National Monument was an important Indigenous ceremonial site.

A couple of hundred miles onward, the road approaches the Twin Cities of Minneapolis and St. Paul. Their location on St. Anthony Falls, the only natural waterfall on the Mississippi, made them an important port in the 19th century. They're still a great place to portage, with restaurants, bookstores, art exhibitions of Indigenous culture, and paeans to native pop star Prince.

ONE RIVER, TWO ROUTES

About half an hour south, the Great River Road becomes the Great River Roads, one on each side of the river, letting you cross back and forth to explore as you like. At Red Wing, head over to the Wisconsin shore to cruise through cute riverside villages like Stockholm, where the Stockholm Pie and General Store serves slices of lingonberry lemon and chocolate cream pie. This stretch of the Mississippi is famed for its towering bluffs, and in La Crosse you can drive to the top of Grandad Bluff for sweeping views. Afterward, commune with the locals, who are enthusiastic about keeping the city's brewing heritage alive.

As the previous name Misi-ziibi suggests, the the route offers up plenty of encounters with Indigenous legacies. Across the border in Iowa, right before you reach Marquette, the Effigy Mounds National Monument preserves more than 200 mounds that Indigenous people

TOP A colorful Minneapolis mural dedicated to Prince

ABOVE Aerial view of La Crosse, dotted with golden foliage

OPPOSITE Downtown Galena, a spot that feels like a film set

one hundred 19th-century buildings have been preserved. It's all impossibly picturesque, the sort of Midwestern hamlet that seems tailor-made for cozy Christmas movies and the all too familiar city-kid-moves-to-a-small-town dramas. Back in Iowa, search out Davenport's Figge Art Museum, which houses a large collection of works by the great Grant Wood, the Iowan who painted America's most famous artwork *American Gothic* (on display in the Art Institute of Chicago).

SHIFTING SOCIETIES

In 1849, three years after the Mormons were forced out of town, Nauvoo, Illinois, welcomed French philosopher Étienne Cabet and his utopian community. They called themselves Icarians and sought to build a society where everything was shared. It didn't work out, and the community split in 1856.

created for burials and other ceremonies roughly a millennium ago, including some in the shape of bears and birds.

As you head south, attractions on either bank give ample reason to skip back and forth across the Iowa–Illinois border. In Dubuque, Iowa, the National Mississippi River Museum and Aquarium provides River Road travelers with background on steamboats and riverine fauna, and the Fenelon Place Elevator funicular railway still shuttles people 189 ft (58 m) up a downtown bluff nearly 150 years after it opened. From the top you can see the river busy at work, with barges moving cargo up- and downriver. Sixteen miles (25 km) east on U.S. 20, tourists photograph their way along Main Street in Galena, Illinois, where over

FROM MORMONS TO MEMPHIS

American visionaries have come in all stripes, and another saw the promised land in the Illinois woodland abutting the Mississippi 100 miles (160 km) south of Davenport. In 1839, Joseph Smith and his Mormon followers arrived in the settlement of Commerce, hoping to create a home for their church. They renamed the settlement Nauvoo and set about constructing a temple. By 1844, Nauvoo had swelled with converts, its population exceeding Chicago's, but simmering conflict resulted in the Mormons being driven out and moving to Utah two years later. Piece together the sect's story from the numerous Mormon historical sites that remain.

Another hour driving through flat Midwestern cornfields brings you to

DUBUQUE

Learn about boats and wildlife at the National Mississippi River Museum and Aquarium.

609 MILES

DAVENPORT

Discover Midwestern, Haitian, and Colonial Mexican art at Davenport's Figge Art Museum.

714 MILES

EXTEND YOUR TRIP

A road so nice they made it twice. If you want the full Great River Road experience, drive it down the Mississippi from source to Gulf on one side of the river, and then drive back up the other side, at least until Hastings, Minnesota/ Prescott, Wisconsin, where it returns to a single route.

the hometown of the Mississippi River's patron saint. The writer Mark Twain grew up in Hannibal, Missouri, and the rowdy river town served as the inspiration for his fictional St. Petersburg. Nowadays, the impression is reversed, with the names of Twain and his characters stamped across town.

After a few days in the backwaters, arriving in St. Louis might give you a hint of how early settlers felt when they came here on their way west. Right on the riverbank, the Gateway Arch commemorates that migration. Elsewhere, Cardinals baseball at Busch Stadium, blues in the Laclede's Landing district, and the sprawling Forest Park (venue for the 1904 World's Fair) are all reasons to pause your journey.

Continue south, through Kentucky, and you'll find yourself in Tennessee before you know it. At Tennessee's southern edge, Memphis is one of the country's great music cities. Stroll down Beale Street, a downtown strip of blues clubs, barbecue joints, and colorful neon signs, and make time to visit Sun Studio, where Elvis cut his first record, and the Stax Museum of American Soul Music, on the site of the label's old recording studio. On the city's southern edge, pay your respects to the King at Graceland, Elvis's over-the-top mansion featuring shag carpeting on the ceilings and an artificial waterfall. More sobering is the National Civil Rights Museum, which recounts Black Americans' struggle for equality. Part of the museum occupies the former Lorraine Motel, where Martin Luther King, Jr. was assassinated in 1968.

INTO THE DEEP SOUTH

Motor onward from Memphis and you enter the Deep South. The magnolias start to bloom bigger, the Spanish moss droops lower, the drawls get thicker, and the heat and humidity slow everything down. If blues licks are still playing in your brain, swing through Clarksdale, Mississippi. The center of the region that birthed the Delta Blues, the city houses the Delta Blues Museum in a 1918 railroad depot. Across the river, Arkansas

EARTHQUAKE EFFECT

Missouri earthquakes between 1811 and 1812 temporarily caused the river to flow backward.

ST. LOUIS

Epic views await from atop the striking Gateway Arch, known as the Gateway to the West.

1,037 MILES

CLARKSDALE

Visit this lively music town for a deep dive into the Delta Blues.

1,518 MILES

1,574 MILES

DALE BUMPERS REFUGE

Ths National Wildlife Refuge is a favorite of birders and hunters alike.

1,976 MILES

NEW ORLEANS

Jazz, zydeco, bounce, and brass bands provide New Orleans' swinging soundtrack.

END

VENICE

Highway 1 provides access to the Dale Bumpers White River National Wildlife Refuge, where alligators, black bears, and roseate spoonbills haunt bottom-land hardwood forest, sloughs, bayous, and some 300 lakes.

Next, find your way to Natchez, a riverside town that grew rich on the trade of cotton and sugar, and on the slave trade. The opulence of its nearly 700 antebellum mansions can be intoxicating, but they shouldn't be viewed as separate from the manacles now displayed at Forks in the Road, the site of what was the second-largest slave market in the Deep South.

ON TO THE SEA

From Natchez, follow U.S. Highways 61 and 10 to New Orleans. Is there a better city to celebrate the end of a cross-country road trip than a place whose unofficial motto is "Laissez les bons temps rouler" (let the good times roll)? Certainly not. So toss back some celebratory shots on Bourbon Street, soak up the ambiance of the French Quarter's brass bands, and watch river barges from Jackson Square. Just don't linger too long, because your drive's not done yet. Finish by taking Highway 23 south to the town of Venice, where your car can literally go no farther, and where the great American river finally delivers itself to the sea.

ABOVE Intricate iron balconies in New Orleans' French Quarter

OPPOSITE Neon lights on busy Beale Street, Memphis

NORTH SHORE SCENIC DRIVE

Duluth ▶ U.S.–Canada border

START/FINISH
Duluth, Minnesota/ U.S.–Canada border

DISTANCE
155 miles (250 km)

DURATION
1–4 days

ROAD CONDITIONS
Paved; snowy or icy conditions possible in winter

THE BEST TIME TO GO
Spring to fall; some businesses close in winter and the weather can be frigid

OPPOSITE Split Rock Lighthouse, standing guard over Lake Superior

When Minnesotans want to get away from it all, there's only one thing to do: head Up North. Make your own escape into the region's boreal forests and historic fishing towns with a drive along the world's largest freshwater lake.

Apologies to Huron, Michigan, Erie, and Ontario, but Superior is the greatest of North America's five Great Lakes. It's the world's largest freshwater lake by surface area, and it holds more water than the other four lakes combined. To get a taste of lake life, travel up Minnesota's North Shore Scenic Drive, which follows Superior's shoreline from Duluth up to the Canadian border.

DULUTH AND BEYOND

No city is tied as tightly to Lake Superior as Duluth, whose pulse is measured in the passing of cargo ships between lake and harbor. On their way to the world's largest freshwater inland port, these behemoths pass beneath the Aerial Lift Bridge, still Duluth's signature sight 120 years after it was built. Abutting the bridge is Canal Park, where folks stroll the Lakewalk, a seven-mile (11-km) trail along Superior's shore. On your way out of Duluth, you'll pass Kitchi Gammi Park, named for the indigenous Ojibwe term for Lake Superior. Follow County Road 61, for now, to Knife River, a town whose fishing heritage stretches back a century and a half. One of the drive's pleasures is the little only-in-this-town shops you stumble upon, and Knife River has a couple of good ones. Russ Kendall's Smokehouse sells Minnesota maple syrup and smoked Lake Superior trout. Just up the road, the family that runs Great! Lakes Candy Kitchen has been making small-batch fudge, toffee, and chocolates for four generations.

The county road rejoins Highway 61 in Two Harbors, where trains load ore from

DULUTH

DULUTH
Dive into the history of Great Lakes shipping at Lake Superior Maritime Visitor Center.

0 MILES

KNIFE RIVER
The family at Great! Lakes Candy Kitchen has been making sweets for over a century.

22 MILES

46 MILES

IONA'S BEACH

Take in the striking expanse of pink-colored sand and rock.

50 MILES

SPLIT ROCK LIGHTHOUSE

Guided tours take you inside the lighthouse and keeper's house in summer.

62 MILES

TETTEGOUCHE STATE PARK

Deer and river otters are just some of the animals that call this large preserve home.

ABOVE Snow-dusted Palisade Head, which offers views of Wisconsin's Apostle Islands

OPPOSITE TOP Cross River Falls

OPPOSITE BELOW Grand Portage National Monument

Minnesota's Iron Range onto cargo ships. Sixteen miles (25 km) from Two Harbors is Iona's Beach. No, you're not wearing rose-colored glasses. The beach actually is pink. A cliff at its north end is made of pink rhyolite, and as Lake Superior storms have battered it over the millennia, pieces have broken off and washed downshore. About 15 minutes up the coast is another wildly colored beach that would seem more at home in Hawaii than northern Minnesota. The well-named Black Beach was formed from taconite tailings.

Between these beaches is the drive's most romantic image. Backed by a thick stand of trees, a towering cliff juts into the water and then plunges straight down, as if the land and lake had sculpted it into a pedestal for the lighthouse that stands atop it. Split Rock Lighthouse is a handsome thing itself: two levels of tan brick capped by a black lantern room and cupola. It was built in 1910, after a 1905 storm.

Not too far from the lighthouse is another, even grander promontory, the 320-ft (98-m) Palisade Head. Created by volcanic eruptions more than a billion years ago, it offers views of the Sawtooth Mountains and Wisconsin's Apostle Islands, some 30 miles (50 km) away. Standing on its edge, you truly come to terms with Superior's enormity.

CHASING WATERFALLS

Continuing north, you'll arrive at Tettegouche State Park, where you can hike through woods populated by moose and black bears or down to a beach with a sea cave. There are waterfalls all along the highway, most requiring at least a short hike, but some 20 miles (30 km) beyond Tettegouche State Park you'll drive over two of them: Cross River Falls in Schroeder and, a mile on, a funneling cascade in Temperance River State Park.

127 MILES

NANIBOUJOU LODGE AND RESTAURANT

Enjoy iconic furnishings across from the Devil's Kettle trailhead.

154 MILES

HIGH FALLS

Wave to the neighbors at High Falls, near the U.S.-Canada border.

END

U.S.-CANADA BORDER

TO THE BORDER

The last town of notable size on the North Shore is Grand Marais, the gateway to the majestic Boundary Waters, a vast tract of wilderness west of Lake Superior. Grand Marais, a noted arts center tucked among the birches, is a good place to overnight, as it has the most lodging and best dining options on the North Shore. The Fisherman's Daughter makes fish and chips with whatever local fishermen catch.

Next up is Judge C.R. Magney State Park. A trail here leads to the Devil's Kettle, where the Brule River splits into two channels, one continuing to the lake, the other pouring into a deep hole in the rock and vanishing.

Just before you run out of America, you'll pull into Grand Portage, the main settlement of a reservation belonging to the Grand Portage Band of Lake Superior Chippewa (Ojibwe). The Grand Portage National Monument commemorates the region's 18th-century fur trade. You can explore both a reconstructed trading post and traditional Ojibwe village, where staff demonstrate skills like bark basketry.

A final six miles (10 km) take you to the Canadian border. Right before reaching it, you'll arrive at a trailhead that leads to High Falls, on the Pigeon River. For centuries, Ojibwe and French-Canadian voyageurs had to bring their canoes ashore and carry them around the falls. The Ojibwe knew the trek as Gichi Onigaming, "the great carrying place," while the French term gives the area its current name: Grand Portage.

WATER, WATER, EVERYWHERE

Were Lake Superior to ever spring a leak, there's enough water in it to cover all of North and South America a foot (30 cm) deep.

OREGON TRAIL

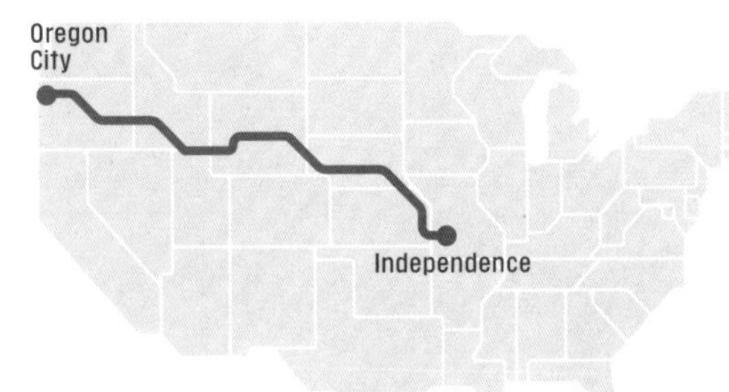

START/FINISH
Independence, Missouri/ Oregon City, Oregon

DISTANCE
2,070 miles (3,330 km)

DURATION
2–3 weeks

ROAD CONDITIONS
Well-maintained paved roads, with optional off-road trails

THE BEST TIME TO GO
Spring or summer for the best weather

OPPOSITE The scenic Columbia River Highway weaving toward the shimmering Columbia River

Follow in the footsteps of pioneers, cowboys, and Indigenous warriors across the heart of America on the Oregon Trail, from the Great Plains to the Rockies to the redwood forests of the Pacific Northwest.

Over 180 years after wagons first rolled west along its route, the Oregon Trail retains its icy grip on America's collective imagination, signalling perseverance and the taming of the frontier. Today, you can trace those early wagons across vast plains, mile-high mountain passes, and thunderous river gorges all the way to the Willamette River.

The Oregon Trail begins in the city of Independence, on the Missouri River, where the first major wagon train left in 1843. Located east of Kansas City, Independence is today part of the suburban sprawl, and is known as the childhood hometown of ex-president Harry Truman. The drive then slices through Kansas City, skirting the Power and Light district, a tourist-friendly area with skyscrapers, buzzing bars, and live music. Continue west across the state line into Kansas, staying on the I-70 until you reach Lawrence, home to the University of Kansas. If time's tight, stay on the road for a farther 30 miles (45 km) to Topeka, the state capital. In addition to a lavish capitol building, the city is home to the Brown v. Board of Education National Historial Park, which honors the landmark decision to end legal segregation in public schools in 1954.

YOU'RE NOT IN KANSAS ANYMORE

At Topeka, cross the winding Kansas River and drive northwest for 300 miles (480 km) across the Great Plains. Once the realm of vast buffalo herds, today it's a seemingly endless farmland, though you'll still pass through patches of undeveloped grasslands, especially

INDEPENDENCE
START

INDEPENDENCE
This small Missouri town is where former president Harry Truman grew up.
0 MILES

TOPEKA
Climb 296 steps to the top of the Kansas State Capitol for epic city views.
85 MILES

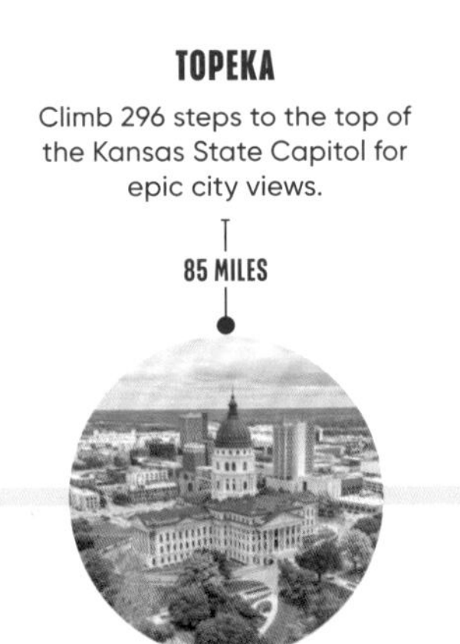

385 MILES

KEARNEY

The city neighbors the Platte River, which attracts migratory birds including sandhill cranes.

650 MILES

SCOTTS BLUFF NATIONAL MONUMENT

This landmark is hard to miss above the Nebraska plains.

THE GREAT EMIGRATION

Though pioneers forged the Oregon Trail in the 1830s, the first wagon train left Independence, Missouri in May 1843. Dubbed the "Great Emigration," it comprised some 120 wagons, 1,000 people, and around 2,000 horses and cattle. It took six months to reach Oregon, which at that time was so sparsely inhabited it doubled the territory's American population.

as you cross into Nebraska. At Kearney you reach the muddy wetlands of the Platte River, a migration spot for sandhill cranes, whooping cranes, and geese in spring. This area has long been a magnet for humans, too—on the other side of the riverbed lies Fort Kearny State Historical Park, which lies on the intersection of three historic wagon routes. A former army outpost, the site includes a replica of the 1848 fort built to protect travelers and gold prospectors.

TRADING RIVERS FOR SEAS OF GRASS

The road continues to shadow the river for over 500 miles (800 km) along what was once called the "Great Platte River Road." By now, you're deep into the Great Plains, a vast sea of grass, wheat, and corn stretching to the horizon. The few landmarks on the route really stick out. Chimney Rock soars over 300 ft (91 m) above the North Platte River, a sharp spearpoint of Brule clay and sandstone. A series of low-lying ridges breaks up the landscape nearby, with Scotts Bluff National Monument preserving the most famous rise, just 30 minutes from Chimney Rock. It's a massive 800-ft (244-m) rampart serving mesmerizing views and exhibits on the Oregon Trail pioneers, Indigenous Americans, and fur traders.

Another fur-trading spot lies across the border in Wyoming: Fort Laramie National Historic Site. Founded in 1834, it served as a fur-trading fort before becoming a military outpost in 1849. The vast grounds are ideal for stretching your legs, while the exhibits on show at the reconstructed buildings are the perfect way to while away a few hours.

Beyond Fort Laramie the route passes through the increasingly wild grasslands of central Wyoming. It's cool and dry here (the initial plateau is 4,300 ft/1,311 m above sea level), and the brown-yellow plains are peppered with sagebrush and juniper. Beyond a handful of small towns, development has been minimal, so it's no surprise that Wyoming contains the best remnants of the Oregon Trail. Hit the road for a farther 15 miles (25 km) to Guernsey, a small community that is home to Register Cliff, a sandstone bluff inscribed with the names of hundreds of trail pioneers. It's also worth detouring 3 miles (5 km) south of Guernsey to visit the Oregon Trail Ruts State Historic Site, which preserves deep gouges carved by original wagon wheels.

CROSSING THE NORTH PLATTE RIVER

The semi-arid plains roll on to Casper, where pioneers made their final crossing of the North Platte River. Today, it's the second-largest city in Wyoming, a modern oasis by the Laramie Mountains. From Casper, head southwest for 60 miles (95 km) on Route 220, rising through plains of grass and scrub to reach Independence Rock. A huge granite monolith, the rounded rock rises some 135 ft (40 m) above the Sweetwater River and is coated in graffiti by pioneers who used the stone as a bulletin board.

The tributaries of the Sweetwater River come to a head at South Pass, which was the only place wagons could easily cross the Continental Divide. Though it's at an elevation of 7,412 ft (2,260 m), the rise is incredibly gradual. Today on Route 28 the "valley" is little more than an extension of the flat, scrubby, grassland you've been driving through for miles, with larger hills far in the distance.

Continue chasing ghosts of pioneers southwest across the vast desert-like wilderness of the Great Divide Basin to Fort Bridger, where there's another

ABOVE Pink clouds gathering above downtown Casper

OPPOSITE LEFT Chimney Rock, fronted by sunflowers

OPPOSITE RIGHT Trading at reconstructed Fort Laramie

REGISTER CLIFF

View the signatures of 19th-century pioneers etched into the sandstone.

720 MILES

INDEPENDENCE ROCK

This large granite rock was regarded by pioneers as the halfway point on the trail.

SODA SPRINGS GEYSER

Witness America's only "captive" geyser blow 70 ft (20 m) into the air every hour.

1,295 MILES

SHOSHONE FALLS

Dodge the spray and enjoy epic, year-round views of the "Niagara of the West."

1,465 MILES

BOISE

The leafy capital of Idaho has excellent festivals, Basque cuisine, and river activities.

1,595 MILES

excellent frontier reproduction—this time the trading post of famed mountaineer Jim Bridger, who set up here in the 1840s.

Now the trail swings abruptly to the northwest, straight into the Rockies, across a series of sun-baked ridges known as the Wyoming Thrust Belt. U.S. 30 eventually delivers you to Soda Springs in Idaho. The main attraction here is the soaring Soda Springs Geyser, which was unleashed in 1937 during a well-drilling accident. It now blows on the hour thanks to a timer valve.

Continue on U.S. 30 west; this is bizarre terrain, high but flat, desert-like valleys surrounded by rounded, arid peaks. Eventually you'll cross the final Portneuf Range and emerge at the Snake River Valley at Pocatello. The route runs rapidly west from here across an increasingly arid landscape, broken by the little city of Twin Falls. The namesake falls have been diminished by dams but they still dazzle and project rainbows in the sunshine. Nearby Shoshone Falls rightfully steal the spotlight here, though. Standing a whopping 212 ft (65 m) high, and framed by the deep Snake River Gorge, they've been nicknamed the "Niagara of the West."

Farther along, stop by Three Island Crossings, one of the few safe places for pioneers to cross the treacherous Snake River. Enjoy a picturesque picnic here or motor on to Idaho's capital, Boise, which serves up excellent pinxtos and paella thanks to its Basque heritage. If you're here in summer, cool off with tubing trips along the Boise River.

FAREWELL IDAHO, HELLO OREGON

The Boise River eventually drains into the Snake River. Say goodbye to this major waterway—and Idaho—at the aptly named Farewell Bend State Recreation Area before cutting through more dry, low-lying hills to the quiet Baker City. This is the parched, eastern half of Oregon, with the Wallowa Mountains to the east and the Elkhorn Mountains over to the west.

The I-84 then continues northwest, traversing the Blue Mountains, where the

SHORTEN YOUR TRIP

Short of time? The most scenic part of the trail is the final portion in Oregon and Idaho: some 775 miles (1,0250 km) between Oregon City and Soda Springs, taking in the Columbia River Gorge, Blue Mountains, and Snake River Canyon (you'll need a minimum of three days).

LEFT The thundering Shoshone Falls, near Twin Falls

OPPOSITE TOP Mount Hood at sunset, in the final stretch

OPPOSITE BELOW Tubing down the gentle Boise River

the scenery shifts to steep, pine-clad slopes. You're spat out again after a winding switchback at Pendleton. Make the 20-minute drive to the Tamástslikt Cultural Institute, which offers a rare Indigenous American perspective on the Oregon Trail, from the local Cayuse, Umatilla, and Walla Walla Tribes.

PORTLAND BOUND

Follow the Columbia River on the I-84 to Portland for the final stretch of the drive, watching the scenery shift from dusty riverbanks to mighty cascades before you. Passing through the town of Hood River, keep an eye out for windsurfers, and the volcanic peak of Mount Hood. Make time to visit one final waterfall: Multnomah Falls. At 611 ft (186 m), it's a stunning multitiered cascade lined with hiking trails and viewpoints.

The route makes a turn south at the Fort Vancouver National Historic Site, following the Willamette River for around 30 minutes through the lively city of Portland before arriving at the End of the Oregon Trail Interpretive Center, which hosts interactive exhibitions including candle making and wagon packing.

End your journey in the enchanting beer garden at Oregon City Brewing Company—with craft breweries in almost every town in the state, it's as fitting a place as any to toast the hardy pioneers that trekked the continent 180 years ago.

Blue Swallow
MOTEL
100%
REFRIGERATED
AIR
VACANCY
TV
LOBBY
OPEN
OPEN

ROUTE 66

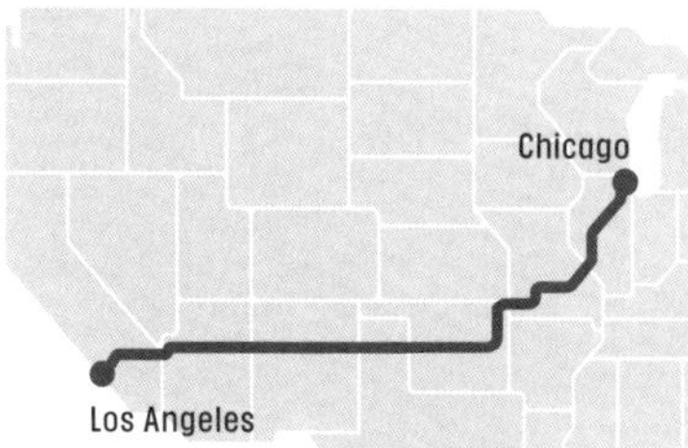

START/FINISH
Chicago, Illinois/Los Angeles, California

DISTANCE
2,170 miles (3,490 km)

DURATION
10–14 days

ROAD CONDITIONS
Well-maintained paved roads

THE BEST TIME TO GO
Spring and fall are the best times of year, to avoid Illinois' harsh winters and California's scorching summer season

OPPOSITE The Blue Swallow Motel in Tucumcari, New Mexico, an iconic overnight stop on Route 66

No other road symbolizes the spirit of America quite like Route 66. The hopes and dreams, struggles and triumphs of a nation have played out on this storied stretch of highway, which links Chicago to California and spans eight states.

Casually cruising along America's most celebrated highway, it soon becomes clear that Route 66 is about the journey as much as the destination. Throughout the twists and turns of its almost 100-year history, Route 66 has constantly shifted gears with the times. In the 1930s, it offered a pathway to a better life for migrants escaping the Dust Bowl. When the car became king during the post-war period, Route 66 again moved lanes, officially entering its golden era. During this heyday, families would pile into the Chevy to drive through cactus-studded landscapes, sipping root-beer floats over Formica tables at mom-and-pop diners along the way, before drifting off to sleep in flickering, neon-lit motels.

These days, Route 66 offers motorists the chance to experience the America of yesteryear, with glowing vintage signs, quirky supersized attractions, and nostalgic motels. And while it remains a beloved pathway for four-wheel enthusiasts, it's also a magnet for groups of leather-clad bikers on Harleys.

RETRO WONDERS

The "Mother Road," as John Steinbeck called the route in his classic novel *The Grapes of Wrath*, starts at the "Route 66 BEGIN" sign on South Michigan Avenue in downtown Chicago. After a quick photo op, rev the engine, pop Nat King Cole's "Get Your Kicks on Route 66" on the car stereo, and answer the siren call of the open road. As the city disappears in the rearview mirror, the scenery morphs to small-town America, and you'll pass by Wilmington's space-age

CHICAGO

CHICAGO
Snap a selfie at the "Route 66 BEGIN" sign, right in front of the Art Institute of Chicago.
0 MILES

WILMINGTON
This 30-ft (9-m) fiberglass astronaut is a survivor from Route 66's glory days.
61 MILES

ABOVE Route 66 Museum in Clinton, Oklahoma

OPPOSITE A roadside statue of a dinosaur in Holbrook, Arizona

Gemini Giant, looming over the curb. He's one of the route's remaining Muffler Men—enormous roadside statues, often cradling burgers or hot dogs, installed by savvy small business owners to lure ravenous motorists to their eateries.

Fields of swaying golden corn wave at passing cars as you head through rural Illinois, headlights facing southward toward the Missouri border. The drive is occasionally punctuated with weird and wonderful curiosities such as the world's largest covered wagon, an enormous pink elephant statue, and a drive-in housed within an ice-cream cone.

BURGERS AND BEATNIKS

A couple of hours into the journey, pull over for a pit stop at Motorheads Bar, Grill and Museum in Springfield, a treasure trove of Americana collectables including several antique automobiles suspended from the ceiling. Pull up a seat at the weathered bar and order the horseshoe sandwich, a signature dish that combines wedges of glistening Texas toast, meaty hamburger patties, and a mountain of fries smothered under a thick blanket of creamy cheese sauce.

Route 66 is dotted with such motor-enthusiast museums, but the Oklahoma Route 66 Museum in Clinton stands out from the pack with its interactive displays that bring the road's myths and legends to life. Before you leave, stop by the well-stocked souvenir shop to pick up a tin Route 66 number plate memento or a copy of Jack Kerouac's *On the Road*, a Beat Generation novel that includes a stretch of the highway.

LINCOLN

Ride the world's largest railsplitter covered wagon in Lincoln, Illinois.

172 MILES

SPRINGFIELD

Feast on a horseshoe sandwich to a soundtrack of rock, at Motorheads Bar.

210 MILES

CLINTON

Brush up your knowledge of the Mother Road at the stylish Oklahoma Route 66 Museum.

886 MILES

1,066 MILES

AMARILLO

Leave a message on one of the tail-finned vintage beauties at the Cadillac Ranch.

1,549 MILES

PETRIFIED FOREST

This national park shelters trees that have turned to stone and a dazzling display of badlands.

EXTEND YOUR TRIP

Built up an appetite for retro architecture while on Route 66? Then extend your trip by powering south from Santa Monica to Palm Springs. The two-hour journey through the serene Mojave Desert ends at the stylish Californian desert town, with its host of mid-century design gems.

KITSCH CLASSICS

Follow the ribbon of asphalt as it gently unfurls through the flat, high plains of northern Texas, leading to the Cadillac Ranch in Amarillo. You really can't miss this stop—it's the row of ten vintage Cadillacs buried nose-first in the ground, decorated in a multicolored riot of graffiti. Originally installed in 1974 by a collective of postmodern artists as a comment on the American Dream, it's since become a pop-culture landmark. Join the throng of curious visitors and snap a surreal selfie against the apocalyptic backdrop.

Another 100 miles (160 km) west, a pastel-blue classic car takes pride of place in front of the iconic, family-owned Blue Swallow Motel in Tucumcari, New Mexico. Beside it, a bedazzlement of neon signs promises potential visitors everything from a color TV to the cool breeze of in-room air conditioning, much needed in the heat of the sun-baked desert. Established in 1939, the motel is exactly the kind of place you would imagine Route 66 regular Marilyn Monroe parking her cherry-red Thunderbird outside, before checking in for the night.

A BREAK IN THE DESERT

From New Mexico, it's into northern Arizona, where the Petrified Forest National Park is an atmospheric spot to get off the beaten track and spend some time in the wilds of nature. The only national park in the country that protects a portion of Route 66, this otherworldly landscape of fossilized prehistoric trees and multicolored badlands is home to burrows of bouncy cottontail rabbits, free-roaming mule deer, and the occasional black bear. If there's time for a break from the route, follow the park's 28-mile (45-km) scenic drive, connecting roadside vistas to historic sites and hiking trails.

From the dramatic panoramas of Petrified Forest National Park, it's just a 30-minute drive through the arid desert, the air scented with the earthy smell of roadside saltbush shrubs, to the Wigwam Motel in Holbrook.

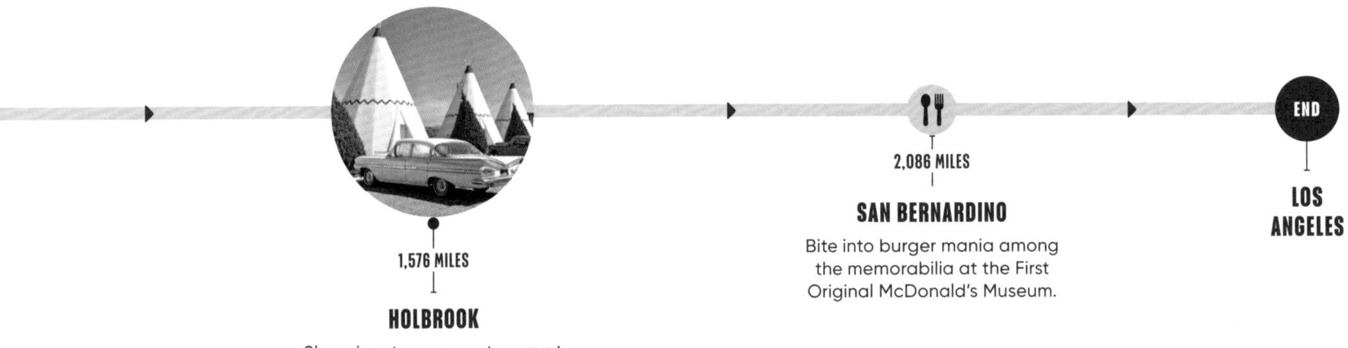

1,576 MILES

HOLBROOK

Sleep in a tepee guest room at the Wigwam Motel, a 1950s classic in the Arizona desert.

2,086 MILES

SAN BERNARDINO

Bite into burger mania among the memorabilia at the First Original McDonald's Museum.

END

LOS ANGELES

ABOVE The First Original McDonald's Museum in San Bernardino, California

A fascinating relic from a bygone era, this cluster of tepee-shaped guest rooms was once part of a thriving hotel chain. Only two of these villages still exist along Route 66 today, one in San Bernardino, California and this 15-lodge camp. When they originally opened, each tepee was fitted out with the latest mod-cons including coin-operated radios so guests could kick back and listen to Elvis crooning over the speakers. Adding to the nostalgic atmosphere, gleaming vintage motors are parked around the property. While in Holbrook, look out for the dinosaur statues around town, once used to advertise a long-closed museum.

THE END OF THE ROAD

You might get the feeling that the best has been saved for last as you slowly roll across the border into California—and it's true, the Golden State has done an excellent job of maintaining its Route 66 attractions. Start with a visit to the birthplace of the Big Mac at the First Original McDonald's Museum in San Bernardino. This is the exact spot where the famous golden arches were first unveiled when the McDonald brothers opened their debut restaurant in 1940. It's since become a museum dedicated to the humble hamburger, where plastic Happy Meal toys and a prototype of a ketchup dispensing gun are displayed as if they were the *Mona Lisa*. There's even a dedicated McDonald's historian on hand to guide visitors through the collection, although sadly he's not dressed as Ronald McDonald.

The twinkling lights of Santa Monica Pier will appear joyfully on the horizon as you drive toward the finish line in Los Angeles. For the final leg of your journey, pull the car over and stroll along the wooden promenade of the pier, seagulls circling overhead as you pose for a commemorative photo beside the "Santa Monica: Route 66 end of the trail" sign. Finish on a high note with a celebratory spin on the retro Ferris wheel, just as previous generations of Route 66 road-trippers did before you.

MUFFLER MEN

America has never lacked for oddballs or their oddities, and a highlight of any road trip is the kitsch you encounter along the way. Among the country's many roadside curiosities, some of the most iconic are the 20-ft- (6-m-) tall fiberglass statues known as Muffler Men. Classic Muffler Men are bland, square-jawed hunks, with outstretched arms holding whatever their owner is trying to sell (often mufflers, hence the name). Variations on the theme have included cowboys, lumberjacks, and Uniroyal Gals—the only Muffler Women.

The roadside reign of Muffler Men was short but glorious. The first Man was built by Bobbie Lee Prewitt, a California rodeo cowboy who made fiberglass cows for dairies and steakhouses. In 1962, the Paul Bunyan Cafe in Flagstaff, Arizona, asked him to craft a giant lumberjack to grab the attention of motorists on Route 66. It also grabbed the attention of Steve Dashew, who purchased Prewitt's business and molds the following year. Dashew's company, International Fiberglass, would go on to make hundreds of Muffler Men over the next decade, but the market for hot dog-bearing colossi soon disappeared, and by the mid-1970s, International Fiberglass had made its last Muffler Man.

Once a common roadside presence, Muffler Men are now elusive, despite their size. As the original site of many giants, Route 66 remains one of the country's more fruitful hunting grounds. The small town of Atlanta, Illinois, is home to the American Giants Museum, which has a collection of six Muffler Men, including a rare Texaco Big Friend. One of America's most unique Muffler Men welcomes customers to Buck Atom's Cosmic Curios on 66, in Tulsa, Oklahoma. Looking like a *Toy Story* casting reject, Buck is half cowboy, half astronaut, with a cowboy hat perched atop a space helmet and a huge shiny rocket in his hands.

The first Muffler Man was built by Bobbie Lee Prewitt, a California rodeo cowboy who made fiberglass cows for dairies and steakhouses.

The most monumental Man of all, though, might just be the one outside the J. Lawrence Walkup Skydome on the campus of Northern Arizona University in Flagstaff. Now a mascot for the NAU Lumberjacks, he's Bobbie Lee Prewitt's first creation, the 1962 Muffler Man all other Muffler Men descend from.

ABOVE A Muffler Man advertising Buck Atom's Cosmic Curios on 66, Tulsa, Oklahoma

LAKE MICHIGAN CIRCLE TOUR

Chicago ▸ Chicago

START/FINISH
Chicago, Illinois/
Chicago, Illinois

DISTANCE
1,100 miles (1,770 km)

DURATION
4–7 days

ROAD CONDITIONS
Paved; snowy or icy conditions possible in winter

THE BEST TIME TO GO
Summer to fall, for outdoor activities and colorful foliage

OPPOSITE: Chicago's Navy Pier, enclosed by the frozen waters of Lake Michigan

There's no salt, but the Great Lakes have just about everything else you'd find on the Atlantic and Pacific shores, from slick cities to sun-kissed beaches. Take a spin around Lake Michigan and uncover the country's Fresh Coast.

Kick your trip off in Chicago, where the skyline rivals New York's, and the first miles along DuSable Lake Shore Drive are an invitation to some serious neck craning. Conveniently, many of the city's marquee attractions are found along Lake Michigan. Jutting out into the water, Navy Pier is a summertime magnet, while directly to the south, Millennium Park, Grant Park, the Museum Campus, and adjacent city blocks host venerable institutions like the Field Museum and Art Institute of Chicago.

As you make your way southwest into Indiana, the glitz of downtown Chicago is quickly forgotten amid a gray expanse of heavy industry. For miles along the coasts of East Chicago and Gary, you'll drive through a strip of shipping ports, coal facilities, generating stations, and the continent's largest integrated steel plant. What comes next feels akin to Dorothy's Technicolor awakening in the land of Oz. The industrial desert suddenly gives way to Indiana Dunes National Park, an idyllic patchwork of beaches, black oak savanna, and wetlands where beavers, coyotes, and green herons carve out a home. The area's dunes have formed over ten millennia; you'll find the largest in the adjacent Indiana Dunes State Park, the king of the hills being the 192-ft- (59-m-) high Mount Tom.

RAISE A GLASS TO MICHIGAN

Almost as soon as you've entered Indiana you're exiting it and sweeping up through Michigan. The state's western shoreline is a delightful series of resort

CHICAGO

START

CHICAGO
The Shedd Aquarium has exhibits on the local Great Lakes environment.

0 MILES

GARY
Michael Jackson's childhood home is on the corner of Jackson Street and W 23rd Avenue.

29 MILES

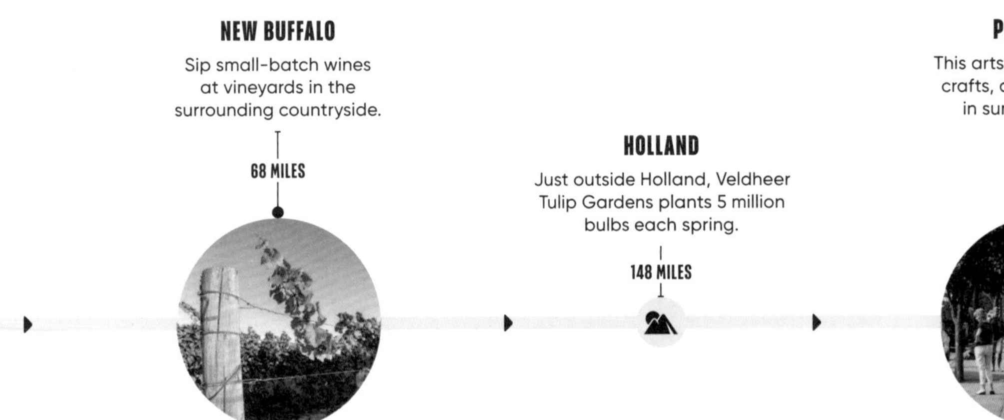

Holland celebrates its Dutch heritage with an authentic windmill, and adjacent gardens where millions of tulips bloom each spring.

ABOVE Holland's colorful Windmill Island Gardens

LEFT Climbing the sand dunes at Sleeping Bear Dunes National Lakeshore

towns, marinas, and beaches. Just across the state line, the New Buffalo area is a sneakily good wine region, with some 20 wineries producing mostly small-batch vintages. Eighty miles (130 km) up the coast, Holland celebrates its Dutch heritage with an authentic windmill, and adjacent gardens where millions of tulips bloom each spring, while halfway up the peninsula, Pentwater is popular for its galleries, antique shops, and summer art fairs. The shoreline scenery reaches its peak half an hour later, at Ludington State Park, where the striking form of the black-and-white Big Sable Lighthouse stands proud.

As you round the Lower Peninsula's northwestern corner you'll come to Sleeping Bear Dunes National Lakeshore, where 450-ft (140-m) sandy bluffs tower over Lake Michigan. You can trek to the lakeshore or explore the forests, lakes, and islands that form the rest of the preserve. Twenty-two miles (35 km) to the north is Leland's historic Fishtown; a hundred years ago, fishing villages lined the Lake Michigan coast, but today few remain. At the bottom of Grand Traverse Bay lies Traverse City, where life is just a bowl of cherries: pass through in summer and the fruit will be everywhere, from roadside stalls to pick-your-own farms.

In Mackinaw City, at the tip of the lower peninsula, bend the road-trip rules and leave your car behind to take the ferry to car-free Mackinac Island, in Lake Huron. The lovely resort island is the site of an 18th-century fort, summer cottages, and irresistible fudge shops.

ABOVE The Milwaukee Art Museum's pavilion, designed by Santiago Calatrava

INTO THE WOODS

Back on the mainland, drive over Mackinac Bridge into Michigan's wild Upper Peninsula (U.P.). The U.P. is 90 percent forested, and towns are few and far between. For the next 200 miles (320 km), your main company will be thick tracts of sugar maples, birches, and ironwoods. If you're passing through in August, swing through the Stonington Peninsula, to see migrating monarch butterflies congregate by the thousands in cedar trees.

From Marinette, take U.S. Route 41 into Wisconsin and trade Lake Michigan sunsets for Lake Michigan sunrises. If you're a sports fan, the Packers Hall of Fame in Green Bay is a good introduction to the city's pro football team and Wisconsin culture. East of Green Bay is the charming Door County, a peninsula frequently compared to Cape Cod. Lighthouses share space with dunes and sea caves, while the bayside towns are filled with boutiques, restaurants, wineries, and, in Sister Bay, goats on the roof. That last one is the signature attraction at Al Johnson's, a Swedish restaurant where the horned "staff" keep the sod roof in check.

Continue south, and from the town of Manitowoc, follow Interstate 43 all the way to Milwaukee. Wisconsin's biggest city is the birthplace of Harley-Davidson but is equally famous for its brewing heritage—Miller, Pabst, and Schlitz were all founded here. Today, the city's beer culture centers on its craft breweries and beer gardens, several of which are right on the lakeshore. And no, it's not the alcohol, that building really did move: on the water downtown, the striking Milwaukee Art Museum's Santiago Calatrava-designed pavilion features giant wings that open and close three times a day.

Leaving Milwaukee, follow the Lake Michigan shore through the small cities, and suburbs that connect it to Chicago until you're back where your adventure began and your circle is complete.

SHORTEN YOUR TRIP

Don't have time to circumnavigate the entire lake? Pick either the northern or southern half and drive a semicircle before hopping aboard the S.S. *Badger*. The car ferry crosses the lake at its midpoint, running between Manitowoc, Wisconsin, and Ludington, Michigan, from June to October.

749 MILES

GREEN BAY

Tour Lambeau Field and visit the Green Bay Packers Hall of Fame.

999 MILES

MILWAUKEE

Cream City gets its nickname from the shade of brick used to construct many of its buildings.

CHICAGO

KENTUCKY BOURBON TRAIL

Louisville ▸ Lexington

START/FINISH
Louisville, Kentucky/ Lexington, Kentucky

DISTANCE
170 miles (270 km)

DURATION
4–7 days

ROAD CONDITIONS
Well-maintained paved roads

THE BEST TIME TO GO
Spring or fall, for quiet roads and perfect temperatures

OPPOSITE Banks of golden leaves bordering a quiet Kentucky road

Sneak into the passenger seat and sip your way across Kentucky's Bluegrass country, taking in the best of the state's bourbon producers amid the rolling farmland, forests, and meadows south of the Ohio River.

Dense oak forests, the rich aromas of smoky wood and corn mash, and no-frills barbecue shacks: welcome to Kentucky bourbon country. This tantalizing trail links the Bluegrass State's best whiskey distilleries, from cosmopolitan Louisville to horse-racing capital Lexington. En route you'll see undulating hills and horse farms, river valleys lined with forests, historic red-brick towns, and great fields of corn and tobacco.

Your journey begins in Louisville, Kentucky's big city on the Ohio River. The Kentucky Bourbon Trail Welcome Center at the Frazier History Museum lies just off the waterfront in the revitalized district of Whiskey Row—many of the old cast-iron warehouses and red-brick buildings here have been converted into museums, boutiques, and cafés. Sample bourbon at distilleries like the Evan Williams Bourbon Experience or Michter's Fort Nelson, before exploring the city's other big attractions: the Louisville Slugger Museum, Kentucky Science Center, and Muhammad Ali Center, which chronicles the life of the city's most famous son.

INTO THE BACKCOUNTRY

Heading south along I-65, beyond Louisville's urban sprawl, your first stop is iconic Jim Beam (also known as the James B. Beam Distilling Co.), in Clermont. Visit the original white clapboard home of Jeremiah "Jerry" Beam (son of founder Colonel Jim), then take a tour of the main distillery, where you can follow your own bottle of Knob Creek through to the bottling line—and add your fingerprint to the wax seal.

LOUISVILLE

START

LOUISVILLE
Discover the bourbon-making process at the Kentucky Bourbon Trail Welcome Center.

0 MILES

CLERMONT
Join a tasting tour at Jim Beam, a distillery that's been open for over two centuries.

28 MILES

Leaving Jim Beam, you'll drive along the northern edge of the tranquil Bernheim Arboretum and Research Forest, a blaze of maple color in the fall, to reach Bardstown, the "Bourbon Capital of the World." Anchored by the circular Court Square and the Old Courthouse, it's a neat, quiet red-brick town, totally dominated by the bourbon industry—the scent of cooked, almost burnt cereal wafting over the whole place. Beyond the green expanse of My Old Kentucky Home State Park sits the modern campus of the Heaven Hill Bourbon Experience, while back in town lie the grand old premises of Barton 1792 Distillery, the enlightening Oscar Getz Museum of Whiskey History, and the creaking floorboards of Old Talbott Tavern, the "world's oldest Bourbon bar."

Trunk now packed with clinking bottles and gifts, head south into more rural backcountry. Just 15 miles (25 km) on, Maker's Mark Distillery stands in a rustic, isolated setting in the heart of Kentucky. It's another small-batch producer with a pedigree that dates back to the 1880s. As you tour the premises, you'll see the aging barrels beneath a stunning Chihuly glass ceiling installed in 2014.

ROSES AND RIVERS

The trail continues east across lush central Kentucky to Danville, one of the first places in the state to be settled by Europeans in the 1780s. Much of the charm here comes from perusing the family-owned businesses on Main Street, and visiting Constitution Square Historic Site, where the first Kentucky constitution was written and signed in 1792. The sprawling premises of Wilderness Trail Distillery, which lies on the edge of town, are just as good a reason to swing by.

From Danville, it's 30 miles (50 km) north along the heavily farmed corridor west of the Kentucky River valley to Lawrenceburg, home to the delightful Four Roses Distillery. Housed in pale yellow Spanish Mission-style premises near the Salt River, the distillery has leafy grounds laced with sweet-smelling rose bushes, and fine views of the hills nearby.

ABOVE RIGHT Fermentation at the Four Roses Distillery

BELOW Dipping whiskey bottles in wax at Maker's Mark Distillery

BERNHEIM ARBORETUM AND RESEARCH FOREST

Take a break from bourbon and get in touch with nature.

29 MILES

BARDSTOWN

Explore whiskey memorabilia at the Oscar Getz Museum of Whiskey History.

43 MILES

DANVILLE

Sample Blüe Heron Vodka and several types of bourbon at Wilderness Trail Distillery.

95 MILES

136 MILES

JO BLACKBURN BRIDGE

Enjoy views of the Kentucky River valley and leaping bungee jumpers.

170 MILES

LEXINGTON

Campbell House hotel was designed to resemble a posh horse farm.

END

LEXINGTON

WHAT IS BOURBON?

Bourbon is a type of American whiskey defined as being distilled from mash containing at least 51 percent corn. The rest is made up of grains, often rye. "Straight" bourbon must be aged—in new charred oak barrels—for a minimum of two years. Not all bourbon comes from Kentucky, though to qualify as Kentucky bourbon it must be both distilled and aged in the state. It's best drunk—as purists insist—either neat or with nothing but a few drops of water to open up the flavor.

Pair even more bourbon with views at the Wild Turkey Distillery. Just 8 miles (13 km) farther on, it sits high above the Kentucky River, with spectacular vistas of the forested valley. Nearby, the soaring Jo Blackburn Bridge runs parallel to rickety old Young's High Bridge, now a popular spot for bungee jumping. Not an adrenaline-seeker? Hop behind the wheel and drive on to Woodford Reserve Distillery, where whiskey has been made since at least 1812. Tours take in the historic stone barrelhouse alongside peaceful Glenn's Creek.

HORSE CAPITAL OF THE WORLD

The final leg of the journey sees increasing traffic as you approach Lexington, so you'll take in America's horse-racing capital at a slower speed, trundling past horse farms and horse "nurseries" before entering the city.

Lexington is a surprisingly dynamic city, home to the International Museum of the Horse, the Hall of Champions, the annual Spirit in the Bluegrass Music Fest—and a smattering of bourbon-related attractions where you can toast to your trip. End your journey with a hunt for rare brands and souvenirs at the Barrel Market, and treat yourself to a night at the venerable Campbell House, a 1950s gem with an on-site tavern that lists a selection of over 300 bourbons and whiskeys—just in case you missed any.

TOP The glass facade of the modern Wild Turkey Distillery

ABOVE Woodfood Reserve maturing in oak barrels

NATCHEZ TRACE PARKWAY

START/FINISH
Natchez, Mississippi/ Nashville, Tennessee

DISTANCE
490 miles (790 km)

DURATION
5–7 days

ROAD CONDITIONS
The highway was opened in 2005, so the roads are excellent

THE BEST TIME TO GO
Fall or spring, for beautiful foliage

OPPOSITE Cypress Swamp, on the Natchez Trace near Jackson, Mississippi

People have been traveling along the Old Natchez Trace for thousands of years. Today, this scenic route captures some of the nation's most beautiful scenery, as well as some of its darkest past.

A place of deep and evocative history, Old Natchez Trace is the official name for the collection of Indigenous-created trails that have been in use for at least 10,000 years. These spiritual paths, later used by European settlers to establish travel corridors and trade routes, have particular significance in Natchez, which sits on the cusp of the modern Natchez Trace Parkway.

Located on the banks of the Mississippi River, the city of Natchez is an architecture lover's dream, with beautiful pre-Civil War buildings. Take a leisurely stroll among the antebellum homes and along the lush tree-lined streets with quaint storefronts. It's easy to be enchanted by the neat and curated city, but its slave-trading past remains front of mind thanks to the Natchez Museum of African American History. Packed with interesting exhibits and artefacts, the museum explores Natchez's past as the second-largest slave port in the south.

Continue as you mean to go on with another deep dive into American history. Hop in the car for the 4-mile (6-km) drive to the Grand Village of the Natchez, a 128-acre (52-hectare) park and museum that preserves the remnants of an important settlement and ceremonial center of the local Natchez people. Another such place is Emerald Mound, about 10 miles (15 km) outside Natchez and the location of a popular hike along the Old Natchez Trace.

SUNKEN TRAILS AND SWAMPLANDS

From Emerald Mound, continue northeast on the parkway through

NATCHEZ

START

NATCHEZ
Take in the city's historic downtown, including Longwood Mansion.
0 MILES

GRAND VILLAGE OF THE NATCHEZ
Marvel at the scope of this old settlment.
4 MILES

49 MILES

SUNKEN TRACE

Trees form a natural roof over the scenic stretch of eroded trail at Sunken Trace.

110 MILES

JACKSON

Learn about the struggle for equality at the interactive Mississippi Civil Rights Museum.

140 MILES

CYPRESS SWAMP

Bring your binoculars and try to spot baby alligators.

ABOVE Sunken Trace, a stretch of the Old Natchez Trace that has eroded away

ABOVE RIGHT Sculpture in the Mississippi Civil Rights Museum

OPPOSITE Tupelo, the birthplace of Elvis Presley

dense green woodlands. If you wind down your window, you'll notice the air is much cooler here, because of the overhang of trees. This effect is even more exaggerated at the next stop on your journey, the Sunken Trace. Here the ground of the trail itself has been eroded by thousands of years of use, creating deep ruts in the landscape that are almost entirely enclosed by trees. The most photographed spot along the Trace, this area is particularly beautiful in the spring, when the green leaves give the trail a magical quality.

After about an hour, the Natchez Trace Parkway loops to the western side of Mississippi's capital, Jackson. The city is an important touchpoint for many cultural and historical moments, but is best known for those from the Civil Rights era, many of which you can learn about by visiting museums such as the Mississippi Civil Rights Museum.

Continue northwest along the parkway for 30 miles (50 km) to Canton, where woodlands give way to swamps. A small pull-off to one side of the two-lane highway marks the trailhead for Cypress Swamp, where you can walk along footbridges to explore this mysterious wetland. It's a great place for wildlife spotting, particularly alligators.

TOWARD NASHVILLE

Leaving the swamp, the landscape transforms into verdant green grasslands, and there are numerous scenic pull-offs and trailheads all the way to Tupelo. The Bynum Mounds at mile marker 232.4 are the oldest Indigenous mounds found along the Trace—the six burial mounds here represent a village that is believed to have been inhabited between 100 BCE and 100 CE.

Once you get to the small city of Tupelo, Mississippi, just 90 minutes from Memphis, pause to pay respects to the King. Elvis Presley, the King of Rock and Roll, was born in Tupelo in 1935, and his childhood home is now preserved as the Elvis Presley Birthplace and Museum. There's also a statue of the musician as a young boy, as well as plenty of opportunities to hear live music here.

From Tupelo, the Trace briefly crosses over into Alabama, a short span of road that holds one of the trip's most mighty views of the Tennessee River, visible as you drive across the John Coffee Memorial Bridge. The tree-lined bank is most impressive in the fall, when the changing leaves put on a free show for drivers on the parkway.

As you travel the hour and a half north toward the Tennessee state line, the landscape becomes hillier and the road more winding. This mountainous landscape is a great place to seek out waterfalls, and Jackson Falls, located within thick foliage just an hour outside of Nashville, is just the spot to soak up a little more nature before heading into the big city.

The Natchez Trace Parkway ends in the urban sprawl of Nashville, Tennessee. While early travelers on the trail would have just been glad to have survived what one milepost on the route calls "a snake-infested, mosquito-beset, robber-haunted forest path," you can celebrate time well spent in more style. Take in a show at the historic Grand Ole Opry or dance the night away at Tootsies Orchid Lounge, the oldest—and probably most atmospheric—honky tonk on Broadway Street.

MERIWETHER LEWIS

Explorer Meriwether Lewis, of Lewis and Clark fame, died under suspicious circumstances along the Natchez Trace in 1809. He'd been staying at Grinder's Stand inn, when he sustained two bullet wounds, one in the head and the other in the stomach. There were no witnesses to the shooting itself, and to this day no one is certain whether the gunshot wounds were self-inflicted or if Lewis was the victim of foul play.

ONE WAY
S. Second St.
Just 90 Minutes from
imagine what you can do here
B.B. KING'S
BLUES CLUB
B.B. KING'S COMPANY STORE
FREE COVER
Have a Coke
SPEED LIMIT 25

BLUES TRAIL

START/FINISH
Jackson, Mississippi/ Memphis, Tennessee

DISTANCE
325 miles (525 km)

DURATION
5–7 days

ROAD CONDITIONS
Roads are modern, but often in need of repair

THE BEST TIME TO GO
Visit Memphis in January, when the International Blues Challenge is held

OPPOSITE Beale Street in Memphis, the end goal for many blues musicians

Follow the Blues Trail north from Jackson, Mississippi and you'll be traveling in the footsteps of the many blues musicians who moved out of the plantations in the South to cities like Memphis and beyond.

In a lot of ways, Jackson feels like it's been plucked from a melancholy blues refrain. Downtown's buildings are in need of repair, and roads like Farish Street, once the main drag for bars and Black-owned businesses, now lie mainly silent. There are a few notable exceptions, like F. Jones Corner, which still plays blues on weekends. Starting here, the Blues Trail whisks you back to the origins of the iconic genre, crisscrossing towns and cities that are indelibly associated with the sound of the South.

Head north for around 35 minutes along the tree-lined Highway 49 into the town of Bentonia. The Blue Front Café, with its slightly peeling paint, is one of the last remaining juke joints (a southern term for an informal music bar) in the Delta. There's no stage here: local musicians play on the floor at the front of the room or on the porch. You'll be perching on folding chairs, if you're lucky (rickety wooden bar stools if you're not), which adds to the old-school ambiance. But don't worry: the quality of the music will help you forget any discomfort.

GREENWOOD AND GREENVILLE

As you head north into Greenwood, the emerald corridor of trees starts to give way to the miles of flat cotton fields that will eventually fill most of your views from the highway. Greenwood itself is a quaint little town full of historic buildings and unique local businesses. Several movies have been filmed here, including the 2011 movie *The Help*. The charming little tree-lined streets are not where you'll find the blues, however. For

JACKSON

START

JACKSON
Sip on cocktails and listen to regional blues musicians at F. Jones Corner bar.
0 MILES

BENTONIA
Hang out with the locals and blues enthusiasts at the iconic, down-home Blue Front Café.
28 MILES

ROBERT JOHNSON

Johnson only made two studio recordings but is considered a master of the Delta blues.

131 MILES

INDIANOLA

Trace the life of the great blues player at the B.B. King Museum and Interpretive Center.

that, you'll have to head to the outskirts. In the back of an overgrown graveyard behind the fading white walls of the Little Zion Church, on a lonely road called Money Lane, is the grave of infamous blues singer Robert Johnson, who, legend has it, sold his soul at a similar crossroads for his musical talents.

Greenwood also makes a good staging ground for a short jaunt west to Indianola. The major draw here is the B.B. King Museum and Interpretive Center, which plays homage to arguably the most famous blues musician in the world. A sprawling modern museum, it explores the singer's incredible life, from his time as the child of sharecroppers, through the Civil Rights era and onto international stardom. The museum also owns the nearby Club Ebony, a mint-green clapboard structure that has hosted musicians such as Howlin' Wolf, a young Ray Charles, and, of course, B.B. King himself, who once owned the club.

Before continuing the northward journey up to Cleveland, Mississippi, consider a secondary stop in and around Greenville, to the west. Here you can finally get a real glimpse of the mighty Mississippi River up close, as well as learn a bit about the original inhabitants of the area at the Winterville Mounds, the remnants of one of several Indigenous cities that were scattered across the South. Though many of these sites were cleared in the 1800s to make

EXTEND YOUR TRIP

Many early musicians, such as the world-famous Muddy Waters, continued the journey north from Memphis along the Mississippi to cities like St. Louis and Chicago, both of which retain their own style of blues to this day.

Dockery Farms was the early 1900s home of Charlie Patton, considered to be one of the very first blues musicians, and thus this spot is seen by many as the birthplace of the art form

room for plantations, several still exist across Southeastern U.S. The Mississippi Mound Trail runs almost parallel to the Blues Trail, and is worth exploring to better understand the domestic lives of the U.S.'s Indigenous peoples.

CLEVELAND AND CLARKSDALE

In Cleveland itself, make a beeline for the interactive GRAMMY Museum of Mississippi, which pays homage to the unique musical talent that has come out of the state. Just outside of town, far beyond the museum's sleek modern feel, lies the ghostly remnants of the cotton gin at Dockery Farms. This former cotton plantation was the early 1900s home of Charlie Patton, considered to be one of the very first blues musicians, and thus this spot is seen by many as the birthplace of the art form. Be sure to watch the documentary that runs on a loop in the window of the old gas station out front, and press the button located in one of the old buildings to hear the haunting strains of early blues music.

In a cotton field just a little north of Cleveland, in Merigold, Mississippi, you'll find Po' Monkey's. Once a famous juke joint, the wooden shack closed down after the death of the owner in 2016. You can still view the site, though, and send up prayers that one of the many plans to reopen it eventually makes good.

The highway meanders 31 more miles (50 km) to Clarksdale, the unofficial center of the Blues Trail—as indicated by the giant crossroads sculpture just as you enter town, a nod to the Robert

BELOW Club Ebony, in Greenwood, Mississippi

OPPOSITE TOP Grave of bluesman Robert Johnson

OPPOSITE BELOW Mural of B.B. King, the B.B. King Museum

CLEVELAND

Take your time to explore the sprawling, interactive GRAMMY Museum of Mississippi.

197 MILES

DOCKERY FARMS

Visit this former cotton plantation, considered the birthplace of the blues.

204 MILES

CROSSROADS MONUMENT

Take a snap of this sculpture, made from three guitars, at the junction of highways 61 and 49.

248 MILES

250 MILES

CLARKSDALE

Get a real juke-joint experience at Red's, a low-key Clarksdale institution.

299 MILES

TUNICA

See the cornet of W. C. Handy, "Father of the Blues," at Tunica's Gateway to the Blues Museum.

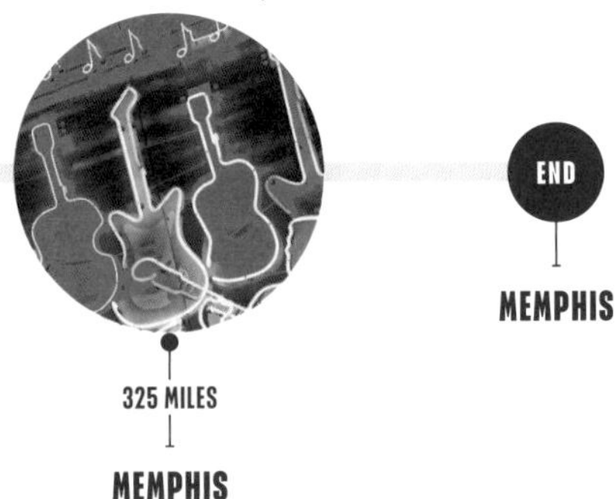

325 MILES

MEMPHIS

Catch blues (and soul R&B and rock) in Beale Street, Memphis's legendary home of music.

END

MEMPHIS

Johnson myth. The town caters to blues enthusiasts, with several music venues, art galleries, and record shops in the downtown area. Many hotels here are blues-themed, although the ethics of staying in replicas of the sharecropper cabins in which many blues musicians lived are dubious at best. Opt instead for the Riverside Hotel, which hosted music greats like Duke Ellington, Muddy Waters, and Howlin' Wolf.

In addition to Clarksdale's downtown shops, be sure to check out the Delta Blues Museum, located in an old freight depot. It would also be a shame to leave town without listening to some live blues at least once–in a place that promises a show every night of the year, there's plenty of music to choose from. Pull up a chair and sip on whatever beer is handy at Red's, a plain building on Sunflower Avenue that has no signage save the faded paint saying "LaVene Music Center." There's a *very* limited bar menu, but the music is fabulous.

ON TO MEMPHIS

If you're feeling inspired to make your own sweet music, hit the road for another 35 miles (55 km) or so, driving past cotton field after cotton field, and make a quick stop at the Gateway to the Blues Museum in Tunica, where you can create and record some simple blues music of your own. Housed in a replica of an old wooden sharecropper's cabin, it's home to memorabilia including W.C. Handy's first cornet.

As you head into Memphis, roll down your window and tune in to the historic WDIA radio station where B.B. King once worked. Head for the flashy neon lights of Beale Street, where you can still listen to live music nearly every night of the week, usually a mixture of blues, soul, R&B, and even rock music, all of which hold a place in Memphis history at one time or another. From the early 1900s through the 1960s, if you'd made it to Memphis, you'd made it to the big time. Park your car, put on your finest dancing shoes, and celebrate your successful trip through musical history.

HOODOO AND THE BLUES

From "mojo hands" to "The Crossroads," the lyrics of blues music are littered with references to African American folk magic, sometimes known as hoodoo. These rituals, charms, and traditions are the remnants of African spirituality passed down to enslaved people and carried into the blues era. Often demonized by the church, references to hoodoo found a home in blues music, which was also frowned upon by more pious members of the community.

ABOVE RIGHT The historic old Riverside Hotel, where many music legends have stayed

ROAD TRIP-INSPIRED ART

If you're an artist, you could hardly ask for a better source of inspiration than the road trip. Throughout history, they have proved irresistible to writers, musicians, and directors. At their most basic, it's the artist themselves taking the "get in the car and go" approach, hitting the road and seeing what they find. This tried-and-true method produced two giants of American literature: Jack Kerouac's *On the Road* (1957), which details the desperate ramblings of Sal Paradise and Dean Moriarty, and John Steinbeck's *Travels with Charley* (1962), a recounting of the author's cross-country trip with his dog from New York all the way to California and back.

What artists and their characters seek on road trips is almost always something they can't find at home. Sometimes that's as simple as the footloose joy Willie Nelson captures in "On the Road Again". Sometimes it's closure, of the sort the Indigenous Oklahoma teens of the TV series *Reservation Dogs* (2021) get from a trip to the Pacific to honor their dead friend. Sometimes it's a romance that could only blossom on the road, like Clark Gable and Claudette Colbert's Model T-assisted, cross-class affair in *It Happened One Night* (1934).

Arguably, the thing that's most sought after, though, is escape. When all's gone to hell at home, hit the road and hope. Bluesman Sleepy John Estes figured that out early, singing in the 1930s that the Model T was the "Poor Man's Friend." In *Thelma & Louise* (1991) , the road is the only place the title characters can find real freedom. In Bruce Springsteen's "Born to Run," it's a release from a "death trap" town. And in Tracy Chapman's classic "Fast Car," it's a last chance, even if the odds are long.

The thing that's most sought after is escape. When all's gone to hell at home, hit the road and hope.

What makes the road trip an inexhaustible subject for American artists is that, no matter what they or their characters are searching for—love, escape, adventure—they're always somehow searching for America itself, too. But that's a slippery subject. As the tagline of that road-trip movie par excellence, *Easy Rider* (1969), put it, "A man went looking for America. And couldn't find it anywhere." Only one thing to do then. Get back on the highway.

ABOVE Thelma and Louise driving their Ford Thunderbird

CIVIL RIGHTS TRAIL

START/FINISH
Atlanta, Georgia/ Memphis, Tennessee

DISTANCE
570 miles (915 km)

DURATION
7–10 days

ROAD CONDITIONS
Well-maintained highways and city roads

THE BEST TIME TO GO
Winter and spring, to avoid hurricane season

OPPOSITE Lorraine Motel in Memphis, where Martin Luther King, Jr. was assassinated; it's now part of the National Civil Rights Museum

Follow in the footsteps of the brave men and women who fought for justice on the U.S. Civil Rights Trail. This thought-provoking road trip shines a spotlight on the important moments in America's ongoing struggle for equality.

A journey along the U.S. Civil Rights Trail is a trip through some of the nation's most painful and triumphant history. Founded in 2018, this sprawling collection of historic sites, museums, and churches, spread across 15 states, highlights the people and places that played a pivotal role in the fight for equality for African Americans in the 1950s and 60s. You could spend months trying to see them all, but—for a more feasible alternative—take this drive from Georgia to Tennessee. Following roughly in the footsteps of the legendary Civil Rights leader Martin Luther King, Jr., it encompasses some of the most iconic places and events in the story of a movement that changed U.S. history.

STORIES OF SWEET AUBURN

Start your journey in Atlanta, Georgia, the most cosmopolitan city in the South and an epicenter in the struggle for Civil Rights since its beginning. Although the city has one of the largest African American communities in the country, it still contends with racial injustice, income inequality, and voting rights disparities, making it a poignant place to immerse yourself both in history and in the community as it is today.

Atlanta is, famously, the birthplace of Martin Luther King, Jr., the Christian minister who inspired the movement. The sprawling National Historic Park named in his honor encompasses mutiple King-related sites, including his restored Birth Home, the Ebenezer Baptist Church, where he was baptized and first ordained, and the King Center, where he is buried alongside his wife,

ATLANTA

MARTIN LUTHER KING, JR. NATIONAL HISTORIC PARK
Find out more about King's life at this park's Civil Rights sights.

0 MILES

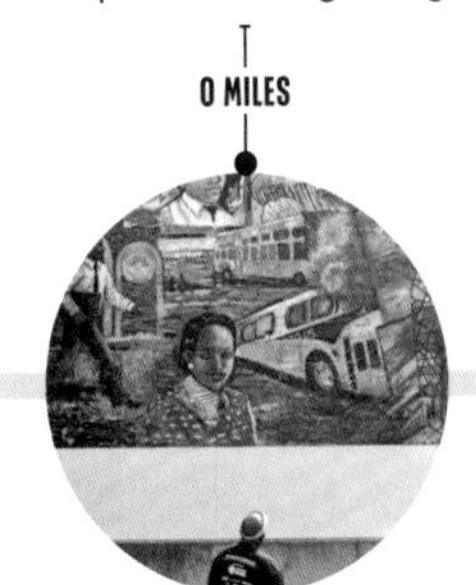

MARTIN LUTHER KING, JR.
In 1964, King became the youngest person to be awarded the Nobel Peace Prize.

306
309
206
207
208

1 MILE

MANGOS CARIBBEAN RESTAURANT

Paintings of Bob Marley adorn the walls of this colorful joint.

2 MILES

NATIONAL CENTER FOR CIVIL AND HUMAN RIGHTS

Learn about the fight for equality at this powerful museum.

Set aside enough time to cover Montgomery's major Civil Rights-related attractions and to reflect on their emotional history.

ABOVE The moving National Memorial for Peace and Justice in Montgomery, Alabama

OPPOSITE Civil Rights activists march across the Edmund Pettus Bridge in 1965

Coretta, in a plain marble tomb. The neighborhood that nurtured King, now known as the Sweet Auburn Historic District, was once a thriving center for Black life in Atlanta and is still home to some first-rate Black-owned restaurants. Tuck into lip-smacking oxtail curry at Mangos Caribbean Restaurant before dropping into the nearby Apex Museum for broader insights into the history and contributions of African Americans.

Last stop is the striking National Center for Civil and Human Rights, a mile (2 km) northwest in downtown. Interactive exhibits span Civil Rights history and the global human rights movement, with highlights including a lunch counter simulation where you can take part in a sit-in protest.

MARCH ON TO MONTGOMERY

Once you've crawled through Atlanta's notorious traffic, it's a little over two hours' drive on the fast-moving I-85 to Montgomery, Alabama. Set aside enough time to cover the city's major Civil Rights-related attractions and to reflect on their emotional history. One of the most evocative sites is the National Memorial for Peace and Justice, a stark collection of hundreds of hanging steel slabs, each engraved with the names, ages, and locations of victims of lynching and racial violence across the nation. The nearby Legacy Museum educates visitors on the ways this grim history is connected to the ongoing racial injustice faced by African Americans today.

Montgomery is perhaps best known for the bus boycott, kicked off on December 5, 1955, by the courageous actions of Rosa Parks, who refused to give up her seat on a segregated bus. You can learn more about Parks and the Montgomery Bus Boycott, which ultimately led to the desegregation of transportation across the country, at the Rosa Parks Museum.

Half a mile to the east is the Dexter Avenue King Memorial Baptist Church, where Martin Luther King, Jr. served as pastor and rose to prominence as spokesperson for the bus boycott. The historic building is beautiful, particularly the luminous stained-glass windows, and the friendly tour leaders here give visitors a valuable insight into King's legacy. It's a powerful place that will leave you with a sense of optimism.

The city is also home to the Alabama State Capitol, the final stop on the infamous Selma to Montgomery march. The march was attempted three times, the first of which became known as "Bloody Sunday" for the violence used by police on the peaceful protestors as they crossed Selma's Edmund Pettus Bridge. To immerse yourself in this pivotal event, take the half-hour drive west to the small city and follow in the footsteps of the activists, from the Selma Interpretive Center across the narrow bridge to the National Voting Rights Museum. Displays tell the full story of the march and the campaign for the voting rights it ultimately achieved.

BOMBS AND BRUTALITY

Back in Montgomery, head north for 90 miles (145 km) to Birmingham, Alabama, whose industrial past has earned the city its nickname "the Pittsburgh of the South." Despite its myriad attractions,

THE RED TAILS

Set in an old training base about 30 minutes' drive from Montgomery, the Tuskegee Airmen National Historic Site celebrates the lives of the first African American military pilots, the Tuskegee Airmen. Known as the Red Tails, these pioneering pilots completed more than 15,000 sorties during World War II.

ROSA PARKS MUSEUM

Find out more about the life of this extraordinary activist.

166 MILES

DEXTER AVENUE KING MEMORIAL BAPTIST CHURCH

Tours of the church focus on the local Civil Rights community.

167 MILES

EDMUND PETTUS BRIDGE

In 1965, activists made three attempts to cross this bridge.

218 MILES

The peaceful, lake-dotted Holly Springs National Forest in Mississippi makes an excellent rest stop for those in need of a moment of quiet contemplation.

ABOVE *I Ain't Afraid of Your Jail*, a sculpture on Kelly Ingram Park's Freedom Walk

OPPOSITE TOP Colorful Beale Street in downtown Memphis

OPPOSITE BELOW Stax Museum of American Soul

including botanical gardens and a fine art museum, the city's inequality is easy to feel, with some neighborhoods full of boarded-up buildings.

Birmingham was notorious for police brutality during the Civil Rights era. During the May 1963 Children's Crusade, city commissioner Bull Connor ordered the use of high-pressure fire hoses, dogs, and cattleprods against hundreds of young protestors in Kelly Ingram Park. Follow the park's Freedom Walk, lined with menacing statues, to tap into the story, and then call into the nearby 16th Street Baptist Church, which stands as a memorial to four Black girls killed by a Ku Klux Klan bomb just four months after the Crusade. Round off with a visit to the Birmingham Civil Rights Institute, which puts these violent events into context.

TO MEMPHIS

It's a three-and-a-half-hour journey to your final destination: Memphis, Tennessee. Along the way, the peaceful, lake-dotted Holly Springs National

EXTEND YOUR TRIP

Two cities at opposite ends of this Civil Rights extension record important moments in the fight for desegregation. In Little Rock, Arkansas, nine Black students famously battled fierce opposition to enroll in the city's Central High School in 1957, paving the way for future integration. And in Columbia, South Carolina, a monument next to the State House commemorates a demonstration by hundreds of protestors against segeregation in 1961.

16TH STREET BAPTIST CHURCH

The bombing of the 16th Street Baptist Church makes the site a solemn but necessary stop.

311 MILES

BIRMINGHAM CIVIL RIGHTS INSTITUTE

Chart the Children's Crusade—and its impressive legacy.

311 MILES

HOLLY SPRINGS

Enjoy the quiet surroundings of Chewalla Lake in the Holly Springs National Forest.

492 MILES

MEMPHIS

568 MILES

LORRAINE MOTEL

The site of Martin Luther King, Jr.'s assassination in Memphis is now preserved as a memorial.

570 MILES

SOULSVILLE

This Memphis neighborhood is home to the Stax Museum of American Soul Music.

Forest in Mississippi makes an excellent rest stop for those in need of a moment of quiet contemplation.

Aside from the bustle of Beale Street, downtown Memphis has a low-key feel. It was here, on the balcony of the Lorraine Motel, that Martin Luther King, Jr. was assassinated on April 4, 1968. The motel now forms part of the National Civil Rights Museum; following the history of the Civil Rights Movement from its beginnings through to King's death, it is one of the most difficult sites on the trail.

Beale Street itself, a center for African American commerce and culture as far back as the Civil War, comes as a welcome respite. In the early 1900s, the district became a gathering spot for blues musicians—the forerunners of the nonstop music that still shakes its joints today. It was also home of the First Baptist Church, headquarters of Ida B. Wells' antisegregationist newspaper, *Free Speech*, and WDIA radio station, the first in the country with programming specifically for African Americans.

South of downtown, make the Stax Museum of American Soul Music your final stop. Telling the story of the iconic music label, it's a fitting place to end your journey with a little soul.

BLUE RIDGE PARKWAY

Rockfish Gap

Cherokee

START/FINISH
Rockfish Gap, Virginia/ Cherokee, North Carolina

DISTANCE
470 miles (755 km)

DURATION
3-5 days

ROAD CONDITIONS
A well-maintained two-lane road

THE BEST TIME TO GO
Fall, for leaf-peeping, or spring for quieter roads and to avoid winter closures

OPPOSITE The winding Linn Cove Viaduct, bordered by colorful fall foliage

Escape the hustle and bustle on "America's Favorite Drive," a slow and scenic national parkway traversing the spine of mountains between Shenandoah and Great Smoky Mountains national parks.

The Blue Ridge Parkway from Central Virginia to the North Carolina/Tennessee border is a rolling, meandering drive through mountains, farmlands, and Appalachian history. You could travel this route along Interstates, but what makes the parkway special is its height—averaging an elevation of 3,000–4,000 ft (915–1,220 m)—and its speed: a slow 45 mph (70 km/h). It's a journey that forces you to sit back and enjoy the scenery.

Construction on the parkway began in the 1930s, partly as an effort by the federal government to curb the level of unemployment during the Great Depression. It was the first paved road in many of the Appalachian counties it traverses, taking travelers on a trip back in time through preserved relics of mountain life: log cabins, country estates, and old blacksmiths' shops.

RIDGE REGION

Enter the parkway at Rockfish Gap, at the edge of Shenandoah National Park—a beautiful stretch of land beloved by day-trippers and Appalachian Trail hikers. Along this northernmost section of the famous byway, known as the Ridge Region, it's easy to see how the Blue Ridge Parkway got its name. Layers of mountains fold up against each other, turning shades of indigo when backlit by the setting sun. The ribbon-like highway hugs the mountain curves, each bend revealing another photo-worthy scene.

Blue-gray signs alert you to pull-offs for overlooks and sites like the dramatic Humpback Rocks or 12 Ridges Vineyard,

ROCKFISH GAP

START

HUMPBACK ROCKS
Dramatic vistas, hiking trails, and an outdoor farm museum all provide reasons to pause.

6 MILES

12 RIDGES VINEYARD
Sample small-batch wines and nibble on charcuterie at this high-altitude winery.

25 MILES

86 MILES

PEAKS OF OTTER LODGE

Picnic by a lake with stunning views of Sharp Top Mountain at this historic lodge.

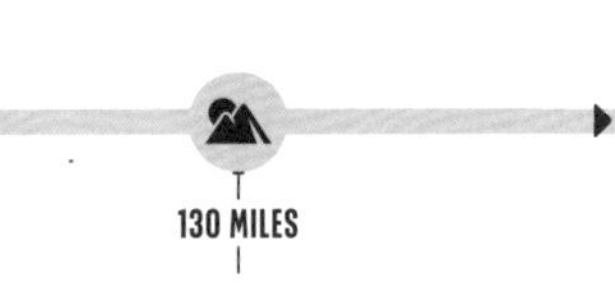

130 MILES

ROANOKE VALLEY OVERLOOK

Reconnect with urban life through a birds-eye view of the largest city on the parkway.

305 MILES

GRANDFATHER MOUNTAIN

With sweeping views, the mountain's swinging bridge sits a mile above sea level.

and visitor centers and rustic lodges—such as Peaks of Otter Lodge—dot the route. It takes a moment to twig exactly what's so different about this road—not a presence, but an absence: no stoplights, gas stations, or large commercial centers. The quiet is refreshing.

PLATEAU AND HIGHLAND REGIONS

You'll trade peaks for pastures and ridgelines for rolling hills as you enter the Plateau Region. Anchored by Roanoke, the largest city on the parkway (which you can view from above at an overlook), it's a storied area. Outdoor museums occupy historic farms, old mills, and family homesteads, giving visitors the chance to explore how people used to live in the 1800s and 1900s. Picture-perfect Mabry Mill charms with Southern cookin' and demonstrations of crafts like handweaving and spinning, and the area's bluegrass, folk, and gospel heritage is celebrated at the Blue Ridge Music Center. A summer concert series is held in its pastoral amphitheater, and local musicians and storytellers take their songs and tales on the road, hosting informal Sunday shows at mileposts along the parkway.

About halfway through the drive, the road crosses the state border into Western North Carolina—home to some of the tallest mountains east of the Mississippi—and the parkway's Highland Region. Past the hippie college town of Boone, Grandfather Mountain is a good place to pause, especially if you've kids in the back, with an easy walk on its mile-high suspension bridge and large enclosures where you can see local wildlife—including cougars and bald eagles—in a natural setting.

From here, follow the Linville River to Linville Gorge, the deepest canyon in the Eastern U.S. This wilderness protected area is rough, wild, and a magnet for avid hikers and climbers. Tumbling 90 ft

It takes a moment to twig exactly what's so different about this road—not a presence, but an absence: no stoplights, gas stations, or large commercial centers. The quiet is refreshing.

ABOVE Looking Glass Rock emerging on the hazy horizon

OPPOSITE TOP Ducks swimming in the waters by Mabry Mill

OPPOSITE BELOW Driving through Boone, a college town

(30 m), spectacular Linville Falls is the most celebrated of the parkway's many waterfalls and numerous hiking trails.

PISGAH REGION

Forty miles (65 km) later, hop off the parkway onto N.C.-128 and drive to the summit of Mount Mitchell, the highest peak east of the Mississippi. An observation deck offers 360-degree, miles-wide views of the mountains in the Pisgah Region below. The air is cool up here, and it smells like Christmas thanks to the Fraser fir on the mountain slopes.

Moving on, the parkway hugs artsy Asheville, the second-largest city on the route. Shop for quilts, baskets, pottery, and jewelry made by local artisans at the nearby Folk Art Center while taking in demos of traditional craftsmanship.

Ears might pop as you climb out of Asheville and head into the Shining Rock Wilderness, a rugged portion of steep slopes, evergreen forests, and craggy rock gardens, with the highest elevations on the parkway. Huge rhododendrons light up with purple blooms, and in the distance, you'll spot Looking Glass Rock, an ominous granite dome that seems to have descended from the moon. Hikers will relish this part of the drive with its endless trailheads. Climb Mount Pisgah, explore the strange landscape of Graveyard Fields, or catch the sunset atop Waterrock Knob, keeping your eyes peeled for black bear and elk.

At Richland Balsam, you pass over the parkway's high point of 6,053 ft (1,845 m) and begin the descent to its southern terminus at Cherokee, capital of the Eastern Band of Cherokee Indians. Your journey on the parkway ends here but you're also on the doorstep of another beautiful national park, Great Smoky Mountains. After stretching your legs at Cherokee's many historic sights, you might opt to continue your adventure into the park and check another state —Tennessee—off your bucket list.

LINVILLE FALLS

Choose between easy and strenuous trails to view this famous three-tiered cascade.

316 MILES

ASHEVILLE

Asheville's Folk Art Center offers retail therapy and the chance to support local artisans.

382 MILES

WATERROCK KNOB

Hike Waterrock Knob, home to wildflowers, elk, and the occasional black bear.

451 MILES

END

CHEROKEE

CIVIL WAR TRAIL

Gettysburg
Charleston

START/FINISH
Charleston, South Carolina/Gettysburg, Pennsylvania

DISTANCE
1,235 miles (1,990 km)

DURATION
9–13 days

ROAD CONDITIONS
Paved; primarily interstates and major highways

THE BEST TIME TO GO
Early July, to catch the reenactment of the Battle of Gettysburg

OPPOSITE A cannon at Lookout Mountain Battlefield, near Chattanooga, Tennessee

Chasing Union and Confederate ghosts on a Civil War tour is the ultimate road trip for military-history buffs. This drive takes in some of the conflict's most important moments, from the first shots to its final surrender.

Taking a Civil War–themed road trip is a fascinating way to explore the hundreds of battlefields, forts, and museums across the country. For the conflict's major sites, try this six-state drive, which takes in the war's beginning, end, and several of the major battles in between.

Start where the war did: Charleston, South Carolina. At 4:30 a.m. on April 12, 1861, Confederate forces fired a mortar shell that exploded above Fort Sumter, a federal redoubt at the entrance to Charleston Harbor. Vastly outnumbered, the Union soldiers vacated Sumter on April 15. Later, they'd lay siege to the now rebel-held fort for 587 days. What remains is a low bunker, squatting on the waves, with 42-pounder cannons, accessible only by passenger ferry. South of the pier, the Old Slave Mart Museum documents Charleston's role in the slave trade and acts as a chilling reminder of the war's stakes.

WEAVING WEST TO ATLANTA

From Charleston, take interstates 26 and 20 inland to Atlanta. During the war, the city was a major rail hub and the South's second-most important industrial and logistical center, after Richmond. That made it a rich prize, and in the summer of 1864, Union General William T. Sherman's army took the city. The North's victory helped President Abraham Lincoln win re-election and set the stage for Sherman's devastating March to the Sea. The war wasn't over, but Atlanta was the beginning of the end. Most battle sites in the city have been built over, but historical markers

CHARLESTON

START

CHARLESTON
The Civil War began here in 1861, when Confederate troops opened fire on Fort Sumter.

0 MILES

ATLANTA
The Union capture of Atlanta laid the ground for General Sherman's March to the Sea.

307 MILES

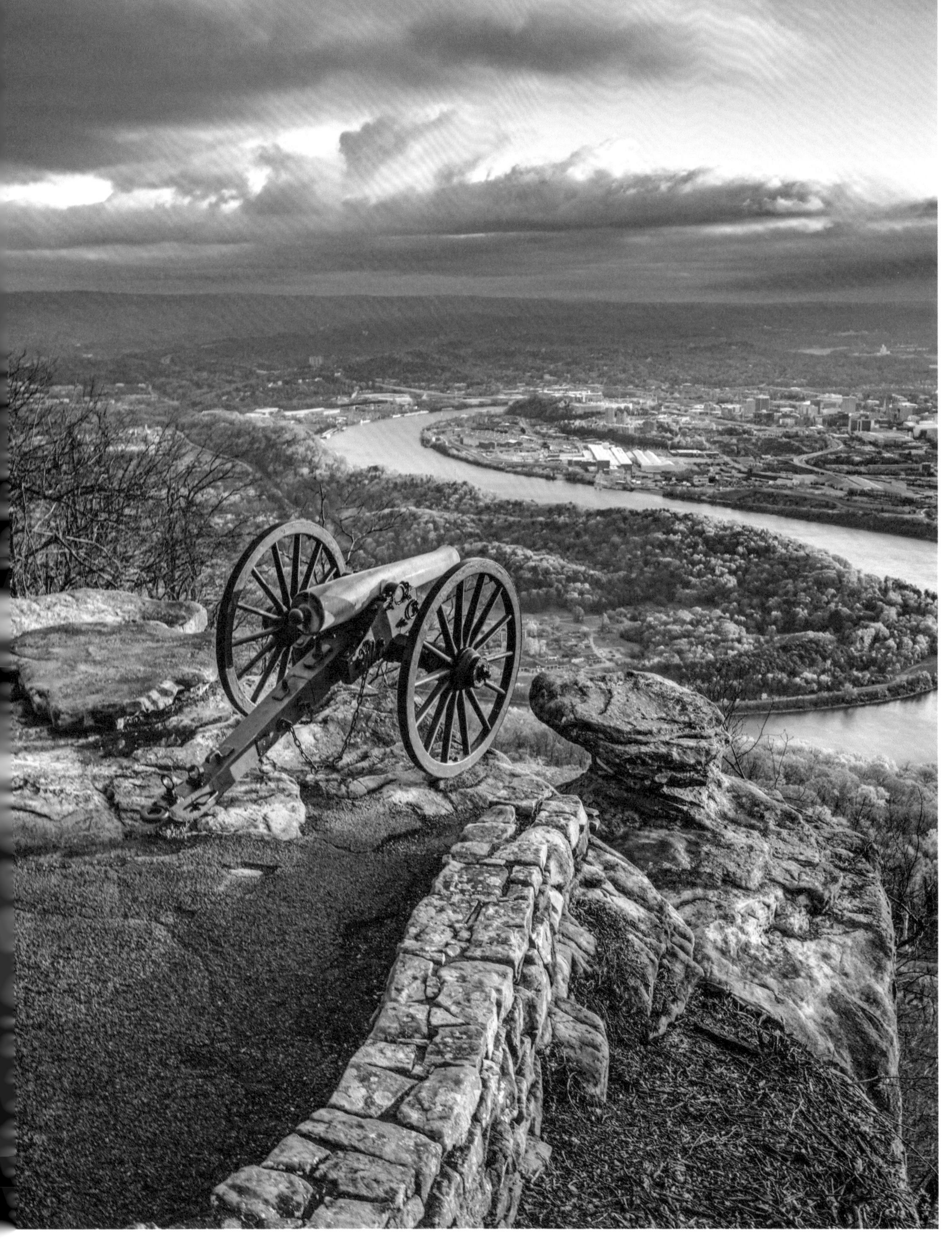

CHICKAMAUGA BATTLEFIELD
The Georgia-based battle was the second deadliest of the Civil War.
417 MILES

LOOKOUT MOUNTAIN BATTLEFIELD
Experience sprawling views of Chattanooga.
430 MILES

FREDERICKSBURG BATTLEFIELD
Take a chilling walk down the infamous Sunken Road.
1,025 MILES

denote key locations, and Tanyard Creek Park preserves some of the Peachtree Creek Battlefield.

For the prelude to Atlanta, drive up I-75 to Chickamauga. Today, the battlefield is a peaceful expanse of forests and fields dotted with various monuments and a rustic wood cabin that served as a busy field hospital; in September 1863, it was the site of the war's second-deadliest battle, behind only Gettysburg. The Confederates won a Pyrrhic victory here but lost two months later in the Battle of Chattanooga, a fight that a rebel soldier deemed "the death-knell of the Confederacy." You'll find battle sites along Missionary Ridge, just east of downtown Chickamauga, and on Lookout Mountain, which provides grand views of the city and a horse-shoe bend in the Tennessee River.

ACROSS TO VIRGINIA

Head northeast on a full day's drive through the Appalachian Mountains to Appomattox Court House National Historical Park. This was where General Robert E. Lee surrendered the Army of Northern Virginia to General Ulysses S. Grant on April 9, 1865. Just outside the park is the American Civil War Museum at Appomattox, which holds the uniform and sword Lee wore to his surrender.

Ninety miles (145 km) east lies the former Confederate capital of Richmond, Virginia. Downtown is the so-called White House of the Confederacy, a drab gray structure that offers guided tours through both public rooms and private quarters. On the banks of the James River are the remnants of the Tredegar Iron Works, which produced most of the Confederacy's battlefield cannons, including those that fired the war's first salvos at Fort Sumter.

Nowhere saw as much fighting during the war as the hundred or so miles (160 km) between Richmond and Washington, D.C. Drive an hour north out of Richmond, and you'll find four major battlefields, all within 20 miles (30 km) of one another: fought in December 1862, Fredericksburg was the largest, and the first urban battle of the war.

BATTLEFIELD ANGEL

Clara Barton was a legendary figure during the war, caring for wounded Union soldiers at Bull Run, Cedar Mountain, Antietam, and other clashes across Maryland, Virginia, and South Carolina, service that earned her the nickname "the Angel of the Battlefield." After the war, Barton opened the Office of Missing Soldiers, which reconnected some 20,000 men with their families. Years later, she founded the American Red Cross.

1,188 MILES

ANTIETAM NATIONAL BATTLEFIELD

Tour locations like Burnside Bridge and the Cornfield.

1,233 MILES

GETTYSBURG NATIONAL MILITARY PARK

This pivotal three-day battle was the Civil War's bloodiest.

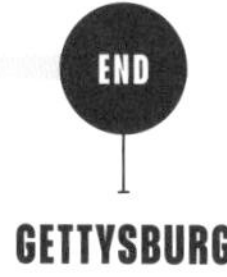

END

GETTYSBURG

ABOVE The Stone House, which was used as a hospital in both battles at Manassas

RIGHT Rows of gravestones at Gettysburg National Cemetery

OPPOSITE American Civil War Museum, Richmond, Virginia

THE LAST LANDMARK BATTLES

Manassas National Battlefield Park, on the outskirts of Washington, D.C, was the site of the Civil War's first full-scale battle, Bull Run, which took place on July 21, 1861. Lincoln was hoping for a quick end to the conflict and sent General Irvin McDowell to capture Richmond, but a Confederate victory here signaled that things wouldn't be so simple.

Following a second clash at Manassas in August 1862, Lee invaded Maryland in the hopes of eventually capturing Washington. On September 17, his army encountered Union soldiers under the command of General George McClellan at Antietam. It would become the single deadliest day in American military history, with some 23,000 men killed, wounded, or missing. Both sides suffered losses, but the result was less devastating for the Union, and the outcome both ended Lee's invasion and gave Lincoln the opportunity to issue his preliminary Emancipation Proclamation. Today, Antietam National Battlefield is one of the prettiest and best-preserved Civil War battlefields in the country, with rolling hills and a monument to the famed nurse Clara Barton, who tended to injured Union soldiers.

End your drive at the Civil War's most famous battlefield, Gettysburg, where you can take tours, visit a museum, and view weapons demonstrations. Lee had invaded the North again in the summer of 1863, this time hoping to compel the Union to sign a peace treaty, but a resounding Union victory here in the first days of July forced the rebels to retreat and shifted the war's momentum in the Union's favor. Four months later, Lincoln would deliver his Gettysburg Address at the dedication of Gettysburg National Cemetery. Together, the speech and the burial ground provide a fitting end for a journey through the country's most harrowing period: a chance to reflect on both the ideals the Union fought for and the terrible sacrifices made to preserve them.

OVERSEAS HIGHWAY

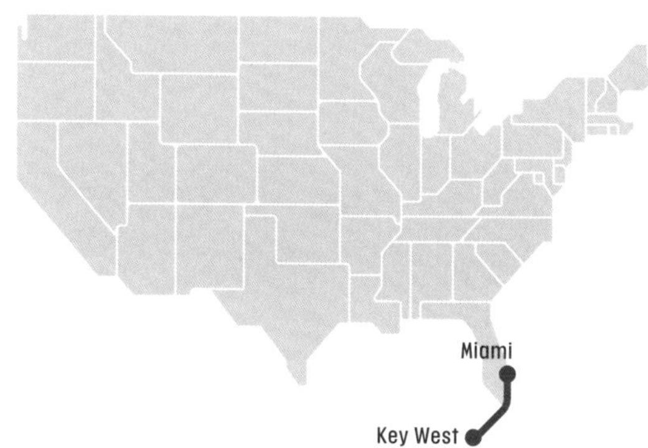

START/FINISH
Miami, Florida/
Key West, Florida

DISTANCE
170 miles (275 km)

DURATION
1–2 days

ROAD CONDITIONS
Well-maintained highway

THE BEST TIME TO GO
Year-round, but avoid hurricane season (June–November)

OPPOSITE Striking Seven Mile Bridge, which runs south of Marathon Key

Make for the pristine turquoise waters of the Caribbean on the Overseas Highway. A marvel of modern engineering, this key-hopping road connects Miami to free-spirited Key West.

Start in the sultry city of Miami, where there's plenty to see and do before you even get behind the wheel–from the Art Deco buildings of Ocean Drive, to the murals and shops that make up Little Havana. Beyond the city lights lies a whole different world. Just a 40-minute drive from downtown Miami, Everglades National Park is the largest remaining subtropical wilderness in the country. This vast swampland can be accessed by detouring west from the city on U.S. 41, but the best way to experience it is by boat–pop out to Coopertown to take a guided airboat tour through this incredible landscape.

As you head south along U.S. 1 through the southernmost tip of the Everglades, your surroundings grow more and more watery until you finally break from the mainland altogether. Welcome to the Florida Keys, a collection of small islands off the southernmost coast of the state. Your first stop, Key Largo, is located only about an hour south of Miami. The island is sometimes called the Dive Capital of the World, as there are so many accessible dive sites here, some just 30 minutes or so from shore.

QUIRKY KEYS

From Key Largo, it's another half an hour south, through miles of subtropical jungle, to the island of Islamorada. Take time to check out the quirky charms of the area, including *Betsy the Giant Lobster*, a 30-ft- (9-m-) tall sculpture of a Florida Spiny Lobster crafted by artist Richard Blaze in the 1980s. There are also a few small but interesting museums

MIAMI

START

MIAMI
Cruise past the Art Deco buildings on buzzing Ocean Drive.

0 MILES

THE EVERGLADES
Detour 28 miles (45 km) west to spot alligators in the swamps of Everglades National Park.

here, including the History of Diving Museum, dedicated to the area's favorite watersport.

The farther south you go along the highway, the more the land succumbs to water. As you leave Islamorada, the small strip of sandy shoreline gives way to open ocean and a picturesque view of Indian Key Historic State Park, a tiny island, accessible only via boat, that regularly draws fishing enthusiasts and snorkelers to its shores. The ruins here are all that's left of Indian Key town, whose community once made a living from salvaging shipwrecks.

WILDLIFE ENCOUNTERS

Manatees and dolphins are a regular sight along the Overseas Highway, and you can brush up on your knowledge of the genteel creatures at the Dolphin Research Center on Marathon Key, just over 30 miles (50 km) south of Islamorada. The insightful center helps support education and research around the area's marine wildlife, particularly dolphins and sea lions.

Once you've reached Marathon Key's downtown area, you're halfway through the drive. The island makes an excellent stopping point, with affordable motels and luxury resorts. There's also plenty to keep you busy here, including the Florida Keys Aquarium Encounters, a

ABOVE Boats lining the waterfront in Marathon Key

RIGHT *Betsy*, Islamorada's enormous lobster sculpture

OPPOSITE Cycling in pastel-painted Key West

ISLAMORADA

The History of Diving Museum highlights sites such as the Christ of the Deep statue.

85 MILES

INDIAN KEY HISTORIC STATE PARK

Kayak the half-mile over seagrass flats to Indian Key.

90 MILES

SOUTHERNMOST POINT MARKER
The end of the continental United States is just 90 miles (145 km) from Cuba.

170 MILES

BAHIA HONDA STATE PARK
With its sugar-soft sand and swaying palm trees, Sandspur Beach is postcard material.

131 MILES

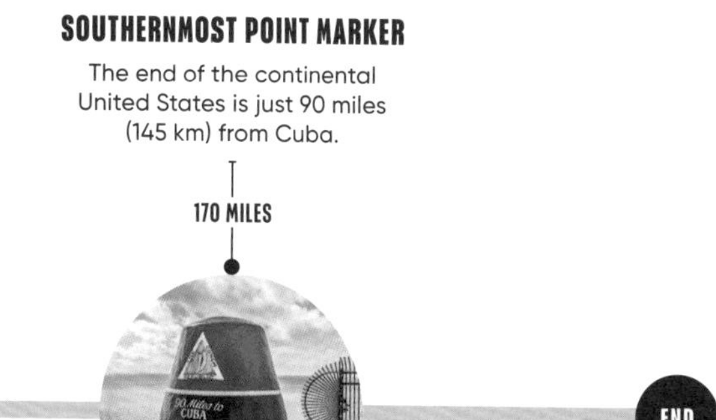

END

KEY WEST

small aquarium that offers opportunities to get up close and personal with the local sea life, and the Turtle Hospital, which is dedicated to rescuing and rehabilitating endangered sea turtles.

Head south out of Marathon across the stunning Seven Mile Bridge, which affords 180-degree ocean views across iridescent Caribbean waters. Nature-lovers should be sure to make a stop on Big Pine Key, to explore the National Key Deer Refuge, home to the diminutive endangered subspecies of white-tailed deer found only here. If sunbathing is more your pace, pull over at Bahia Honda State Park, home to what's considered one of the best beaches in the entire country.

THE END OF THE ROAD

The highway finally runs out at Key West, the most populated island in the Florida Keys. Much of downtown retains its unique and historic architecture, particularly so on Duval Street, where neon lights shine like beacons from the wooden balconies of the area's many bars. This is the party section of town, known for its raucous atmosphere, but there's a quieter, more artistic side to the island as well. It's here that you'll find the house where author Ernest Hemingway lived between 1931 to 1939. Now the Hemingway Home & Museum, the gorgeous white building, with distinctive lime green shutters, retains many of the touches that Hemingway installed. As well as its connection to the writer, the museum is known for its many cats, said to be descendents of Hemingway's own pet.

Before starting the northward journey back to the mainland, be sure to check out the Southernmost Point marker. This red-and-black buoy, which marks—you guessed it—the southernmost point of the continental United States, is a popular photo-op, although the deep-blue ocean beyond is the real star here, especially when bathed in the golden glow of sunset.

THE GREEN FLASH

Every evening, people gather at Mallory Square in Key West to watch the horizon. They're looking for the "green flash," a rare atmospheric refraction of light that happens most often at sunset and over water. Although the phenomenon is real enough, there are quite a few myths associated with it, including that seeing it will bring good luck and that it signifies a soul that has returned from the dead.

TRANSAMERICA TRAIL

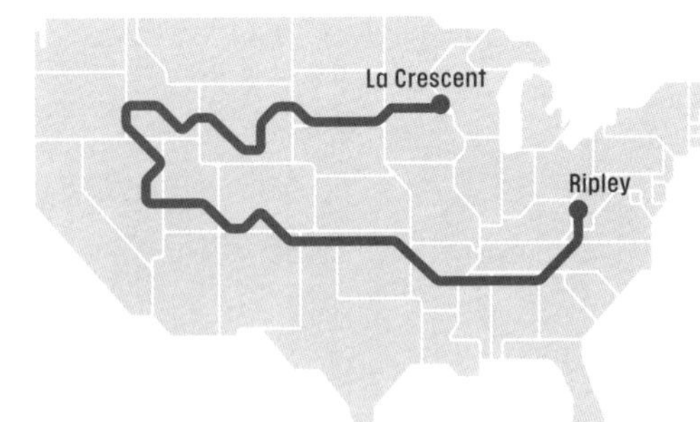

START/FINISH
Ripley, West Virginia/ La Crescent, Minnesota

DISTANCE
Approx. 5,000 miles (8,000 km)

DURATION
4–5 weeks

ROAD CONDITIONS
Mostly off-pavement (dual-sport motorcycle required; also passable in a 4WD vehicle)

THE BEST TIME TO GO
Late June to early September (to avoid snow in the Rockies)

OPPOSITE A luggage-laden motorbike, parked up outside Oark General Store, Arkansas

America's longest motorbike adventure winds across the U.S. on a blend of dirt and minor paved roads. A gargantuan ride, it races through the Appalachians and the Rockies, taking in sunbaked deserts and vast pine forests en route.

Riding the TransAmerica Trail (TAT) means getting off the highways and reconnecting with the U.S.'s rural byways. Expect trees smothered in creeping green kudzu vines, apple orchards, and isolated woods—it's the small things that make this journey unique, as much as the mesmerizing mountain ranges, vast deserts, and national monuments.

ACROSS THE APPALACHIANS

The trail begins just beyond Ripley in West Virginia, with a tranquil ride of around 160 miles (260 km) through rolling hills and the spruce, fir, and mountain-ash woods of the Monongahela National Forest—particularly stunning in the fall, when bathed in bright colors. You then run along the lush banks of the Williams River, eventually emerging at the town of Marlinton in the Greenbrier Valley.

Over the border in Virginia, the TAT curves south along the line of the Blue Ridge Mountains, through increasingly hilly terrain. Two of the most beautiful stretches lie, ironically, just beyond Bland: the first is a 20-mile (30-km) gradual ascent with numerous switchbacks up to the bowl-like valley of Burkes Garden. A little farther along, the aptly named "Back of the Dragon" (also known as Route 16), comprises a gut-churning 438 curves, slaloms, and hairpins through wooded valleys often shrouded in mist.

The trail enters North Carolina just south of tiny Damascus, into the Cherokee National Forest and ever deeper into Appalachia. There's a break from jarring dirt roads here on the Blue Ridge Parkway (pp184–187). Make a stop

RIPLEY

START

WILLIAMS RIVER
Deep in the Monongahela National Forest, this river is home to native brook trout.

135 MILES

BACK OF THE DRAGON
Ride the curves and hairpin bends in the heart of Virginia's Appalachian Mountains.

300 MILES

CAFE
EST. 1890
SELF SERVICE
NON
ETHANOL
87
OCTANE
MISFITS OFF-ROAD
BLUE ice CHIP
MOSKO
HINSON

450 MILES

LITTLE SWITZERLAND

Chow down on hickory smoked pork at Switzerland Café smokehouse.

500 MILES

MOUNT MITCHELL

Enjoy trails and 360-degree views at the highest point east of the Mississippi River.

ABOVE Fiery foliage lining the road in Pisgah National Forest

LEFT Vintage bikes at the Wheels Through Time Museum

OPPOSITE TOP A creek flowing through Ozark National Forest

OPPOSITE BELOW Slicing through Oklahoma farmland

at Little Switzerland at 3,468 ft (1,057 m). This tiny community is home to the Switzerland Café smokehouse, celebrated for its Applewood smoked trout, and pulled pork. The state prides itself on its barbecue traditions—you'll be able to compare rival "Cue" from Tennessee later on the ride.

Not far from here you should detour up a well-paved road to the summit of Mount Mitchell—at 6,684 ft (2,037 m), the highest peak east of the Mississippi River. The route continues through the Pisgah National Forest—ablaze in the fall—to the Cataloochee Ski Area then down to the town of Maggie Valley and the Wheels Through Time Museum. This is a popular stop for riders thanks to its rare American motorcycles and memorabilia, including 1936 Harley-Davidson Knuckleheads.

Continue southwest through the Nantahala National Forest south of Great Smoky Mountains National Park before turning north into Tennessee along the Tellico River Gorge—the forest here is incredibly dense, an emerald-green carpet stretching for miles. The gorge is peppered with waterfalls and smothered in wildflowers in the spring.

VAST PLAINS AND THICK WOODLANDS

After Tellico Plains, the route cuts in and out of Georgia and Alabama as it bypasses Chattanooga, traversing busy farmlands of corn and cattle.

The Great Plains and big skies beckon in Oklahoma, where you ride fast, open roads passing little more than free-range cattle.

You eventually reach the Tennessee River at the Pickwick Landing Dam and The Outpost at Pyburns, a faux pioneer village of timber shacks that serves superb Southern food. The dam itself, completed in 1938, holds back Pickwick Lake, a sportfishing paradise thanks to its smallmouth bass and catfish.

South of the river, red-clay dirt roads whip though pine forests in Mississippi, home to herds of white-tailed deer. The kudzu is everywhere here, especially in the Holly Springs National Forest, sometimes so thick it smothers the route. You then cross the Mississippi River at the Helena Bridge just north of Clarksdale—the spiritual heart of Delta Blues.

Now in Arkansas, you pass catfish ponds and rice fields en route to the dense woodlands of the Ozark Mountains. As the route snakes through gorgeous Ozark National Forest, there's a surprise: the Oark General Store. Not much has changed since it was built in 1890—fill up your tank and restore energy levels with some country cooking, and fruit pies.

The Great Plains and big skies beckon in Oklahoma, where you ride fast, open roads passing little more than free-range cattle. The TAT intersects Old Route 66 near Tulsa before reaching the small plains town of Bartlesville. You'll spot its main claim to fame long before you reach it: Price Tower, architect Frank Lloyd Wright's only skyscraper, is a 1950s cantilevered copper-green oddity that looms over the pancake-flat plains like something from *The Wizard of Oz*. Beyond Bartlesville the landscape really flattens out, with fast, straight stretches of road—this is "open range" cattle country, so look out for livestock crossing. Boise City, at the end of the long Oklahoma Panhandle, is home to some interesting remnants of the Santa Fe Trail, including rocks inscribed with the names of travelers from its heyday.

RIDING THE ROCKIES

Next, the TAT makes a brief foray into New Mexico before crossing over to Branson, Colorado. This is where it gets more challenging—the route corkscrews up and down the Rocky Mountains, circling sapphire blue lakes and wind-blown peaks. At first it climbs gradually, crossing the Continental Divide at Marshall Pass, before dropping down to laid-back Lake City. From here into Utah,

CLARKSDALE

Feel the rhythm and make a pit stop at the birthplace of the Delta Blues.

1,200 MILES

BARTLESVILLE

Tour the 19-storey Price Tower and learn more about the architect Frank Lloyd Wright.

1,800 MILES

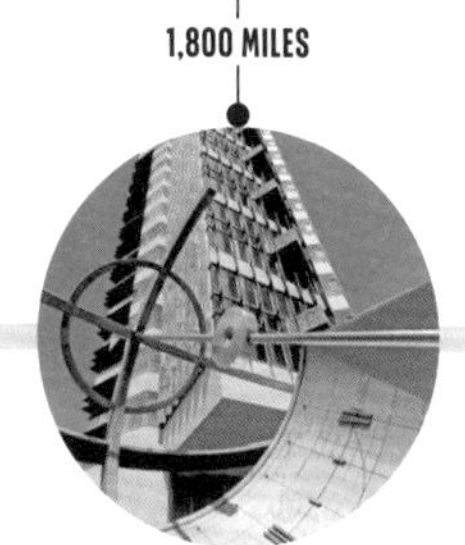

BOISE CITY

This small Oklahoma town was accidentally bombed by the U.S. military on July 5, 1943.

ANIMAS FORKS
Capture the ruins of a mining ghost town deep in the Rockies at over 11,000 ft (3,350 m).

2,700 MILES

BONNEVILLE SALT FLATS
Admire the desert vistas and endless skies across the gleaming Utah salt flats.

3,200 MILES

CREATING THE TRAIL

First scouted in 1984, the TransAmerica Trail is the brainchild of dual-sport motorcycle enthusiast Sam Correro, who spent 12 years riding and mapping the route, using only publicly accessible roads and trails. Now in his 80s, Sam still monitors the route, updating resources regularly on the website.

the TAT twists and turns over range after range, tackling ever gnarlier terrain: the Cinnamon, California, and Corkscrew passes across to the Million Dollar Highway, then up and over the treacherous Ophir Pass, with huge drop-offs, giant boulders, and switchbacks. You'll see derelict mine works all over, including the 1870s Animas Forks camp, abandoned in the 1920s.

DESERT TRACKS, DIRT ROADS

You're eventually spat out on the west side of the Rockies, into the high plains of Utah, a byword for long, lonely stretches of trail broiled by the sun. First, the route cuts due north into the La Sal Mountains, crossing the range at Geyser Pass before dropping down to outdoor sports hub Moab. It then continues west to the Nevada border where you turn north across its most desolate section: the sagebrush plains of the Snake Valley and Great Basin Desert. The sense of being on another planet increases when you hit the shimmering Bonneville Salt Flats, the vast salt pans west of the Great Salt Lake itself—it's a burning furnace here, the sun making everything seem white and shiny. The trail continues around the lake, passing Golden Spike National Historic Site, which commemorates the completion of the U.S.'s first transcontinental railroad in 1869.

Potato farms really do stretch to the horizon in Idaho, where the TAT makes a huge loop through the southern half of the state. The first section follows dirt-based roads across rich farmland. The Pacific Ocean Spur splits from the main route at Emmett, which now turns decisively east across Idaho's mountainous interior and the Sawtooth National Forest before taking in the desolate lava landscapes of Craters of the Moon National Monument and Preserve.

You cross into Wyoming some 100 miles (160 km) south of Yellowstone National Park before making a 785-mile (1,260-km) zig-zag across the state. This is very isolated country—only

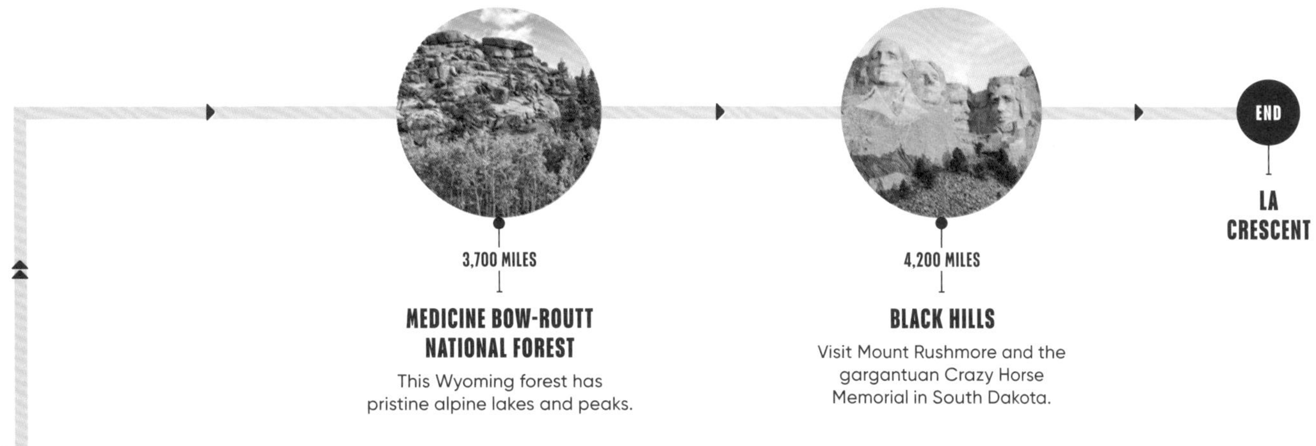

Indigenous ranches, tiny gas stations, and small settlements break up the sagebrush steppe grasslands. You'll wind through the Teton National Forest, the Shoshone and Arapaho Wind River Reservation, the mountains and alpine lakes of Medicine Bow-Routt National Forest, and the vast prairies of the Thunder Basin National Grassland, home to masses of pronghorn and black-tailed prairie dogs. Most of the roads are rarely traveled dirt tracks—dusty in the sun and mud baths when wet.

MARCH TO BIG MUDDY

A dark, high mass on the horizon, you'll see the Black Hills long before you cross into South Dakota. The trail slices right through this pine-scented upland: spot buffalo herds and burros in Custer State Park, plus hordes of elk and mule deer.

After the Black Hills, it's back to the Great Plains once more, with dead-flat prairies and fields of corn and wheat all the way across South Dakota and into Minnesota. Rolling country returns as the route approaches the Mississippi for the second time, where the TAT officially ends in La Crescent, right on the banks of the river, opposite the larger town of La Crosse, Wisconsin. America's Big River—the "Big Muddy"—makes a fittingly epic conclusion for you and your dusty, dirt-splattered vehicle.

ABOVE The sparse Craters of the Moon National Monument and Preserve

RIGHT Biking through the Corkscrew Pass, Colorado

OPPOSITE An abandoned mine disintegrating at Animas Forks

MIDLAND TRAIL SCENIC BYWAY

Kenova ▸ White Sulphur Springs

START/FINISH
Kenova, West Virginia/ White Sulphur Springs, West Virginia

DISTANCE
175 miles (280 km)

DURATION
2–4 days

ROAD CONDITIONS
Paved; some hairpin bends in the mountains

THE BEST TIME TO GO
Spring to fall, for the best hiking conditions

OPPOSITE A boat traveling the New River from Hawks Nest State Park

Trace ancient rivers through scenic valleys and switchback your way across the untamed Appalachians—land so wild and beautiful that by road's end you'll be joining the Mountaineer chorus proclaiming "West by God Virginia!"

Those country roads John Denver sang so wistfully about? Well, this is them. Part of U.S. Route 60, the Midland Trail Scenic Byway runs from border to border across West Virginia, winding along country hollows and over rumpled mountains, taking you straight through Appalachia's rugged heart.

EXCHANGING COAL FOR COLLEGE

The byway starts on the banks of the Big Sandy River in Kenova. While it later envelops you in West Virginia's ample natural beauty, these first miles do something like the opposite. The state is rightly proud of its blue-collar identity, but its economy has long been extractive, and as you set out, you drive past fields of oil storage tanks and towering hills of coal. Just up the road, however, is Huntington, a pleasant college town on the Ohio River. In the hills south of town, the Smithsonian-affiliated Heritage Farm Museum introduces Appalachian history through its re-creation of a 19th-century home and interactive folk crafts. A short drive away, the Huntington Museum of Art displays a more contemporary legacy, that of the state's glass-making tradition.

Downtown, Highway 60 runs by Heritage Station, an 1887 railroad depot that now houses shops, a yoga studio, and the Red Caboose Regional Artisan Center, where you'll find locally made jewelry, honey, and pins shaped like pepperoni rolls, a favorite miner's lunch. Stop here to browse the trinkets, or to grab a caffeinated beverage, before hitting the road once more.

KENOVA

KENOVA
Kenova's Big Sandy River marks the border between West Virginia and Kentucky.

HUNTINGTON
The college town comes to life on Marshall University football game days.

8 MILES

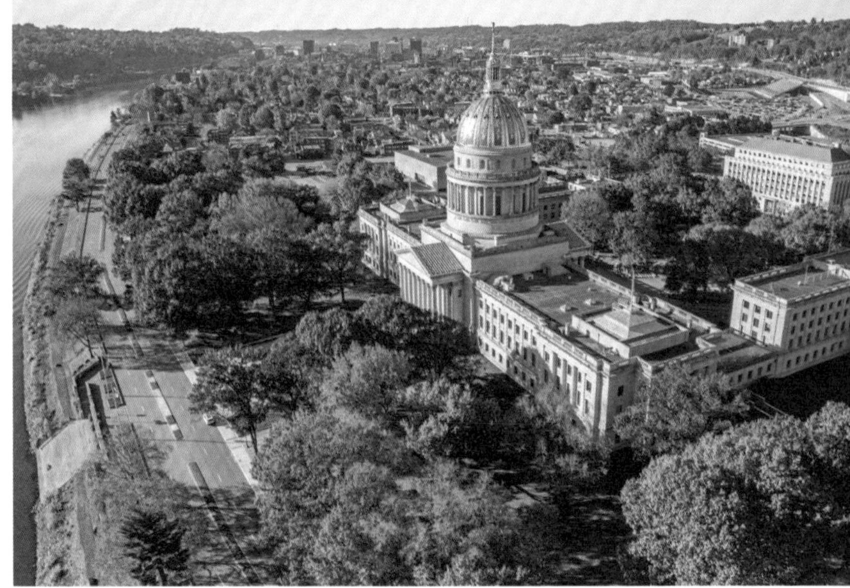

MODERN-DAY CHARLESTON

An hour from Huntington is Charleston, the state's capital and biggest city, despite having a population of fewer than 50,000 people. Even though you haven't been on the road very long, there's more than enough here to warrant pausing your drive for a day. On the city's east side is the handsome state capitol building, its dome covered in copper and gold leaf. And if you liked one reimagined, century-old train depot, hey, how about another? Charleston's houses the fantastic Capitol Market, which sells seasonal produce from in-state farmers and has a very good wine shop, butcher, and café to boot.

Charleston is also a good place to witness how young West Virginians are reclaiming Appalachia from the hoary stereotypes. Near Capitol Market, Base Camp Printing uses hand-set wood and metal blocks to make stylish West Virginia-themed art prints, while over in the trendy Elk City Historical District, Kin Ship Goods stocks clothing, stickers, and housewares whose aesthetic is best described as "hipbillie."

COUNTRY ROADS, TAKE ME HOME

Departing Charleston, the byway follows the Kanawha River southeast, and you can see just how much geography dictates things in West Virginia. Squeezed into what little flattish land exists between the water and the mountains, the towns you pass are all long and thin, just a few blocks deep. They mostly grew around former mines or chemical plants, and almost all of them have seen better days.

About 40 miles (65 km) from the capital is Glen Ferris, home to one of the country's most historic hotels: the Glen Ferris Inn, which has been hosting travelers since 1839. Right in front is Kanawha Falls, where the river tumbles and crashes over a smattering of low, flat rocks. Soon after Glen Ferris, the byway makes a long, curvy ascent up Gauley Mountain—lots of fun if you're

MILLION DOLLAR SMILE

One of Huntington's favorite daughters is "Diamond Teeth" Mary McClain. Born in the city in 1902, she boarded a train at age 13, joined the circus, and eventually sang at Carnegie Hall and the White House. She earned her nickname in the 1940s after she had diamonds taken out of a bracelet and set in her front teeth.

56 MILES

CHARLESTON

Buy new art for your walls back home from Base Camp Printing, near Capitol Market.

95 MILES

GLEN FERRIS INN

This historic hotel has hosted four presidents since opening its doors in 1839.

driving; less if you're a passenger. On the way, drop into the Mystery Hole, a delightfully goofy roadside attraction featuring retro decor, a room where gravity allegedly no longer exists, and a whacky souvenir shop. The climb ends at Hawks Nest State Park, where a viewpoint showcases the valley into New River Gorge National Park.

OLD BUILDINGS AND A "NEW" RIVER

Three 19th-century structures make the neighboring town of Ansted worth a quick stop. Right on Highway 60 is the Contentment Museum. Once the home of a former Confederate colonel, the whitewashed house now displays the county historical society's collection. A couple of blocks off the byway is the Tyree Tavern/Halfway House, which welcomed travelers before serving as a base for both Union and Confederate troops during the Civil War. You can still see the carving of the Union's Chicago Gray Dragoons made above the door. The youngest of the bunch is the Page Vawter House, built in 1890 for a local coal company president and featuring 11 fireplaces. Today, it's an inn.

The crown jewel of the drive, if not the entire state, is New River Gorge National Park. The preserve flanks a long stretch of the New River, which, despite its name, is one of the oldest rivers in the

RIGHT The horseshoe bend of the turquoise New River

BELOW The unusually decorated Mystery Hole

OPPOSITE Charleston's grand capitol building in the fall

HAWKS NEST STATE PARK

Hike or take a jet boat ride at this 270-acre (109-hectare) recreational area.

104 MILES

ANSTED

The Contentment Museum gets its name from the moniker given to it by the former owner's wife.

105 MILES

EXTEND YOUR TRIP

You can just about turn U.S. Route 60 into a cross-country drive if you feel like it. From West Virginia, the road continues east to the Atlantic coast, terminating at Virginia Beach, Virginia. Heading west, it runs through Kentucky, Missouri, Oklahoma, Texas, and New Mexico before ending in western Arizona.

world. The evenly sloping walls of the gorge and the Appalachian peaks beyond are the realm of bobcats and black bears, while giant Hellbender salamanders slip through cold New River tributaries. Dozens of hiking trails wind through the wilderness to scenic overlooks or abandoned mining towns, and there's also world-class white-water rafting and rock climbing on offer.

New River Gorge deserves at least one full day, and its location at the drive's halfway point makes it a natural place to pause your trip. The byway skirts the park's northern edge, but you'll need to detour off Route 60 to explore. The simplest way is to drive southwest on U.S. Route 19 to the show-stopping New River Gorge Bridge, which crosses the gorge 876 ft (267 m) above the river and is the longest single-arch bridge in the Western Hemisphere.

As the road leaves the national park behind and runs through rural mountain greenery, it often does feel more like a trail than a highway, cutting back and forth, finding its way through the terrain. Every few miles, a town pops up, often not much more than a post office, church, and a few worn down houses.

BACK INTO THE CITY

Just when you've gotten used to that countryside rhythm, you arrive in Lewisburg, a quaint little city that could hardly feel more different from the last 50 miles (80 km). Its downtown streets are lined with elegant brick buildings, art galleries, gourmet grocers, and French restaurants. Art lovers come here to catch shows at the Greenbrier Valley Theatre and to watch the West Virginia Symphony Orchestra perform at Carnegie Hall, a 1902 venue built with a donation from steel magnate Andrew Carnegie. More history awaits across the street at the Old Stone Presbyterian Church, which has been in use since 1796, save a brief interruption during the Civil War. But if natural history is more your scene, grab your torch and head just

NEW RIVER GORGE BRIDGE

This impressive steel arch stretches 3,030 ft (923 m) across the New River below.

117 MILES

LEWISBURG

Shop for art and antiques or restaurant-hop in this charmer of a small city.

163 MILES

LOST WORLD CAVERNS

Detour 3 miles (5 km) out of town and head underground to view giant stalagmites.

175 MILES

WHITE SULPHUR SPRINGS

The Greenbrier resort has a renowned spa, falconry lessons, and multiple golf courses.

WHITE SULPHUR SPRINGS

LEFT The landscaped grounds of the Greenbrier resort

BELOW Window-shopping in White Sulphur Springs

OPPOSITE Driving across the New River Gorge Bridge

outside town, where Lost World Caverns runs cave tours that explore the Appalachians from the inside.

FIT FOR THE PRESIDENT

Wrap up your drive in White Sulphur Springs, whose mineral springs have been soothing weary souls since the 1770s. Nearly that entire time, visitors, including no fewer than 28 presidents, have been calling at the Greenbrier. One of the country's premier resorts for almost 200 years, it was also the location of a secret bunker, constructed during the Cold War, in the event of a nuclear strike. Today, the Greenbrier offers tours behind the 25-ton blast door, giving you a peek of the facility's dorms, and emergency Congressional chambers.

The byway reaches its end a couple of miles from the Greenbrier resort, giving you just enough time to decide if John Denver was right about West Virginia, if it is "almost heaven." The obvious answer is that, if anything, he undersold it. No need for that "almost."

OUTER BANKS SCENIC BYWAY

START/FINISH
Beaufort, North Carolina/ Nags Head, North Carolina

DISTANCE
155 miles (250 km) (including ferries)

DURATION
1–3 days

ROAD CONDITIONS
Mostly paved

THE BEST TIME TO GO
Year-round; though hurricanes can occur between June and November

OPPOSITE Beach houses at Rodanthe, home to the Chicamacomico Life-Saving Station Historic Site

The Outer Banks may be a vacation hot spot, but there's something wild about this place, too. With pelicans for company, a drive along these barely there barrier islands will reveal windswept beaches, wildlife, and a unique culture.

Hanging off the North Carolina mainland like a necklace, the Outer Banks divide the open Atlantic from Pamlico Sound. They're a favorite of sunseekers, who come for the usual beachy charms, but a drive along the Outer Banks Scenic Byway also opens up their rich maritime heritage and many natural blessings.

Before it gets to the Outer Banks, though, the byway snakes through a part of the mainland that North Carolinians call Down East. Bays and estuaries poke greedy fingers into the land, and lives are lived half on the water; hunters watch for waterfowl from marsh blinds, while crab traps sit stacked in front yards.

DECOY DETOUR

The byway starts north of Beaufort, where U.S. Route 70 turns east at Merrimon Road. Follow the road until you get to Harkers Island Road, a spur that leads to the eponymous island. As you head south, watch for egrets swooping through the loblolly pines and pelicans standing sentry on dock pilings.

At the far end of Harkers Island is the Core Sound Waterfowl Museum, which focuses on Harkers' long tradition of decoy carving. The island and Core Sound have attracted duck hunters for more than a century—President Franklin D. Roosevelt and baseball great Babe Ruth included—and the homegrown art form has endured in spite of mass manufactured alternatives. Upstairs, an observation tower lets you gaze across the sound at Cape Lookout Lighthouse,

BEAUFORT

BEAUFORT
The byway starts at the intersection of U.S. Route 70 and Merrimon Road.
0 MILES

HAWKERS ISLAND
Take a look at the local craft of decoy carving at the Core Sound Waterfowl Museum.
14 MILES

CEDAR ISLAND NATIONAL WILDLIFE REFUGE

A habitat for minks, bald eagles, and other animals.

40 MILES

OCRACOKE ISLAND

Dolphins can sometimes be spotted in the water off the idyllic Ocracoke Beach.

73 MILES

HATTERAS

Converging currents mean this village offers some of the country's best sport fishing.

94 MILES

built in 1859 and affectionately known as the Diamond Lady for its patterning.

Back on Route 70, continue west to join North Carolina Highway 12 and drive through Cedar Island National Wildlife Refuge, where forests and marshes hide deer, mink, and muskrats. Along the road, vast fields of reeds run to the horizon, interrupted only by the occasional fallen tree.

HIGHWAY TO HIGH TIDE

On the opposite side of the refuge, your road trip temporarily turns into a cruise. Here, a car ferry links the mainland with Ocracoke Island, its route still considered part of Highway 12. You come ashore in Ocracoke Village, home to cheery inns and beach-bum bars. If you didn't already notice it on the mainland, listen out for the "Ocracoke Brogue," a unique accent that retains Scots-Irish inflections. It's sometimes called Hoi Toider for its pronunciation of "high tide."

BLACKBEARD

Treacherous shoals and proximity to trade routes made the Outer Banks a hive of piracy in the 17th and 18th centuries. The most famous buccaneer of all was Blackbeard, who often anchored just off Springer's Point in what is now Ocracoke. He was killed here in a naval battle in November 1718.

Ocracoke's lighthouse, built by hand in 1823, is the second-oldest continuously operating beacon in the country. A short walk away is the 122-acre (49-hectare) Springer's Point Nature Preserve, where trails run between moss-flecked oak down to the water. While you can't visit all of Outer Banks' beaches, Ocracoke Beach is a must. On the island's Atlantic side, it has white sand as fine as pixie dust and dunes that shield the road, so it's just you and the ocean.

A second ferry takes you from Ocracoke Island to Hatteras Island. If you'd come here in early 1846, the boat wouldn't have been necessary, but that year a hurricane blew a hole right through a beach and created the inlet that now separates the two. Hatteras Village is a major fishing center. That once meant small commercial fleets, but today the focus is recreational. Trucks loaded up with surfcasting rods line local beaches, and marinas are filled with sport-fishing boats.

From the village, drive east to Buxton, at the island's elbow, where it's just a mile to Cape Hatteras Lighthouse, which

guides ships through one of the East Coast's most dangerous stretches; a small museum occupies the former keeper's quarters.

It hasn't just been lighthouse keepers who've watched over sailors along the Outer Banks. Continue on north to Rodanthe, where you'll find the Chicamacomico Life-Saving Station Historic Site and Museum. Consisting of the original 1874 station building, its 1911 replacement, and several other structures, it's one of the best-preserved such stations in the country. It was staffed by members of the U.S. Life-Saving Service, a precursor to the U.S. Coast Guard. Their finest hour came on August 16, 1918, when a German U-boat torpedoed the British tanker SS *Mirlo*, when the men of Chicamacomico rescued 42 of the *Mirlo*'s 51 sailors.

INTO THE FINAL STRETCH

After Rodanthe, the highway swings out onto the Jug Handle Bridge, giving you a chance to take in the Outer Banks from the water. The next several miles run past wetlands, low scrub, and sand dunes that sometimes run right up to—and, if the wind's been blowing the right direction, over—the road.

The north end of Hatteras Island is taken up by the Pea Island National Wildlife Refuge, which provides habitat for nearly 400 species of birds. Another bridge carries you to Bodie Island and Bodie Island Lighthouse Road, which takes you, predictably, to Bodie Island Lighthouse. Painted black and white, the lighthouse is tucked away in brackish marsh; the adjacent boardwalk leads to a viewing platform where you can look for crabs and herons.

The byway ends just up the road in Nags Head at Whalebone Junction, the intersection with U.S. Route 64. It's almost a shame to finish your drive here, as both the Outer Banks and Highway 12 continue north for several dozen miles and have so much more to explore, such as "*Dune*"-esque Jockey's Ridge State Park. The mainland can wait.

TOP A boardwalk leading to Bodie Island Lighthouse

ABOVE Chicamacomico Life-Saving Station

OPPOSITE The white sands of Ocracoke Beach

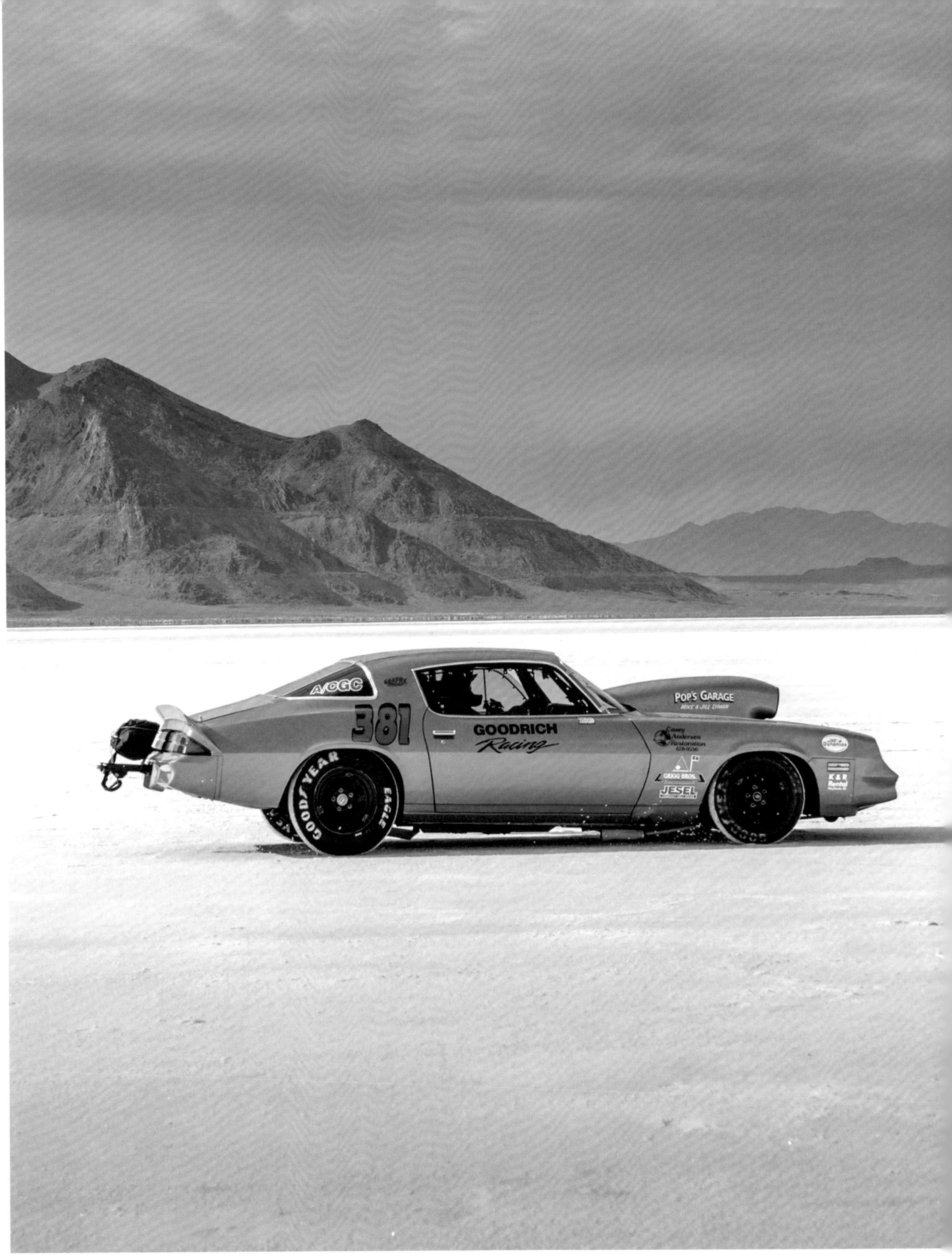

A/CGC
381
GOODRICH
Racing
POP'S GARAGE
GRIGG BROS.
JESEL
K&R
Rental
GOODYEAR
EAGLE

LINCOLN HIGHWAY

START/FINISH
New York City, New York/ San Francisco, California

DISTANCE
3,345 miles (5,385 km)

DURATION
1–3 weeks

ROAD CONDITIONS
Paved; possible hazardous conditions in mountainous areas in winter

THE BEST TIME TO GO
Spring to fall, to see the cornfields in full glory

OPPOSITE Vintage race car at the Bonneville Salt Flats International Speedway, Utah

To truly experience America, skip the plane and embark on an epic road trip from the Atlantic to the Pacific—through alabaster cities, mountain majesties, and amber waves of grain. You've never seen the country like this.

For the ultimate road trip, buckle up and hit the Lincoln Highway, America's original coast-to-coast road. Dedicated in 1913, it ran for nearly 3,400 miles (5,470 km) across the heart of the country, connecting New York City with San Francisco and opening up the land to four-wheeled exploration. Its exact route has changed over the years, with newer roads providing alternatives, but it remains a trusty framework to structure a cross-country trip around.

The road begins in Times Square, at the corner of 42nd and Broadway. If you're setting out on a journey of national discovery, what better place to start than the country's biggest and most important city? A spin through its five boroughs offers an inexhaustible list of things to do. Just one piece of advice: stick to the subway, and save the driving till you're ready to move on.

When the original Lincoln Highway left town, it employed a ferry to cross the Hudson River, but that's long gone, so take the Lincoln Tunnel before heading southwest through New Jersey. This first stretch of the drive—through Hoboken, Newark, and Trenton—passes through early America (the colonial version at least), carrying you past Revolutionary War battlefields and towns that trace their history to the 17th century, inviting you to reflect on where the country came from, and where it's going.

PHILADELPHIA FREEDOM

After crossing the Delaware River, the route continues into the heart of Philadelphia and makes a beeline for

NEW YORK CITY

NEW YORK CITY
Take a bite out of the Big Apple before setting out from New York City's Times Square.

0 MILES

PHILADELPHIA
Onetime capital of the U.S., this exciting city is a living museum of American history.

95 MILES

City Hall, a sumptuous Second Empire structure that's the largest municipal building in the country. The city offers a good chance to get out of the car for a while, so grab a cheesesteak and marvel at its history: the Liberty Bell; Independence Hall, where the Declaration of Independence was signed; the home of Betsy Ross, seamster of the first American flag.

LEFT Pittsburgh, set on the Allegheny River

BELOW *Mapping Courage*, a mural in Philadelphia

OPPOSITE A storm lights up the sky over cornfields in Iowa

STEEL CITIES

From Philadelphia, take U.S. Route 30 into the Appalachian Mountains, whose peaks and valleys you'll surf for 300 miles (485 km) across to Pittsburgh. The Steel City boomed and then busted with the rise and fall of American industry, but in recent decades it's enjoyed a resounding comeback, with a winning combo of blue-collar charm, boundary-pushing art, and one of the best natural settings of any American city.

Follow the Ohio (river) out of town, and point your compass west across Ohio (state) and Indiana. The big cities and mountains are now behind you, giving way to smaller towns, rolling hills, and flatlands. The next 400 miles (640 km) or so run through farming communities and smaller Rust Belt cities like Canton, Ohio, and Fort Wayne, Indiana. Deindustrialization has taken its toll, but national attractions like the Pro Football Hall of Fame and rejuvenating

PITTSBURGH

Pittsburgh is home to an exciting arts scene, both avant-garde and homespun.

395 MILES

CANTON

Rub shoulders with gridiron greats at the Pro Football Hall of Fame.

490 MILES

FORT WAYNE

Indiana's second city combines Rust Belt grit with refined riverside parks.

705 MILES

870 MILES

CHICAGO

Gawk at lakeside towers in the country's most architecturally exciting city.

1,860 MILES

CHEYENNE

Wyoming's state capital is home to the world's biggest rodeo.

riverside parks speak of these places' resilience. If you find yourself on rural roads outside the cities, keep an eye out for traditional horse-drawn buggies carrying Amish families, members of a Mennonite sect who largely reject modern technologies.

After Fort Wayne, the Lincoln Highway veers northwest. It skirts the Chicago metropolitan area, but you may want to detour to Lake Michigan to squeeze a bonus coast into your trip. That will also give you the chance to spend some time getting to know the nation's third-largest city. Home of the world's first skyscraper and America's best hot dogs, Chicago is both ambitious and down-to-earth. The enormous Art Institute of Chicago, raucous blues clubs, and the dazzling Magnificent Mile all make worthwhile diversions before hitting the road again.

ACROSS AMERICA'S HEARTLAND

Escape Chicago's sprawl, and you soon find yourself wrapped in the Heartland, the vast expanse at the nation's middle where corn and wheat fields line the roadsides and rural hamlets are anchored by churches and bar-and-grills. People on the coasts may deride this as "flyover country," but when you're on the ground, the hypnotically empty miles invoke a revelatory sense of America's enormity. This is a stretch of the journey where the rewards are found in the simple things: bacon sizzling in a country diner; towering thunderheads hurling down rain and lightning; the sense of freedom that comes with being the only car on the road.

Every so often, a larger imposition on the landscape interrupts the meditative drive. The mighty Mississippi River marks the unofficial divide between eastern and western United States; the charming university town of Ames, Iowa, serves up college culture; and the cosmopolitan city of Omaha, Nebraska, offers history, art, and refined dining.

As you cross Nebraska, watch as the east's greenery gradually gives way to the arid High Plains. For a long while, the Lincoln Highway parallels the broad curve of the Platte River but then, around Ogallala, it parts ways and takes you to Cheyenne. Despite being Wyoming's state capital, Cheyenne remains, stubbornly, a

BERNIE QUENEAU

Motorists who drive the entire Lincoln Highway receive the Bernie Queneau Coast-to-Coast Lincoln Highway Recognition Award, named for a onetime Boy Scout who, aged 16, completed the route in an REO Speed Wagon in 1928.

2,475 MILES

SALT LAKE CITY

Salt Lake City offers endless opportunities for hiking and skiing.

2,585 MILES

BONNEVILLE SALT FLATS

The Bonneville Salt Flats are where daredevils go to set land-speed records.

2,820 MILES

GREAT BASIN

Stargaze at the dark skies that blanket the vast empty spaces of the Great Basin.

ABOVE The Wasatch Mountains in northern Utah

LEFT Highway 50 sign, Nevada

OPPOSITE Chinese lanterns decorating a street in San Francisco's Chinatown

frontier town: home of the world's biggest rodeo and the kind of place where even the governor wears a cowboy hat.

An hour from Cheyenne, the highway turns north and then heads west for hundreds of desolate miles, with little around save scrubland and sky. The peaks and canyons of northern Utah's Wasatch Mountains then come as a welcome distraction, and Salt Lake City can feel like an urban oasis after days in America's less-peopled places. Squeezed between the Great Salt Lake and some of the country's top ski resorts, the city is a good place to park up and put some miles on your legs instead.

DESERT AND DARK SKIES

Leaving Salt Lake City, the original Lincoln Highway route zigzags through some extremely isolated terrain, so you may want to take I-80 across the desert instead. This has the added benefit of traversing the Bonneville Salt Flats, an ancient lake bed that may be the flattest spot on earth and is the place people chasing land-speed records come when they want to go faster than anyone's ever gone before.

If you're traveling by yourself, make sure you've loaded up on podcasts, because you're soon headed across the heart of the Great Basin on Highway 50, often dubbed "the loneliest road

If you're driving at night, pull over, cut the engine, and look up at a firmament strewn with stars. Virtually untouched by light pollution, the basin has some of the country's darkest skies.

in America" (p73). The surroundings are stark, to be sure, but they also hold hot springs, fossil beds, and ghost towns. And being this alone has its benefits. If you're driving at night, pull over, cut the engine, and look up at a firmament strewn with stars. Virtually untouched by light pollution, the basin has some of the country's darkest skies.

It's the complete opposite at the far end of the basin, when you reach Reno and its strip of casinos, less luminescent than Las Vegas's, but still plenty bright.

INTO THE GOLDEN STATE

As you wave your goodbyes to Reno, the Lincoln Highway gives you a choice: west through Tahoe National Forest, or south past crystal-clear Lake Tahoe and through Eldorado National Forest. You can't go wrong either way. The two legs meet up in Sacramento. The capital of the U.S.'s most glamorous state can feel surprisingly rural, but it does sit at the heart of California's Central Valley, and the next 70 miles (115 km) of the drive head south through this gloriously fecund region.

Just past Stockton, the highway turns west in a final push to the coast. After negotiating the Diablo Range, it passes through Oakland, crosses San Francisco Bay, and arrives in San Francisco itself. If you can't quite bring yourself to end the journey just yet, the city provides plenty of ways to procrastinate. When it's finally time, follow El Camino del Mar into Lincoln Park, where the Lincoln Highway terminates with views of the Golden Gate Bridge and the mighty Pacific.

THE LINCOLN LINK

The Lincoln Highway was created in 1913 by Carl G. Fisher, who also built the Indiannapolis Speedway. It was named after Abraham Lincoln, one of Fisher's heroes.

LAKE TAHOE

With a depth of 1,645 ft (500 m), this picturesque lake is the second-deepest in the U.S.

3,100 MILES

SAN FRANCISCO

The road finally ends in San Francisco's Lincoln Park, on the Pacific Coast.

3,345 MILES

END

SAN FRANCISCO

ATLANTIC COAST TRAIL

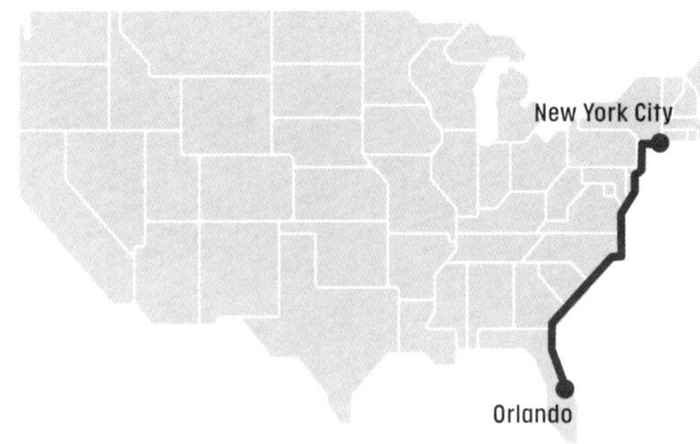

START/FINISH
New York City, New York/ Orlando, Florida

DISTANCE
1,325 miles (2,130 km)

DURATION
1–2 weeks

ROAD CONDITIONS
Excellent 4-lane interstate highway

THE BEST TIME TO GO
Spring, to catch Washington, D.C.'s cherry blossom

OPPOSITE New York City, the starting point of your journey down the Atlantic Coast

The Atlantic Coast Trail takes you from the heart of New York City to the theme parks of Orlando, ticking off many of the country's most exciting and important cities, with fascinating history and culture waiting at every exit.

Begin your journey in cosmopolitan New York City, taking time to explore the largest city in the U.S. before hitting the road. It's busy and loud and crowded, but New York has some of the best museums (and theaters) in the world. Grab a bagel to go or enjoy a leisurely breakfast before whiling away the hours in one of the city's top museums—the Metropolitan Museum of Art, home to Monet's famous *Water Lilies*, is a great choice—or swinging to the top of the skyscraping Empire State Building, where you can take obligatory selfies on the observation deck and view the King Kong exhibits inside. Follow the crowds to dazzling Times Square, located in the heart of New York's Theater District, before tucking into an early dinner and attending a Broadway musical.

INTO NEW JERSEY

Leave the bright lights and big dreams of New York City behind you and head toward New Jersey, just across the Hudson River. While the sight (and smell) of the industrial plants doesn't make a good first impression, keep the faith. Jersey is well known for its beautiful landscapes, from the beaches of the Jersey Shore to the Pine Barrens that spread across a million acres inland. Even urban Atlantic City, a world-famous spot for gambling, lies within a block of the boardwalk and the beach, with stunning sunsets over the Steel Pier Amusement Park.

The next stop along I-95, just over 60 miles (95 km) northwest of Atlantic

NEW YORK CITY
START

NEW YORK CITY
Whizz to the top of the iconic Empire State Building for shots of the city's skyline.
0 MILES

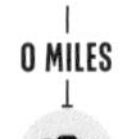

ATLANTIC CITY
Try your luck at the casino slots or enjoy sunset by the retro Steel Pier.
129 MILES

FULL HING TRADING INC
TEL: 349-7036
ONE WAY

No trip would be complete without ordering a signature Philly Cheesesteak, an indulgent grilled steak sandwich layered with cheese and onions.

City, is Philadelphia, Pennsylvania. The "Birthplace of America," the city hosted the signing of the Declaration of Independence in 1776 at Independence Hall, declaring America's freedom from the British Empire. Around a decade later, the Constitutional Convention was drafted in the same building, which can be toured today. The food in Philadelphia is as rich as its history, and no trip would be complete without ordering a signature Philly Cheesesteak. This indulgent grilled steak sandwich, layered with cheese and onions, can be enjoyed 24 hours a day at either Pat's King of Steaks or Geno's Steaks—just be prepared to loosen your seatbelt before hitting the road again.

DRIVING INTO DELAWARE

It's easy to pass right through the tiny state of Delaware. However, the city of Wilmington, just 30 miles (50 km) from Philly, is worth at least a quick stop for

BRITISH COLONIES

With the exception of Florida, which was a Spanish colony, all of the states on this road trip were part of the original 13 British colonies set up in the Americas.

PHILADELPHIA

Dive into America's history and see where the Declaration of Independence was signed.

191 MILES

DELAWARE

The first state of the United States, Delaware belies its diminutive size.

223 MILES

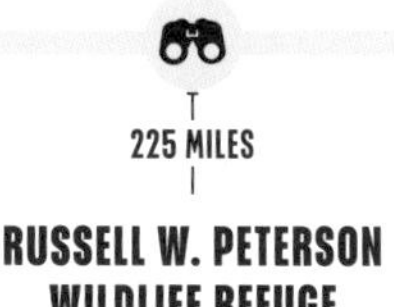

225 MILES

RUSSELL W. PETERSON WILDLIFE REFUGE

Keep an eye out for beavers and birds in this urban reserve.

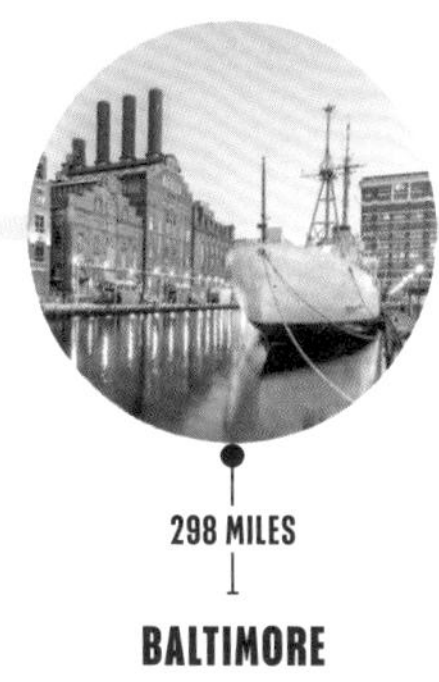

298 MILES

BALTIMORE

Check out the historic ships –and Maryland's maritime history–on Baltimore's wharf.

342 MILES

WASHINGTON, D.C.

Tour the capital's many Smithsonian museums and impressive monuments.

its stately homes and miles of sandy beaches bordering the Atlantic Ocean. Delaware was the first state to ratify the Constitution, which is detailed at the First State National Historical Park.

As you head toward Maryland, the scenery around I-95 grows in interest. Just beyond the city limits, the highway passes through the Russell W. Peterson Wildlife Refuge, offering views of the peaceful wetland area that beavers, ducks, and ospreys call home. Farther down the road, you'll get another gorgeous view, this time of the Susquehanna River, as you pass over the Tydings Memorial Bridge. The river is one of the longest on the U.S.'s Eastern Seaboard.

Baltimore has an industrial feel that can be unnerving at first–it's fair to say that some areas of the city have seen better days. However, there's plenty to see and do here, particularly along the Inner Harbor, or waterfront area. Even if you don't spend the night, it's worth taking a stroll along the river. If time allows, stop at the Historic Ships Museum to explore Maryland's interesting maritime history.

AMERICA'S CAPITAL

Just another 40 miles (65 km) south will bring you to the nation's capital, Washington, D.C. The city is renowned for its museums: 17 Smithsonians alone call Washington home. The best of the bunch is the National Museum of Natural History, which has dinosaur fossils, mummies, and marine specimens. You could easily spend a day here, but make time to stroll the streets. There are dozens of terrific monuments and memorials to visit, including the Washington Monument, the Lincoln Memorial, and the Martin Luther King, Jr. Memorial, all within walking distance of the White House. Springtime is particularly special, when the city's cherry trees come into beautiful bloom.

ABOVE Exploring D.C's National Museum of Natural History

OPPOSITE TOP Geno's Steaks, famous for Philly Cheesesteaks

OPPOSITE BELOW One of many fine beaches in Delaware

MOUNT VERNON

Take a 10-mile (15-km) side trip to visit the home of former president George Washington.

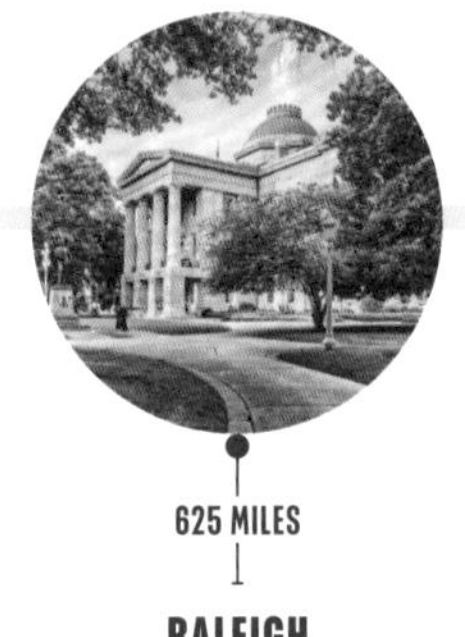

625 MILES

RALEIGH

Catch a live show and enjoy a spot of shopping in North Carolina's leafy capital.

Aside from visiting museums and monuments, dive deeper into the city's Black American culture by taking a tour through the U-Street corridor, a historically Black neighborhood near Howard University, one of the country's premiere historically Black colleges.

As you leave downtown D.C., make a quick stop in historic Old Town Alexandria, located right across the Potomac River, to explore the shops and museums, and take a walking tour. Mount Vernon, the former home of George Washington, is 10 miles (15 km) south; its furnishings reflect how the house was decorated during his presidency (1789–97).

BALMY VIRGINIA

Edging south, you'll leave the D.C. Metro Area, where the road opens up and pine and poplar trees hug the highway. The two-hour drive to Richmond, Virginia, might even nudge you to turn on the air-con–the landscape grows lusher and the weather becomes more humid the farther south you go.

Richmond makes the most of its "Goldilocks climate" (not too hot or too cold), with outdoor activities aplenty. Stop off to rock climb or hike, or even raft down the James River, which runs through the city. There's also a burgeoning beer and wine scene, with several craft breweries and an official "beer trail." If you're here for the history, you might prefer to make a short detour to nearby Colonial Williamsburg and Jamestown settlements, both of which explore the area's colonial history through living history museums.

Just two and a half hours away, the next major city on the route is Raleigh, North Carolina, known as the "City of Oaks" for the plethora of beautiful oak trees that line the city's streets. Though not the biggest city in the state, Raleigh is the capital, and part of a larger area known as the "Research Triangle," which includes some of the most renowned

RESEARCH TRIANGLE

The metropolitan area enclosed by Raleigh, Durham, and Chapel Hill gets its nickname from its proximity to three major research universities: Duke University, North Carolina State University, and the University of North Carolina at Chapel Hill.

universities in the country. This vibrant college town is also known for having the most music venues in all of North Carolina and is a great place to see both local and national acts.

Though Charleston, South Carolina, is technically about an hour east of I-95, the city has won so many "World's Best" awards that it's well worth the detour. It's easy to see why so many people visit—Charleston is truly beautiful, with church steeples piercing the sky, well-preserved antebellum houses, and a picturesque waterfront that glows orange at sunset. The city is also known for its Southern hospitality and impeccable food scene: there are three James Beard award-winning restaurants to be found here.

FROM TAFFY TO DAFFY

Another picturesque Southern city along I-95 is Savannah, Georgia, with its cobblestone streets, elegant architecture, and landscaped parks. Lively River Street is lined with bars, restaurants, and shops, perfect for picking up some local taffy or boarding a riverboat cruise on the Savannah River. Savannah is also said to have resident ghosts–it's regarded as one of the country's most haunted cities.

The road south becomes more industrial again as you head across the state line into Jacksonville, Florida, named after General Andrew Jackson. From here you can continue all the way to Miami, but for a more whimsical end to your trip, take a southeasterly turn onto I-4 to Orlando. This is, of course, the home of the Walt Disney World Resort®–exchange the highway for a roller coaster and start exploring America's history through the lens of movies and entertainment instead.

ABOVE Early morning in a peaceful park in Savannah

OPPOSITE The James River flowing through Richmond

1,013 MILES

SAVANNAH

Prepare to get goosebumps on a ghost tour of Savannah's cemeteries.

1,307 MILES

WALT DISNEY WORLD RESORT®

Rub shoulders with Mickey Mouse and Daffy Duck in Florida's famous theme park.

ORLANDO

LAKE CHAMPLAIN BYWAY

Mount Independence ▸ Alburgh

START/FINISH
Mount Independence, Vermont/Korean War Veterans Memorial Bridge, Alburgh, Vermont

DISTANCE
120 miles (195 km)

DURATION
2–3 days

ROAD CONDITIONS
Well-maintained paved roads

THE BEST TIME TO GO
Fall, for the New England foliage at its russet best

OPPOSITE Gazing out over Lake Champlain from the waterfront in Burlington

The Lake Champlain Byway takes in the best of Vermont's folksy, New England charms: dairy farms, clapboard villages, and gorgeous lakes framed by distant peaks. In the fall, the whole region erupts in fiery colors.

The Lake Champlain Byway charts a leisurely course along the eastern shore of New England's largest body of water. A harmonious blend of rural and urban, it passes bucolic islands, apple orchards, and Vermont's "big city" of Burlington as it winds its way to the Canadian border. Your only struggle will be keeping to a schedule, with plenty of trails to lure you out from behind the wheel.

Your journey begins at Mount Independence on the lake's southern shore. There's not much left of this crucial Revolutionary War fortification, but you can explore 6 miles (10 km) of trails that take in the ruins. You'll also get fine views of the lake from here, and of Fort Ticonderoga on the New York side.

ALONG THE EASTERN SHORE

Mount Independence Road takes you to the tiny colonial village of Orwell, with its pretty English-style green surrounded by clapboard homes, a colonial church, and the stately town hall.

Moving on, along Route 74, you'll lose the lake for now and reach the busy college town of Middlebury, driving through the landscaped colonial campus of posh Middlebury College as you enter. Stretch your legs in the compact downtown, taking in the ornate white church on Middlebury Town Green, and the shops and restaurants in the old mill area. Here, the Otter Creek Falls cascade some 18 ft (5 m) below Main Street Bridge.

Hop back behind the wheel and leave town on U.S. 7. At Vergennes, there are more waterfalls on Otter Creek, best captured alongside the

MOUNT INDEPENDENCE

START

MOUNT INDEPENDENCE
Explore the enigmatic ruins of this strategic American fortress from the Revolutionary War.

0 MILES

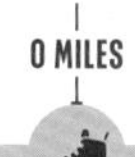

ORWELL
Admire the clapboard homes and church on the historic village green.

5 MILES

SPADE FARM COVERED BRIDGE

Stop for a snap of this gloriously photogenic ivy-cloaked bridge.

45 MILES

DOWNTOWN BURLINGTON

Vermont's "big city" has shops, markets, cafés, galleries, and a scenic lakefront promenade.

63 MILES

old sawmills from Vergennes Falls Park. Camera roll full, continue north on U.S. 7, passing the Spade Farm Covered Bridge, a short, ivy-smothered wooden beauty alongside the main highway. Just five minutes ahead lies a turning up to Mount Philo State Park. Trails at the top lead to an astonishing panorama across the valley of rich farmland, with the lake and New York's Adirondack range far to the west.

After passing through Shelburne you'll hit the suburbs of Burlington, Vermont's biggest city (population: 45,000). The route takes you into the relatively laid-back downtown, where Main Street gradually slopes down to the lake from City Hall Park. Surprisingly cosmopolitan, Burlington is a youthful college town, with fun brewpubs, diverse restaurants, and lots of cafés. Lake Champlain is at its widest point here, with yachts, cruisers, and motorboats zipping over its glassy surface on clear days and the mountains peeking through the haze on the western horizon.

TO THE ISLANDS

After a brief stint in the city, it's back to nature. Leave Burlington on U.S. 2, cutting through pine and maple forest and crossing over the Lamoille River, before heading straight for the lake. The road passes through marshy

ABOVE Taking in the view of the lake from Mount Philo State Park

RIGHT Summer fun on Lake Champlain

OPPOSITE The chapel of Saint Anne's Shrine, on Isle La Motte

VIVA LA REPUBLIC

Founded in 1777, the Vermont Republic was an independent state for 14 years—and the first to abolish slavery. It was never diplomatically recognized by any foreign country and eventually joined the United States in 1791.

wetlands before going over the old Sandbar Causeway to South Hero, the first of the Champlain Islands. Stop at the parking area on the causeway to enjoy the view or take a break from the road at Sand Bar State Park, where there's a small stretch of sugary beach.

From here, the byway cuts north through the sparsely populated islands in the heart of Lake Champlain: mostly flat, they feel like tranquil oases, peppered with apple trees that blossom in spring, and a hub for ice fishing and lake skating in the winter.

Woods and hayfields accompany the route as it enters the center of South Hero, also known as Grand Isle. Make a short detour at the main village to Allenholm Farm, to pick your own apples in late summer or simply load up on fruit pies and fresh berries. Back on the main road, you'll pass the Rest Stop, a popular summer food truck for indulgent lobster rolls and smashburgers. Alternatively, pack your own picnic and take it to the forest trails at Grand Isle State Park Beach.

Continuing on, you'll emerge at the lake again to cross a short bridge to North Hero, where the highway hugs the shore and the Green Mountains shimmer in the distance. Soak up the views at the handsome North Hero House Inn and Restaurant, an 1890s gem that's a lovely place to eat or stay.

NORTH TO THE BORDER

For your final stretch, follow the route across a narrow channel back to the mainland—a peninsula known as the Alburgh Tongue—where you can detour to the sandy beach at Alburgh Dunes State Park or cross another causeway to bucolic Isle La Motte. A loop around this tiny island takes in Saint Anne's Shrine, vineyards, orchards, and community museums. There are also remnants of the 450-million-year-old Chazy Fossil Reef, an ancient rock outcrop.

Back on the main route, U.S. 2 cuts across the northern end of the lake at the impressive Korean War Veterans Memorial Bridge. End your journey at the parking area on the Vermont side for a last glimpse of Lake Champlain: the surrounding maple forest seems completely untouched here, emerald green in summer but an especially gorgeous blaze of color in the fall.

VERMONT ROUTE 100

START/FINISH
Massachusetts state line, near Stamford, Vermont/Newport, Vermont

DISTANCE
220 miles (355 km)

DURATION
2–4 days

ROAD CONDITIONS
Well-maintained paved roads

THE BEST TIME TO GO
The fall for leaf peeping season, or spring to avoid the crowds

OPPOSITE Leaves changing color around scenic Stowe, overlooked by Mount Mansfield

Fiery fall foliage, rustic red barns, and softly scented maple sugarhouses; Vermont's Route 100 runs through the Green Mountains, all while taking in the best this quintessential New England state has to offer.

Known as the "The Skier's Highway," Vermont Route 100 is one of America's most picturesque roads with swaths of gorgeous beech, birch, and maple woods. Snaking across the length of the state, it takes in country stores, craft breweries, charming clapboard villages, and, true to its nickname, some of the best ski resorts in New England.

WINDING ROADS AND THICK FORESTS

The highway—officially known as the Scenic Route 100 Byway—starts at the Massachusetts state line near Stamford. At first the byway makes a gentle zigzag across the southern part of the state—weave through a lush country of forest and small farms down the Deerfield River Valley, across to Lake Whitingham, and then finally north again to the delightful town of Wilmington. Lined with craft and culinary stores, it's also a good place to enjoy a hot drink at cafés like Dot's before strolling over to Reardon's Crossing, a blossom-covered footbridge at the west end of town with the best views of the Deerfield River.

North from Wilmington, the byway starts to climb up into the Green Mountains proper. Ski shops and outfitters along the road mean you've reached Dover, the gateway to Mount Snow ski resort—the main slopes and ski runs are easy to spot to the west. Continue north through the Green Mountain National Forest, winding down the forest of Wardsboro Valley. Emerald green in summer, it transforms into a mesmerizing blend of amber, red, and gold in the fall.

MASSACHUSETTS STATE LINE

START

LAKE WHITINGHAM

Enjoy views of Lake Whitingham, one of the largest and clearest in the state.

17 MILES

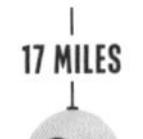

WILMINGTON

Peruse the arts and crafts stores, and pop into cafés in this charming town.

28 MILES

Though nature steals the spotlight on this drive, the quaint towns aren't far behind. Farther up the valley of the West River delivers you to Jamaica, one of the prettiest villages on the drive, with brightly painted clapboard homes. Source snacks at West Provisions and stretch your legs at Jamaica State Park where you can stroll along the river or tackle the hike to Hamilton Falls, a 125-ft (40-m) series of cascades and rockslides.

FOODIE TERRITORY

Another 20 minutes on the road will bring you to Londonderry, where it's worth straying off the main route for a couple of miles east to visit Taylor Farm, a working farm with horse-drawn sleigh rides in winter and a shop that sells homemade bread, artisan cheeses, and maple syrup. From Londonderry, it's a short drive to Weston, another idyllic village, home to one of the biggest Vermont Country Stores in the state, a labyrinth of Vermont-made products. The Weston Village Store opposite, established in 1891, is a creaky delight and is similarly crammed with souvenirs, fudge, and maple syrup.

Treats secured, drive 10 miles (15 km) north of Weston where Route 100 finally tops the West Valley and drops down to the Black River. Forests give way to suburbs as you approach Ludlow, the gateway to Okemo Mountain Resort and neighboring Jackson Gore. If blood sugars have crashed, restore them at the red-roofed Green Mountain Sugarhouse, a short drive away. Located on the picturesque shores of Lake Pauline, it's the place to sample maple "creemee" (maple-flavored soft ice cream) while taking in the lake views.

Back on the road, ascend the Black River Valley, skirting a series of lakes before arriving at tiny Plymouth Notch. This small town is where you can find the President Calvin Coolidge State Historic Site, which preserves the childhood home of the 30th president of the United States. It's also where Coolidge took the presidential oath of office in 1923.

Continuing north along the Ottauquechee River, the byway bypasses Killington Resort, one of the state's top ski centers and the halfway

MAPLE SYRUP

Vermont is the largest producer of maple syrup in the U.S. (a record 2.55 million gallons/9.65 million liters in 2022). The smaller, traditional sugarhouses usually provide tours, and make everything from maple-coated almonds to maple lollipops, in addition to quality syrup. The sap-collecting season starts in February in southern Vermont and lasts into April in the north, but many sugarhouses are open year-round.

TAYLOR FARM

Take a short detour east from Londonderry to buy Vermont cheeses and maple syrups.

PLYMOUTH NOTCH

Visit the President Calvin Coolidge State Historic Site, home of the 30th U.S. president.

93 MILES

KILLINGTON RESORT

The halfway point offers skiing in winter, and a wide range of outdoor activities in summer.

105 MILES

point on your journey. Trundle ahead for 45 minutes to Moss Glen Falls, a stunning 30-ft (10-m) cascade worthy of a pit stop and a couple of selfies.

Once you've passed Granville Notch, the highway sinks into the Mad River watershed, hugging the river through the artsy village of Waitsfield to Waterbury. Best known for its culinary outlet stores, Waterbury is home to Ben & Jerry's Ice Cream Factory, where you can take a tour and sample the newest flavors.

NORTHERN END POINT

Drive north for 10 miles (15 km) to the 19th-century village of Stowe, another major ski resort. The alpine scenery around Stowe Mountain attracted the real Von Trapp family in the 1940s (of *The Sound of Music* fame) and you can still stay at the Trapp Family Lodge today.

From Stowe the byway edges away from the mountains into Vermont's Northeast Kingdom, a fertile region with rolling farmland and maple-rich shores along Lake Eden. The drive officially ends without fanfare at Route 105 just before Newport, a small town on Lake Memphremagog. A glacial lake that spans the Canadian border, it's the perfect location to gaze across at the Quebec mountains and reflect on this sugary-sweet drive through Vermont. Perhaps a Canadian road trip is next?

LEFT The peaceful Moss Glen Falls, near Granville Notch

BELOW Still waters across Lake Eden in northeast Vermont

OPPOSITE The historic blue Weston Village Store

163 MILES

WATERBURY

Tour the Ben & Jerry's Ice Cream factory and sample classic and new flavors.

220 MILES

NEWPORT

Gaze across Lake Memphremagog, which shadows the Canadian border.

END

NEWPORT

KANCAMAGUS HIGHWAY

Lincoln ▸ Conway

START/FINISH
Lincoln, New Hampshire/ Conway, New Hampshire

DISTANCE
35 miles (55 km)

DURATION
2–4 hours

ROAD CONDITIONS
Well-maintained paved roads

THE BEST TIME TO GO
The fall for spectacular foliage; or spring to avoid the crowds

OPPOSITE A tree-lined switchback on the Kancamagus Highway

Welcome to the Kancamagus Highway, a snaking route through the forests of New Hampshire's White Mountains, featuring rushing waterfalls and lofty viewpoints all ready to lure you away from the driver's seat.

The Kancamagus Highway (commonly known as "The Kanc") cuts through an untouched slice of New Hampshire's White Mountains. Nature puts on an impressive show here all year round, but you'd be forgiven if you wanted to prioritize the fall when the air is crisp and the foliage explodes with color.

The highway officially begins as Route 112 in North Woodstock, New Hampshire, but the best place to start is the White Mountains Visitor Center, which has exhibits and information on the latest road conditions. The center lies on the edge of Lincoln, with a strip of restaurants, malls, and condominium lodgings, but don't let this concrete first impression deter you—adventure awaits.

INTO THE WOODS
The drive gains momentum on the edge of town, where the highway enters the White Mountain National Forest. Follow the densely wooded East Branch of the Pemigewasset River for a few miles until there's a break in the canopy and Loon Mountain comes into view. You'll also be able to see the popular Loon Mountain ski resort on the opposite bank of the river, which has activities for all seasons, including hiking and mountain biking in summer months. Alternatively, sit back and take in the views on a gondola ride to the top of Loon Peak (2,733 ft/833 m).

Hit the road for another 5 minutes to reach Lincoln Woods Scenic Area, where more outdoor activities await. Pack your swimsuit and take the easy hike along the river to Franconia Falls—there's plenty of swimming holes on the way, though the water can be icy cold, even

LINCOLN

LOON MOUNTAIN
This ski resort offers summer activities too, from hiking to mountain biking.

3 MILES

LINCOLN WOODS SCENIC AREA
Stretch your legs and enjoy views of the cold and calming Franconia Falls.

6 MILES

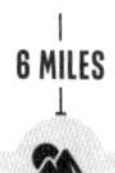

The woods finally open here for a sweeping panorama back down the Pemigewasset Valley and over to the rugged Osceola Range in the west.

ABOVE Crossing the stream on the Greeley Ponds Trail

OPPOSITE Taking a dip in the Swift River, near Conway

in July. At Lincoln Woods the river splits, with the highway continuing southeast along the Hancock Branch of the Pemigewasset for another 8 miles (13 km), steadily rising through the forest.

Toward the top of the valley there's a parking area for the Greeley Ponds Trail, a 4.5-mile (7-km) round-trip hike to two small dark blue pools deep in the mountains. But if this doesn't float your boat, stay on the road and tighten your seatbelt. The route switchbacks up to your first major viewpoint, the Hancock Overlook. The woods finally open here for a sweeping panorama back down the Pemigewasset Valley and over to the rugged Osceola Range in the west.

TAILING THE SWIFT RIVER

From here, the highway twists and turns on its ascent, with a couple of hairpin turns thrown in for good measure. Trees shield the road until the Pemigewasset Overlook at 2,810 ft (855 m), which offers epic views of contoured mountains. Less than a mile later, you'll reach the top of Kancamagus Pass at 2,855 ft (870 m), marked by a sign. Stay on the road and you'll be rewarded at the next viewpoint: the C.L. Graham Wangan Overlook. Just a few yards down, it provides a gorgeous vista northeast along the Swift River Watershed and another excellent excuse to hop out the car.

GREELEY PONDS TRAIL

This challenging 4.5-mile (7-km) hike leads to a couple of tarns deep in the forest.

11 MILES

KANCAMAGUS PASS

This is the highest point on the Kancamagus Highway (2,855 ft/870 m).

14 MILES

C.L. GRAHAM WANGAN OVERLOOK

Drink in views of the Swift River Valley and hazy mountains.

14 MILES

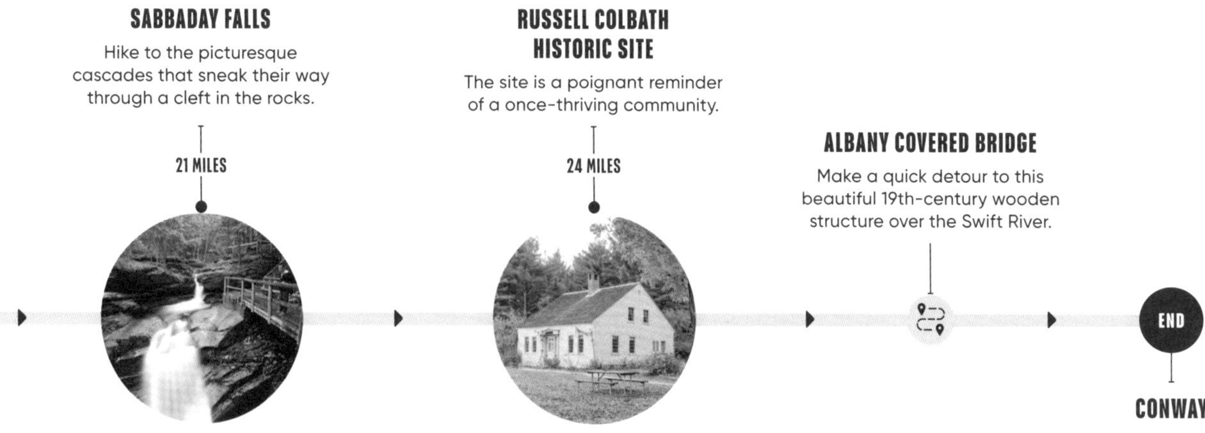

CHASING WATERFALLS

It's all (literally) downhill for the remaining 20 miles (35 km), but that doesn't mean the views are any less impressive. Before long, you'll arrive at the Sugar Hill Scenic Vista, a popular overlook frequented by seasonal leaf-peepers and locals alike, with panoramic views of the Swift River Valley, Sugar Hill, and Potash Mountain. From here the highway is once again enclosed by thick groves of maple, spruce, and beech, but the ever-near Swift River provides plenty of waterfalls and worthy distractions. Two miles (3 km) beyond the Sugar Hill overlook, Sabbaday Falls is an easy half-mile (800-m) hike featuring a 25-ft (8-m) series of plunging cascades. It's another 3 miles (5 km) to the enigmatic Russell Colbath Historic Site. This white clapboard homestead, built in 1832, is all that remains of the once-flourishing lumberjack community of Passaconaway, founded around 1790. The falls aren't over yet though—hit the road for a few more minutes to reach wispy Champney Falls, named after the artist Benjamin Champney.

Back on the highway, the valley narrows at the Rocky Gorge Scenic Area, where you can view the trusty Swift River and stroll around the tranquil, spruce-lined Falls Pond. Two miles (3 km) on there's a final cascade: a series of rocky rapids known as the Lower Falls. A popular swimming spot in the summer, it also charms in the fall. Just beyond the falls, you can take the two-minute detour down narrow Passaconaway Road to the Albany Covered Bridge, a timber structure built over the Swift River in 1858 and still in use today.

Some 6 miles (10 km) beyond the bridge the Kancamagus Highway comes to a sudden end at the junction with Route 113, on the western edge of Conway. It's a short drive into the center of town, which may seem incredibly busy after your ride through the woods. End your journey at the impressive Saco River Covered Bridge, where the Swift runs into the Saco, and wave farewell to the river that's been your trusty sidekick along the Kancamagus Highway.

THE FEARLESS ONE

Kancamagus (meaning "The Fearless One") was the grandson of Passaconaway, a chief who united over 17 Indigenous groups of Central New England into the Penacook Confederacy. Kancamagus was the last chief of the Confederacy, leading the peoples against the English during King William's War. After his family were captured, the chief was forced to move his peoples to French Canada in 1691.

NEW ENGLAND LIGHTHOUSE TRAIL

Cape Neddick
Old Saybrook

START/FINISH
Cape Neddick, Maine/Old Saybrook, Connecticut

DISTANCE
355 miles (570 km)

DURATION
7–8 days

ROAD CONDITIONS
Well-maintained paved roads

THE BEST TIME TO GO
May–October, as many lighthouses close in low season

OPPOSITE Pastel sunrise skies illuminate the Boston Light on Little Brewster Island

Take an illuminating drive along New England's Lighthouse Trail, which connects the East Coast's most scenic coastal communities. Meet witch covens, delve into maritime history, and feast on lobster rolls along the way.

With its windswept wilderness and beaming lighthouses, it's easy to see how driving New England's Lighthouse Trail stirs the romantic core. This spectacular route strings together the rugged coastal edges of the states of Maine, New Hampshire, Massachusetts, Rhode Island, and Connecticut. Lighting the way, you'll find almost 200 historic watchtowers dotting the shoreline, many of which have been reimagined as niche museums, upscale restaurants, and unique overnight stays.

THE MAINE SHORE

Begin your adventure at the summer resort town of York at Cape Neddick, in New England's most northern state. As one of the country's oldest English settlements, this sprawling town is filled with seaside homes loaded with period charm, along with a new wave of fashionable boutiques and coffee shops.

Take the coastal path a couple of miles east, past crisp, blue waters and creamy sand beaches. Perched atop a craggy islet at the north end of Long Sands Beach, Cape Neddick Light, known locally as Nubble Light, has been guiding boats to safety since 1879. It's no longer open to visitors but the proud tower crowned with an ornate iron balcony and red-roofed lightkeeper's cottage nestled next to it make for a perfect photo opportunity. Before leaving town be sure to pay a visit to the nearby Lobster Cove, where a bounty of fresh clams, scallops, and glistening lobster is served with a side order of Atlantic Ocean views.

CAPE NEDDICK

START

CAPE NEDDICK LIGHT

Enjoy the fresh ocean air and snap a selfie at Maine's most photogenic lighthouse.

2 MILES

LOBSTER COVE

Tuck into a buttery lobster roll or order the Captain's Platter to share—you won't leave hungry.

4 MILES

62 MILES

SALEM

Let the town cast its spell on you with a visit to the Salem Witch Museum.

84 MILES

LITTLE BREWSTER ISLAND

Located in Boston Harbor, the island is home to the first lighthouse in the U.S.

BEWITCHED IN SALEM

Driving an hour south on roads specked with sun-bleached vintage motels, you may notice the mood shift as you arrive in Salem. This popular Massachusetts city is infamous for its role in the witch trials of 1692 in which 200 people were accused of witchcraft. Delve into this haunting chapter of New England history at the Salem Witch Museum, housed in a former church, before picking up some potions at the witch-themed shopping mall in Salem. Around Halloween, the spookiness is cranked up a notch with gardens and front porches decorated with increasingly extravagant displays. All-black costumes, pointy hats, and broomsticks can be spotted on the cobbled side streets, too.

Beyond the witch hunts, Salem also has a rich maritime history, best explored on a boat trip from the harbor. Cruising past protected coastlines, private islands, and the occasional seal, a 90-minute ride offers the opportunity to spot five working lighthouses in action, while sipping steaming mugs of hot chocolate from the blustery deck.

From Salem, follow the curve of land 20 miles (30 km) south to Boston Harbor. A stone's throw from the hustle and bustle of downtown Boston, Little Brewster Island is home to Boston Light—a 1783 replacement for the first

You may notice the mood shift as you arrive in Salem. This popular Massachusetts city is infamous for its role in the witch trials of 1692.

ABOVE Walking down historic Derby Street, Salem

RIGHT Holding a rare, freshly caught blue lobster

OPPOSITE The Boston Tea Party Ships & Museum

ever lighthouse built on U.S. soil, erected in 1716. As with many of New England's steadfast stations, Boston Light became automated in the 1990s, although a keeper still lives on the island to offer visitors guided tours in the summer months. Expect close-up views of Long Island Light, Graves Light, and Boston Light, three of the area's most beloved pioneering beacons.

No visit to the Massachusetts capital would be complete without diving into the revolutionary events that occurred here in 1773. At the Boston Tea Party Ships & Museum, a tour guide dressed head-to-toe in period costume steers visitors through the collection of historic artefacts and hands-on exhibits. Walk the creaking floorboards of a full-scale replica of an 18th-century sailing vessel, similar to the boats from which American colonist rebels hurled 342 chests of tea into Boston Harbor as a caffeinated protest against imposed taxes.

R&R IN RHODE ISLAND

From Boston, inland roads speed 60 miles (100 km) south to Newport, Rhode Island, but set your compass for the leisurely route along the coast. Pause to soak up the glamorous seaside treats of Martha's Vineyard along the way, an upscale vacation island favored by the Kennedys and Clintons that's accessible via a short but rewarding ferry ride across choppy waters.

Arriving into Newport Harbor, you'll be greeted by the sound of masts jingling on the superyachts moored in Newport's ultra-exclusive harbor. You might notice a lonesome island set adrift on the horizon. Rose Island has no permanent residents but the keenest of lighthouse fans can book in a once-in-a-lifetime castaway experience by staying overnight in its lighthouse. After being whisked across in a tiny speed boat, you'll bed down for the evening in a cozy apartment, furnished with

SHORTEN YOUR TRIP

If time is of the essence, condense this trip into its star attractions. Start by admiring the Boston Light before heading 80 miles (130 km) south for an overnight stay at the lighthouse on Rose Island, remembering to pack your own food supplies as there's no catering on-site.

BOSTON

Take part in a seriously fun history lesson at the Boston Tea Party Ships & Museum.

85 MILES

MARTHA'S VINEYARD

Hop on the ferry to Martha's Vineyard to admire the imposing Gay Head Light.

175 MILES

ROSE ISLAND
Sleep overnight in a working lighthouse, on your own castaway island.
270 MILES

STONINGTON
Delve into seafaring archives at the Stonington Lighthouse Museum.
318 MILES

KATHARINE HEPBURN CULTURAL ARTS CENTER
Catch a dance performance or comedy show while in town.
352 MILES

antique oak floorboards and a timeworn typewriter. Life on the island is dictated by the ebb and flow of the tides, which roll back to reveal a pebbly beach covered in driftwood. Overnight lighthouse guests can haul a canoe into the icy waters, joining the fleet of sailboats floating past, or climb to the tip of the light-house tower for a bird's-eye view of the American oystercatchers, blue herons, and Canada geese that also call this sliver of paradise home.

CRUISING INTO CONNECTICUT

Back on the mainland, continue the scenic route south along the ocean road. The route snakes alongside the rugged coastline, past remote archipelagoes and cutting through verdant nature reserves. An hour from Newport, a web of winding streets leads through the historic town of Stonington to Stonington Point, where the small but mighty Stonington Lighthouse Museum keeps watch. This mid-19th-century stone lighthouse saw off attacks from the British navy in 1775 and again in 1814, and has since been resurrected as a quirky museum that throws light on the area's seafaring history. Visitors today can also climb the 29 stone steps up the tower for picturesque harbor views.

Driving on, past colorful clapboard summer homes adorned with star-spangled banners and wooden picket fences, it's another 35 miles (55 km) along the Connecticut shore to Old Saybrook, where the small-town charm reaches its climax and the Connecticut River meets the Long Island Sound. Jam-packed with quaint cottages, this is one of the oldest hubs in the state. As you glide through the quiet town, keep an eye out for the Katharine Hepburn Cultural Arts Center, a performance space dedicated to the Hollywood actress who spent many of her childhood summers here.

On the horizon you may also spot the Saybrook Breakwater Light, one of the few remaining spark-plug lighthouses.

IDA WILSON LEWIS

New England's most famous female lighthouse keeper was the fearless Ida Wilson Lewis. Tending the Lime Rock Light near Newport, Lewis made her first rescue aged 12, coming to the aid of four men who capsized their small sailboat. She went on to save an estimated 18 people, plus one very lucky sheep, from an early watery grave. For her exploits she was dubbed "The Bravest Woman in America" by the press.

LEFT Rose Island, an idyllic lighthouse retreat

353 MILES

SAYBROOK BREAKWATER LIGHT

This beloved lighthouse is easily spotted on the horizon, and all across the town's merch.

355 MILES

SAYBROOK POINT RESORT & MARINA

Capture a romantic sunset over the beautiful marina.

END

OLD SAYBROOK

This handsome tower has become the town's symbol, and you'll find its silhouette splashed across postcards and cotton tea towels in its many seaside gift shops.

THE FINAL BEACON

Saybrook Breakwater Light is far from the only beacon in these parts. Pulling into the car park at Saybrook Point Resort & Marina—once frequented by the high-rolling Rat Pack on gambling sprees—you can't miss the whimsical lighthouse situated in the heart of the marina complex. Overnight stays are offered in the lighthouse apartment, where a tiny balcony opens out onto fiery orange sunset views, reflected in the water below. It's also the perfect place to watch the moored boats bob gently with the tide, from luxury yachts to chartered fishing boats.

New England's seafood is the stuff of legends, so take a deep dive with a final supper by the crackling log fire at the resort's Fresh Salt restaurant. This local institution is renowned for its creamy clam chowder, oysters plucked straight from the sea, and indulgent lobster rolls smothered in warm butter. As you glance across the dock, your private lighthouse will wink back at you. It's offering you sanctuary, just as New England's lighthouses have done for generations.

TOP Saybrook Point Resort & Marina's lighthouse apartment

ABOVE Maine oysters, a New England seafood specialty

MAINE'S ROUTE 1

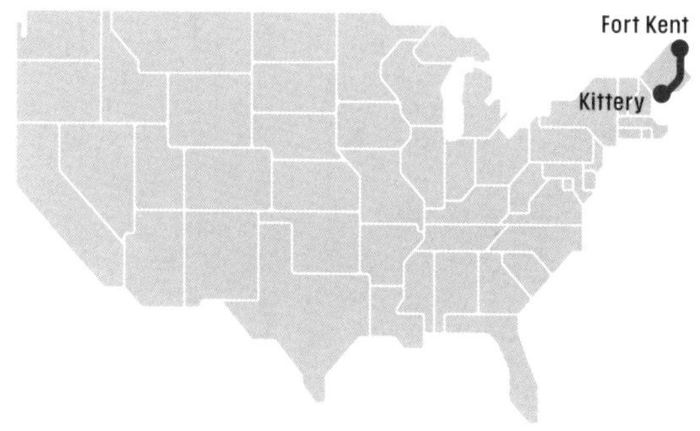

START/FINISH
Kittery, Maine/
Fort Kent, Maine

DISTANCE
525 miles (845 km)

DURATION
1–2 weeks

ROAD CONDITIONS
Well-maintained paved roads

THE BEST TIME TO GO
Summer and fall; to avoid heavy traffic, visit between Labor Day and mid-October

OPPOSITE The craggy shoreline of Acadia National Park

Lobsters, lighthouses, and rugged coastal beauty—Route 1 is the perfect introduction to America's "Vacationland." From the southern beaches to the Canadian border, this is New England's ultimate adventure.

Created in 1926, Route 1 (U.S. 1) was the country's first interstate highway, with its most northerly, and most hauntingly beautiful, sections in Maine. The route parallels the crinkled coast of the Atlantic Ocean—a land of lobster shacks, fishing villages, and pristine beaches fringed by pine woods. At the Canadian border, it then runs north along the St. Croix and St. John rivers, deep into the forested interior.

Your journey begins in the south of the state on the World War I Memorial Bridge connecting Maine with New Hampshire. Spanning the glistening Piscataqua River, the bridge delivers you into the workaday port town of Kittery. Maine's oldest town, Kittery is home to the Portsmouth Naval Shipyard and features several historic forts, including Fort McClary, established in 1808.

SANDY SHORES

Heading north, the highway runs through wooded, flat country, but only a few miles inland from the coast—sea views are never too far away. You can answer the ocean's call at York Harbor, with its golden beaches and picturesque lighthouses. Stock up on saltwater taffy at The Goldenrod, an old-fashioned establishment from 1896, or stretch your legs on the scenic path to the Wiggly Bridge along the York River.

If you want a few more miles under your belt before pulling over, keep on north to Ogunquit Beach, a long barrier island of dunes and sugary sand perfect for sunbathing. Wells, a few miles farther, is another good option. Considered

KITTERY

START

YORK HARBOR

Admire views of York River while taking to the aptly named Wiggly Bridge.

7 MILES

OGUNQUIT BEACH

Paddle in the Atlantic, grab a lobster roll, or just enjoy lounging on golden sands.

16 MILES

24 MILES

RACHEL CARSON NATIONAL WILDLIFE REFUGE

Spot migratory birds from the salt-marsh boardwalk.

53 MILES

PORTLAND

Sample the craft beers of Bissell Brothers, Shipyard Brewing, and many others.

TOP Buoys decorating a lobster shack in Maine

ABOVE Biddeford's Palace Diner, housed in a 1920s railcar

Maine's "Antique Capital," its main road is lined with stores selling all sorts of knickknacks. Wells is also a great foodie spot. Stop at the 1960s Maine Diner for lobster pie or clam chowder, and work off the calories with a stroll on the boardwalk at Rachel Carson National Wildlife Refuge, five minutes to the north.

The highway leans more inland as it approaches Kennebunk, but if time allows, stop by Kennebunkport, a beautiful little town with chic shops and restaurants. It's also the location of the "Bush Compound," the summer home of the late president George H. W. Bush and still owned by the Bush family.

Outside of Kennebunk, the roadside scenery runs through woodlands of oak, maple, and birch, though beaches are always on hand. It's just a short detour to Old Orchard Beach, a lively family-friendly summer retreat, with pristine sandy stretches, an old wooden pier, and the Palace Playland amusement park. The Palace Diner, in nearby Biddeford, is a great place to eat, housed in a 1920s railcar, while in Scarborough, 10 miles (15 km) on, kids can enjoy the sweet treats and giant chocolate moose at Len Libby Candies.

SHOPPING AND SHIPBUILDING

Beyond the Fore River, the highway enters Portland, Maine's biggest city. Perched on Casco Bay Peninsula, the historic waterfront and revitalized Old Port district are redolent of the city's glory days as a major shipbuilding hub. Portland is best explored on foot, not least because of all the shops you'll want to visit, so park up and splash the cash at the red-brick antiques stores and clothing boutiques. Venturing on foot also gives you a chance to enjoy the craft breweries, and explore the Portland Observatory—this octagonal red-brick signal tower has loomed over the city streets since 1807.

If you've caught the shopping bug, Freeport, your next stop, will scratch that itch. Thirty minutes beyond Portland, this once rustic village became the home of outdoor clothes and equipment specialist L.L. Bean in 1912. Today, the original Bean store rubs shoulders with other clothing outlets that line a mile-long stretch.

MIDCOAST TO DOWNEAST

Back on the road, trunk stashed with hiking gear, you'll soon reach historic Brunswick on the Androscoggin River, home to the Harriet Beecher Stowe House (this is where the 19th-century author wrote her anti-slavery novel, *Uncle Tom's Cabin*). At Brunswick, the U.S. 1 heads northeast through the region dubbed MidCoast Maine. Here, the beaches are replaced by long, deep inlets and estuaries, with rocky, forested peninsulas that break off into windswept islands dotting the Gulf of Maine.

A short drive ahead lies Wiscasset and the next big crossing, over the Sheepscot River. It's generally a lot quieter up here, but the long lines you'll see in summer are for the lobster rolls at Red's Eats and Sprague's Lobster, two of the state's most famous food shacks.

The highway emerges at the shoreline proper in Rockland. Home to the Maine Lobster Festival, this lively port town has plenty of seafood restaurants, and an illuminating collection of American art at the Farnsworth Art Museum. From here, follow the edge of Penobscot Bay, through increasingly hilly country, arriving at the enchanting colonial town of Bucksport on the Penobscot River. Be sure to take in the view of the forest and glimmering ocean from the Observatory at the Penobscot Narrows Bridge, an architectural wonder that stands 420 ft (130 m) above the river.

ABOVE A float at the Maine Lobster Festival

Home to the annual Maine Lobster Festival, Rockland is a lively port town with plenty of seafood restaurants and an illuminating collection of American art at the Farnsworth Art Museum.

FREEPORT

Shop till you drop at L.L. Bean and numerous other fashion outlet stores.

70 MILES

WISCASSET

Chow down on fresh seafood, clam cakes, and sumptuous lobster rolls at Red's Eats.

98 MILES

ROCKLAND

Admire the artwork in the Farnsworth Art Museum, known for its paintings by N.C. Wyeth.

131 MILES

Motor on to Downeast Maine, the halfway point of your journey. This is the drive's final coastal section—a remote, far less-traveled region of small villages and tranquil bays.

From Bucksport, U.S. 1 cuts inland again, to Ellsworth, gateway to Mount Desert Island and Acadia National Park. Bar Harbor, Acadia's main hub, lies slightly to the south of your route, but it's worth making time for New England's only national park to take in its fjords, craggy headlands, and gorgeous coastal scenery. You can work off all that Rockland lobster on the various cycle paths and mountain trails here.

Back behind the wheel, motor on to Downeast Maine, the halfway point of your journey. This is the drive's final coastal section—a remote, far less-traveled region of small villages and tranquil bays where you'll often have the road to yourself. Be sure to stop at Helen's, a 1950s diner in Machias, for blueberry pie, before continuing on, with just the occasional glimpses of inlets or the sea.

SHADING THE BORDER

U.S. 1 makes a decisive turn to the north at Passamaquoddy Bay. Here, the St. Croix River begins its long, snaking journey inland, forming the border with

RIGHT Bar Harbor, the jumping-off point for New England's only national park

BELOW The rocky coastline of Acadia National Park

ACADIA NATIONAL PARK

Venture 20 miles (30 km) off U.S. 1 to explore these forested inlets.

MACHIAS

Savor the wild blueberry pie at Helen's, Machias, the heart of Downeast Maine.

253 MILES

ST. CROIX RIVER

The French made camp here a year before establishing their first colony in America.

LEFT Sunrise over the banks of the St. Croix River, St. Croix Island

Canada. Stop by the St. Croix Island Visitor Center to learn about Pierre Dugua's early 17th-century expedition—a reminder that this part of North America was settled by the French long before the Pilgrim Fathers. The highway passes through the busy border town of Calais before cutting inland through the Passamaquoddy Indian Township Reservation—a reminder that the Indigenous people of Maine were here long before any Europeans, period.

U.S. 1 rejoins the St. Croix Valley at Aroostook County, also known as "The County." Famed for its potato crop and wind farms, much of this region is actually an untrammeled wilderness of pine forest and windswept lakes, little changed since writer Henry Thoreau canoed through in the mid-1800s and wrote *Maine Woods*.

END OF THE HIGHWAY

Farther north, allow your car to transform momentarily into your own personal spaceship as you look out for the "Maine Solar System," a series of scale models of the planets that spans a 100-mile (160-km) section of U.S. 1. Back on earth, follow the highway as it plunges ever deeper into the forest before suddenly emerging in the St. John River Valley.

From here, wind your way along the river's lush banks, tiny farms and villages breaking up the otherwise dense groves of spruce and fir. Fort Kent marks the end of the road; just across the bridge is New Brunswick and Québec. Check out the lonely blockhouse that constitutes the Fort Kent State Historic Site and end your journey at the historical marker raised here in 1926, overlooking the bridge: "America's First Mile."

EXTEND YOUR TRIP

U.S. 1 extends south from Kittery and the New Hampshire border all the way to Key West, Florida—some 2,370 miles (3,810 km) from Fort Kent. It takes in some spectacular scenery, notably the rugged coastlines of Rhode Island and Massachusetts, and the Overseas Highway across the Florida Keys.

408 MILES

MAINE SOLAR SYSTEM

As you drive through Aroostook County, look out for the roadside planet models.

525 MILES

FORT KENT STATE HISTORIC SITE

Explore the blockhouse and take a photo at "America's First Mile."

END

FORT KENT

INDEX

N

O

P

Q

R

S

T

U

V

W

Y

Z

ACKNOWLEDGMENTS

The publisher would like to thank the following for their kind permission to reproduce their photographs:

(Key: a-above; b-below/bottom; c-centre; f-far; l-left; r-right; t-top)

2 Travel South Dakota. 5 Getty Images / iStock: SpVVK (c). **6 Unsplash:** Heidi Kaden (c). **7 Getty Images / iStock:** franckreporter (ftr); piola666 (fbr). **9 Getty Images / iStock:** monkeybusiness images (ftr). **Unsplash:** Jametlene Reskp (fcrb). **10-11 Unsplash:** Dino Reichmuth (c). **14 Amine Abassir:** (c). **15 Alamy Stock Photo:** Ray Bulson (fbr). **16 Alamy Stock Photo:** Kevin G Smith (tr); Ray Bulson / Alaska Stock (tc); Tim Plowden (fcla). **17 Alamy Stock Photo:** Robert Valarcher / Biosphoto (fcra); Westend61 GmbH (tc). **Getty Images:** Brett Maurer (fbr). **18 Dreamstime.com:** Rena Tan (bl); Victoria Ditkovsky (br). **19 William Frohne:** (c). **20 Alamy Stock Photo:** Design Pics Inc (ftl); RGB Ventures / SuperStock (ftr). **Dreamstime.com:** David Crane (fbl). **21 Alamy Stock Photo:** H. Mark Weidman Photography (fcra); Ray Bulson (fbl). **Getty Images / iStock:** Chansak Joe (ftl); DCrane08 (fbr). **22 Getty Images:** Matteo Colombo (c). **23 Getty Images:** John Seaton Callahan (fbr). **24 Alamy Stock Photo:** Hawaii (fbl). **Getty Images / iStock:** paula cobleigh (tl); Wirestock (cl). **Shutterstock.com:** Joshua Rainey Photography (br). **25 Alamy Stock Photo:** Lisa123456 / Stockimo (ftl). **Dreamstime.com:** Paul Topp (fbr). **Getty Images / iStock:** Ryan Tishken (tc). **26 Getty Images / iStock:** 7Michael (bc). **Hawaii Tourism Authority (HTA):** Tor Johnson (bl). **27 Getty Images:** Matteo Colombo (c). **28 Dreamstime.com:** Exposurestonature (tc). **Getty Images / iStock:** Adam-Springer (ftl). **Getty Images:** Kjell Linder (fbl). **29 Alamy Stock Photo:** Kjell Linder (tc). **AWL Images:** ClickAlps (fbr). **Getty Images / iStock:** VaisualCommunications (tr). **Hawaii Tourism Authority (HTA):** Tommy Lunberg (fcr). **30 Kyle Fredrickson:** (c). **31 Dreamstime.com:** Blueenayim (fbr); Edmund Lowe (bc). **32 Getty Images / iStock:** Francisco Blanco (tc); Sean Pavone (tr); Wirestock (fcr). **33 Alamy Stock Photo:** Jared Hobbs (fbl). **plainpicture:** DEEPOL (fcl). **34 Alamy Stock Photo:** Cindy Shebley (br). **35 Alamy Stock Photo:** Darrell Gulin / Danita Delimont Creative (c). **36 Getty Images:** Dale Johnson / 500px (fclb). **Getty Images / iStock:** SEASTOCK (fcla). **Shutterstock.com:** J Bradwin (br). **37 AWL Images:** Danita Delimont Stock (fbr). **Dreamstime.com:** Denise P. Lett (ftl). **Getty Images:** James O'Neil (tc). **Shutterstock.com:** Jacquelynn Brynn (ftr). **38 AWL Images:** Christian Heeb (fbl). **Getty Images / iStock:** franckreporter (tc). **39 Alamy Stock Photo:** ML Harris. **Getty Images:** Steve Satushek (ftl). **Shutterstock.com:** Edmund Lowe Photography (fcl). **Unsplash:** Josh Hild (ftr). **40 Getty Images / iStock:** 4nadia (br). **41 Justin Bailie:** (c). **42 Getty Images / iStock:** BirdImages (tc); Boogich (fcl); davemantel (br). **Getty Images:** Boogich (fbl). **43 Alamy Stock Photo:** Valery Companiytsev (tl). **Dreamstime.com:** Emily Wilson (fbr). **Getty Images / iStock:** benedek (tc). **44 Getty Images / iStock:** Zhiling Zheng (c). **45 Alamy Stock Photo:** Emily Riddell (bc). **46 Alamy Stock Photo:** Ian Dagnall (tc); Larry Geddis (cl). **Getty Images / iStock:** kojihirano (ftl). **47 Alamy Stock Photo:** David R (tc); Lev Mergian (br). **Dreamstime.com:** Lehmanphotos (tr). **Getty Images / iStock:** Grant Wylie (fcrb). **48 Dreamstime.com:** Gifttogive (bl). **49 4Corners:** Massimo Ripani (c). **50 Alamy Stock Photo:** Ian Dagnall (cl). **Castello di Amorosa:** (ftl). **Dreamstime.com:** Allard1 (fbl). **Rombauer Vineyards:** (bc). **51 Alamy Stock Photo:** Gary Crabbe (cr). **Auberge du Soleil:** (tl). **Getty Images / iStock:** 4kodiak (tc). **52 Humberto Portillohportilor35@gmail.com:** (c). **53 Dreamstime.com:** Svetlana Day (fbl). **Getty Images:** Artur Debat (bc). **54 Getty Images / iStock:** Paul James Campbell (ftl); Paul James Campbell (fbr). **55 Alamy Stock Photo:** Noriko Walters (c). **Depositphotos Inc:** Sooner (tr). **Getty Images / iStock:** Bartfett (br); Ziga Plahutar (tl). **56 Getty Images / iStock:** halbergman (bl); stellalevi (br). **57 Getty Images:** Ian.CuiYi (c). **58 Alamy Stock Photo** (tl). **Alamy / Zoonar / Giovanni** (tr). **Getty Images / iStock:** nata_rass (fcl); benedek (fclb). **59 Alamy Stock Photo:** Hanna Tor (fcra); Sandra Foyt (fcrb). **Getty Images / iStock:** Disco Flye Dai (bl); ehughes (br). **60 Getty Images / iStock:** Edu Borja (tr); Gomez David (ftl); simonkr (fbl). **61 Alamy Stock Photo:** heyengel (fbr). **Dreamstime.com:** Mkopka (ftl). **Getty Images / iStock:** minddream (tc). **Unsplash:** Tim Mossholder (fcr). **62 Getty Images / iStock:** dancestrokes (bl). **63 AWL Images:** Christian Heeb (c). **64 Alamy Stock Photo:** Efrain Padro (fcl); Hugh Mitton (ftl). **Getty Images / iStock:** benedek (br); Name_Thats_Not_Taken (bl). **65 Alamy Stock Photo:** Jeffrey Isaac Greenberg 19+ (fbl). **Getty Images / iStock:** peeterv (tc). **Shutterstock.com:** EWY Media (tl). **66 Capricorn Sounds Studios and Museum:** (fbl). **Getty Images:** joe daniel price (ftl). **Shutterstock.com:** Ruth Peterkin (br). **67 plainpicture:** Alex Treadway / Robert Harding (fcra). **68 Getty Images / iStock:** ClaudineVM (fbr). **69 Getty Images / iStock:** LPETTET (c). **70 Alamy Stock Photo:** Jeremy Nixon (br); Witold Skrypczak (tc). **Depositphotos Inc:** Hackman (fbl). **71 Dreamstime.com:** Chon Kit Leong (tc). **Getty Images:** Sumiko Scott (fbr). **Shutterstock.com:** BrianPIrwin (tl). **Travel Nevada:** Devon Blunden (fcr). **72 Travel Nevada:** (c). **73 Travel Nevada. 74 Alamy Stock Photo:** ZUMA Press, Inc (fbr). **Travel Nevada** (ftl); (ftr). **75 Travel Nevada. 76 Getty Images / iStock:** Avatar Knowmad (fcl). **Travel Nevada** (fcl). **77 Alamy Stock Photo:** Spring Images (ftr). **78 Alamy Stock Photo:** Leon Werdinger (fbl). **Minam Store:** (bc). **79 Getty Images / iStock:** thinair28 (c). **80 Alamy Stock Photo:** Arpad Benedek (bc); Leon Werdinger (tc). **Getty Images / iStock:** egiadone (fcl). **Z'S BBQ:** (fbl). **81 Alamy Stock Photo:** John Lambing (ftr). **Dreamstime.com:** Davidrh (fbr). **Getty Images / iStock:** benedek (fbl). **82 Dreamstime.com:** Mkopka (c). **83 Alamy Stock Photo:** America (bl). **Dreamstime.com:** Acareylau (fbr). **84 Alamy Stock Photo:** Chuck Haney / Danita Delimont (c); Janet Sheppardson (ftl). **Depositphotos Inc:** (tr). **Getty Images / iStock:** kanonsky (fbl). **85 Getty Images / iStock:** brytta (ftr); JeffGoulden (fbl). **Shutterstock.com:** Sherry Conklin (br). **86 Depositphotos Inc:** Wirepec (fbr). **87 Kyle Fredrickson:** (c). **88 AWL Images:** Danita Delimont Stock (fbl). **Dreamstime.com:** Sean Pavone (tr). **Getty Images / iStock:** Andrew Soundarajan (ftl). **89 AWL Images:** Jan Miracky (c). **Dreamstime.com:** Rita Robinson (ftl). **Getty Images / iStock:** kojihirano (fbr); Paul Maguire (tr). **90 Getty Images:** Adrian Studer (c). **91 Alamy Stock Photo:** Jesse Kraft (fbr). **92 Alamy Stock Photo:** Regis Burek (ftl). **Getty Images / iStock:** John Morrison (bl). **Getty Images:** Universal Images Group Editorial (fcl). **93 Alamy Stock Photo:** rollie rodriguez (bc). **Dreamstime.com:** David Burke (ftr); Jim Parkin (tc). **Shutterstock.com:** melissamn (ftl). **94 Alamy Stock Photo:** Jennifer Magnuson / Cavan Images (bl). **AWL Images:** Jason Langley (fbr). **95 AWL Images:** Peter Adams (c). **96 Alamy Stock Photo:** Andrew Bain (fbl); H. Mark Weidman Photography (ftl). **Shutterstock.com:** Atmosphere1 (ftr). **97 Alamy Stock Photo:** Bryan Mullennix (fbr). **Dreamstime.com:** Ronniechua (tc). **Getty Images / iStock:** Inger Eriksen (ftl). **Shutterstock.com:** Diegomezr (fcr). **98 Getty Images / iStock:** ranckreporter (c). **99 Getty Images / iStock:** claire codling (bl); imv (fbr). **100 Alamy Stock Photo:** Michael Lingberg (ftl). **Getty Images / iStock:** JimVallee (fbl); lightphoto (bc). **101 Alamy Stock Photo:** David Tomlinson (tl). **Getty Images / iStock:** sdbower (fbl). **Getty Images:** Suzanne Stroeer / Aurora Photos (fbr). **Shutterstock.com:** Robert Atkinson (tc). **102 Alamy Stock Photo:** john norman (tl). **Shutterstock.com:** Checubus (br); orxy (tc). **103 Getty Images / iStock:** Jessica Harrison (ftr). **104 Getty Images / iStock:** Sean Pavone (bl); williamhc (br). **105 www.westwindairservice.com**: (c). **106 Alamy Stock Photo:** Sébastien Lecocq (tc); Wendy White (fcla). **Getty Images / iStock:** fdastudillo (fclb). **Getty Images:** John Elk III (bl); Jon Hicks (fbr). **107 Getty Images / iStock:** Nirian (fbl); wanderluster (cra). **108 Getty Images / iStock:** Wilsilver77 (c). **109 Alamy Stock Photo:** Mark Summerfield (br); Rawf8 (bl). **110 Alamy Stock Photo:** Luc Novovitch (bl). **Getty Images / iStock:** Jim Ekstrand (fcl); jjwithers (fcla). **111 Alamy Stock Photo:** Mark Summerfield (ftl). **Getty Images / iStock:** ablokhin (tr); miroslav_1 (fbr). **112 Alamy Stock Photo:** Stars and Stripes (bl). **Shutterstock.com:** Kit Leong (bc). **113 Shutterstock.com:** haveseen (c). **114 Alamy Stock Photo:** Martin Shields (fcl); Paul Hamilton (ftl). **Getty Images / iStock:** Takako Phillips (tr). **115 Alamy Stock Photo:** David Spates (tc); Pat & Chuck Blackley (fcr); Faina Gurevich (fbl). **116 AWL Images:** Danita Delimont Stock (c). **117 Getty Images / iStock:** dszc (bc). **118 Alamy Stock Photo:** Don Johnston (bc); Stephen Saks Photography (fcl). **Getty Images / iStock:** Raul Rodriguez (tc). **Shutterstock.com:** Alyh M (ftr).

119 Alamy Stock Photo: Jack Plunkett (bc). **Getty Images:** Bill Heinsohn (ftr). **Visit San Marcos :** Meadows Center (fbr). **120 Alamy Stock Photo:** Stephen Saks Photography (br). **Getty Images / iStock:** Dee Carpenter Photography (bl). **121 Alamy Stock Photo:** Marek Uliasz (c). **122 Alamy Stock Photo:** Chuck Haney / Danita Delimont (bc). **Kinkaider Brewing:** (fbl). **Nebraska Tourism Commission:** (tl). **Sandhills Journey Scenic Byway Visitor Center:** (fcl). **123 Alamy Stock Photo:** Chuck Bigger (br); Jim West (fcr). **Getty Images / iStock:** GaryAlvis (tl). **124 Getty Images / iStock:** Cheri Alguire (c). **125 Alamy Stock Photo:** Danita Delimont (bl). **Dreamstime.com:** Geoffrey Kuchera (br). **126 Alamy Stock Photo:** CNMages (br); Dominique Braud / Dembinsky Photo Associates / Alamy (fcr); Glenn Nagel (bc). **Getty Images / iStock:** DeniseBush (ftl). **127 Alamy Stock Photo:** Paul Brady (ftl); Walter Bibikow / Jon Arnold Images Ltd (br). **Travel South Dakota. 128 Alamy Stock Photo:** Serhii Chrucky (bl). **Travel South Dakota:** Chad Coppess (br). **129 Travel South Dakota:** (c). **130 Alamy Stock Photo:** James Schwabel (tr); John Dambik (tc). **Travel South Dakota:** Byron Banasiak (fbl). **131 Alamy Stock Photo:** John Dambik (cr). **Travel South Dakota. 132 Getty Images:** Danita Delimont (c). **133 Alamy Stock Photo:** WireStock (bc). **134 Dreamstime.com:** Thomas Kelley (fbl). **Getty Images / iStock:** Art Wager (ca). **135 Alamy Stock Photo:** Philip Scalia (ftl); Tom Bean (fcrb). **NPS:** (fcr). **Shutterstock.com:** Traveller70 (ftr). **136 Alamy Stock Photo:** Emily Marie Wilson (tc); Jocelyn Catterson (fbr). **Getty Images / iStock:** varkdvr (ftl). **137 Alamy Stock Photo:** GL Archive (cra). **138 Alamy Stock Photo:** John Elk III (br). **Shutterstock.com:** JB Manning (bl). **139 Getty Images / iStock:** jimkruger (c). **140 Alamy Stock Photo:** Clint Farlinger (tr); Independent Picture Service (cr). **Dreamstime.com:** Wirestock (cb). **Getty Images / iStock:** AndreyKrav (ftl). **141 Alamy Stock Photo:** Dawid Swierczek (tl). **National Mississippi River Museum & Aquarium:** Mike Burley (bl) **Shutterstock.com:** Sam Wagner (br). **142 Alamy Stock Photo:** BHammond (ftl); Frifet Patrick / hemis.fr (br). **Getty Images:** Michael S. Lewis (bc). **143 Alamy Stock Photo:** Enrico Della Pietra (tr). **Jim Chamberlain - U.S. Fish & Wildlife Service:** Ray Patera (ftl). **Getty Images / iStock:** travelview (cr). **144 Shutterstock.com:** Andrew Marek (c). **145 Alamy Stock Photo:** imac (bl). **Dreamstime.com:** Mkopka (br). **146 AWL Images:** Danita Delimont Stock (tc). **Getty Images:** Jeff La Frenierre / 500px (fcl). **147 Alamy Stock Photo:** Daniel Thornberg (fcl); Todd Strand (tc); Stephen Taylor (fbr). **148 Alamy Stock Photo:** Matt Gush (bl). **Getty Images / iStock:** DutcherAerials (fbr). **149 Getty Images / iStock:** DaveAlan (c). **150 Alamy Stock Photo:** Heebphoto (br). **Getty Images / iStock:** Chris Boswell (fbl); Jim Glab (tl); zrfphoto (tr). **151 Alamy Stock Photo:** Jim West (fbl). **Getty Images / iStock:** DenisTangneyJr (tr). **152 Alamy Stock Photo:** Steve Bly (tr). **Getty Images:** Jan Butchofsky (ftl). **Getty Images / iStock:** powerofforever (fbl). **153 Dreamstime.com:** Charles Knowles (bl). **Getty Images / iStock:** estivillml (ftr); Haizhan Zheng (fcl). **154 AWL Images:** Christian Heeb (c). **155 Getty Images / iStock:** StockPhoto Astur (br). **156 Alamy Stock Photo:** Eva Worobiec (tc). **AWL Images:** Walter Bibikow (br). **Dreamstime.com:** Brian Scantlebury (fbl). **157 AWL Images:** Danita Delimont Stock (br). **Dreamstime.com:** Jonmanjeot (tc). **Shutterstock.com:** Andrey Bayda (ftl). **158 Getty Images / iStock:** MichaelGordon1 (fcl). **Shutterstock.com:** Alberto Loyo (tl). **159 Alamy Stock Photo:** BDP (tr). **160 Alamy Stock Photo:** Cavan Images (bl). **Dreamstime.com:** Benkrut (br). **161 Getty Images:** darekm101 (c). **162 Alamy Stock Photo:** Jess Merrill (tc); Jim West (fcl). **Dreamstime.com:** Oseland (fbl). **Getty Images / iStock:** groveb (ftl). **163 Alamy Stock Photo:** Timothy Mulholland (ftr). **Getty Images / iStock:** Starcevic (bc). **164 Getty Images:** Adam Jones (c). **165 Frazier History Museum:** (fbl). **Getty Images / iStock:** Althom (fbr). **166 Alamy Stock Photo:** Daniel Dempster Photography (fbl). **Kentucky Distillers' Association:** (br). **167 Kentucky Distillers' Association** (fcra); (fcrb). **The Campbell House, Curio Collection by Hilton, Lexington, Ky.:** (tr). **168 Alamy Stock Photo:** Stephen Saks Photography (bl); Stephen Saks Photography (br). **169 Marc Muench:** (c). **170 Alamy Stock Photo:** BHammond (tc); K.D. Leperi (fcr). **Getty Images:** Alan Majchrowicz (fcl). **Shutterstock.com:** Dennis MacDonald (ftr). **171 Alamy Stock Photo:** BHammond (bc); Chad Robertson (ftl); Jennifer Wright (ftr). **172 Getty Images / iStock:** FangXiaNuo (c). **173 Alamy Stock Photo:** BHammond (bl); BHammond (br). **174 Alamy Stock Photo:** FRILET Patrick / hemis.fr (fbl); Nigar Alizada (tc); Rob Crandall (fcla). **175 Alamy Stock Photo:** Carmen K. Sisson / Cloudybright (bc); Rogelio V. Solis (bl). **Wikimedia Commons:** CC BY-SA 4.0 DEED (fcr). **176 Alamy Stock Photo:** FRILET Patrick / hemis.fr (tc); FRILET Patrick / hemis.fr (ftl); Tetra Images (tr). **Getty Images:** John van Hasselt - Corbis (fcra). **177 Alamy Stock Photo:** Maximum Film (fcra). **178 Alamy Stock Photo:** Mark Waugh (br). **179 Alamy Stock Photo:** Allen Creative / Steve Allen (c). **180 Alamy Stock Photo:** Allen Creative / Steve Allen (tr). **Getty Images:** Bob Miller (fclb). **181 Alamy Stock Photo:** Everett Collection Inc (fbl). **Getty Images / iStock:** Dennis Rosario (fbr). **Getty Images:** Flip Schulke Archives (ftr); Image Source (bc). **182 Alamy Stock Photo:** Allen Creative / Steve Allen (bc); Incite Photography (fcla). **Dreamstime.com:** Calvin L. Leake (fbl). **183 Alamy Stock Photo:** Jim West (tc); Roy Johnson (ftl). **Getty Images / iStock:** benedek (fcr). **Getty Images:** Bloomberg (bc). **184 Getty Images / iStock:** alex grichenko (c). **185 Getty Images / iStock:** Montes-Bradley (fbl). **186 Getty Images / iStock:** Chansak Joe (ftr); LaserLens (fcl); J. Michael Jones (fclb). **Shutterstock.com:** Malachi Jacobs (ftl). **187 Alamy Stock Photo:** Randy Duchaine (bc). **Getty Images / iStock:** chrisncami (fbl); Sean Pavone (ftl). **188 Getty Images / iStock:** Noah Densmore (fbr); Shunyu Fan (fbl). **189 Getty Images / iStock:** Kruck20 (c). **190 courtesy of the National Park Service:** (ftl). **Shutterstock.com:** Alexandre Tziripouloff (br); Mkopka (tr). **191 Alamy Stock Photo:** H. Mark Weidman Photography (fbr). **Getty Images / iStock:** BackyardProduction (fcl); ggustin (ftl). **Getty Images:** Daniel Grill (tr). **192 Getty Images / iStock:** FilippoBacci (c). **193 Getty Images / iStock:** emson (bl); Mark Kostich (br). **194 Alamy Stock Photo:** James Schwabel (fcrb). **Getty Images / iStock:** felixmizioznikov (bl); Ryan Tishken (ftr). **Getty Images:** Stephen Frink (bc). **195 4Corners:** Susanne Kremer (fbr). **Dreamstime.com:** Buurserstraat386 (ftl). **Getty Images / iStock:** Nancy Pauwels (tc). **196 Getty Images:** Westend61 (fbr). **197 @rtwPaul:** (c). **198 Dreamstime.com:** Margaret619 (ftr). **Getty Images / iStock:** Sean Pavone (fcl). **Shutterstock.com:** Jose Medeiros (fbl). **199 Alamy Stock Photo:** Heidi Besen (bl); Terry Smith Studios (ftl); Jim West (fclb); John Elk III (bc). **200 Dreamstime.com:** Natalia Bratslavsky (tr); Paul Brady (fbl). **201 Alamy Stock Photo:** Witold Skrypczak (tl). **Getty Images / iStock:** Joshua McDonough (tc); Sundry Photography (fcl). **@rtwPaul. 202 Alamy Stock Photo:** James Schwabel (c). **203 Alamy Stock Photo:** Sholten Singer (br). **204 Alamy Stock Photo:** Savanna Shriver (bl). **Getty Images / iStock:** Wirestock (tc). **205 Alamy Stock Photo:** Emanuel Tanjala (fcr). **Getty Images / iStock:** wanderluster (ftr). **Shutterstock.com:** Jon Bilous (bl). **206 Alamy Stock Photo:** Brenda Kean (br). **Getty Images:** Reynold Mainse / Design Pics (ftl). **207 Alamy Stock Photo:** Jeffrey Isaac Greenberg 16+ (fbr). **Getty Images / iStock:** ablokhin (fcl). **Shutterstock.com:** Andriy Blokhin (tr). **208 VisitNC.com:** Ryan Donnel (fbl). **209 Getty Images / iStock:** Kyle Little (c). **210 Alamy Stock Photo:** Jeffrey Isaac Greenberg 19+ (fbl). **Getty Images / iStock:** Malven (ftr). **Getty Images:** Teresa Kopec (ftl). **211 Alamy Stock Photo:** Spring Images (fcrb). **Getty Images / iStock:** Joesboy (ftl). **Shutterstock.com:** Cvandyke (cr). **212 Alamy Stock Photo:** (c). **213 Getty Images / iStock:** Eloi Omella (fbl). **Shutterstock.com:** f11photo (fbr). **214 Alamy Stock Photo:** Craig Jack Photographic (cr); rudi1976 (tc); Naum Chayer (fbl). **Getty Images / iStock:** Chris Boswell (fbr). **215 Alamy Stock Photo:** Xinhua (tc). **Getty Images / iStock:** Aerial Views (ftl). **Shutterstock.com:** Laura Hedien (bc). **216 Getty Images / iStock:** Boogich (fbl); Joey Ingelhart (fcl). **Getty Images:** Eric A Norris (tr). **Unsplash:** Ryan Crisman (tc). **217 Alamy Stock Photo:** Prisma / Malherbe Marcel (bc). **Getty Images:** Alexander Spatari (ftr). **Getty Images / iStock:** photoquest7 (fbl). **218 Getty Images / iStock:** Chris Boswell (br). **219 Getty Images:** Alexander Spatari (c). **220 Alamy Stock Photo:** Krzysztof Sawicki (ftl). **Getty Images / iStock:** DenisTangneyJr (br); DenisTangneyJr (fcl); Krapels (bl). **221 Alamy Stock Photo:** Stu Gray (fcr); Wasin Pummarin (tl). **Getty Images / iStock:** PatriceO (tr). **222 Getty Images / iStock:** fotoguy22 (tr); traveler1116 (br). **223 Alamy Stock Photo:** Greg Balfour Evans (bc). **AWL Images:** Danita Delimont Stock (bl). **Getty Images / iStock:** zimmytws (ftr). **224 Caleb Kenna:** (c). **225 Getty Images:** DEA / M. BORCHI (fbr). **226 Alamy Stock Photo:** Everyday Artistry Photography (tc). **Tom Dempsey / www.photoseek.com:** (c). **Getty Images:** Robert Nickelsberg (fbr). **227 Alamy Stock Photo:** Susan Pease (fbr); Tom Croke (tc). **Getty Images / iStock:** vgajic (tl). **228 Alamy Stock Photo:** Vespasian (fbr). **229 AWL Images:** Jon Arnold (c). **230 Alamy Stock Photo:** Anna Wagner (tc); Robert F. Bukaty (br). **Shutterstock.com:** (bl). **231 Alamy Stock Photo:** Kumar Sriskandan (fcr). **Getty Images / iStock:** DenisTangneyJr (bc); PictureLake (tc). **232 Alamy Stock Photo:** Cavan Images (c). **233 Shutterstock.com:** FashionStock.com (bl). **234 Alamy Stock Photo:** Kumar Sriskandan (ftl); Wangkun Jia (bc). **235 Alamy Stock Photo:** Erin Paul Donovan (tc); Jim West (fbr). **AWL Images:** Michele Falzone (ftl). **236 Getty Images / iStock:** Nicholas Klein (bl). **237 Getty Images / iStock:** C_Cherdchai (c). **238 Dreamstime.com:** Jiawangkun (tr), Pierrette Guertin (tl); Jon Bilous (cr). **Getty Images / iStock:** Rixipix (br). **239 Dreamstime.com:** Cheri Alguire (fbr); Dejan Baric (ftr). **240 Alamy Stock Photo:** Rachel Boucher / Stockimo (tr). **Dreamstime.com:** Lei Xu (tc). **Getty Images:** Archive Photos (fbl). **241 Alamy Stock Photo:** Harry Collins (fcr). **Getty Images:** Brandon Rosenblum (crb). **James Robertson:** (tc). **242 Getty Images / iStock:** Ultima_Gaina (c). **243 Getty Images / iStock:** Oleg Albinsky (br); pictus photography (bc). **244 Alamy Stock Photo:** James Kirkikis (cl). **Getty Images / iStock:** peeterv (tc). **Greta Rybus:** (fbl). **Shutterstock.com:** Joseph Sohm (ftl). **245 Alamy Stock Photo:** Randy Duchaine (fbr); Richard Ellis (fcr). **Dreamstime.com:** Chicco7 (fbl). **246 Alamy Stock Photo:** Danita Delimont (bc). **Getty Images / iStock:** mirceax (fcrb); Paula andreaonline (fcra). **247 Alamy Stock Photo:** Robert F. Bukaty. **Getty Images / iStock:** fdastudillo (tl). **Shutterstock.com:** EWY Media (br)

Cover images: *Front:* **Jake Guzman**; *Back:* **AWL Images:** Christian Heeb (fcla); **Getty Images / iStock:** Zhiling Zheng (ftl) **Getty Images:** Matteo Colombo (fbl); **iStockphoto**/kojihirano (fcrb)

Main Contributors Charles Usher, Stephen Keeling, Zoey Goto, Kristen Shoates, Adam Karlin, Jacqui Agate, Lisa Voormeij, Maxine Sheppard, Lynn Brown
Project Editor Sarah Allen
Senior Editors Keith Drew, Zoë Rutland
Editors Edward Aves, Alex Pathe
Senior Designer Adrienne Pitts
Designer Kei Ishimaru
Proofreader Kathryn Glendenning
Indexer Hilary Bird
Picture Researcher Adam Goff
Publishing Assistant Simona Velikova
Cartographic Editor James Macdonald
Cartographer Animesh Pathak
Jacket Designer Gemma Doyle
Senior Production Editor Tony Phipps
Image retoucher Adam Brackenbury
Senior Production Controller Samantha Cross
Managing Editor Hollie Teague
Managing Art Editor Gemma Doyle
Art Director Maxine Pedliham
Publishing Director Georgina Dee

First edition 2024

Published in Great Britain by Dorling Kindersley Limited, DK, One Embassy Gardens, 8 Viaduct Gardens, London SW11 7BW, UK

The authorized representative in the EEA is Dorling Kindersley Verlag GmbH. Arnulfstr. 124, 80636 Munich, Germany

Published in the United States by DK Publishing, 1745 Broadway, 20th Floor, New York, NY 10019, USA

24 25 26 27 28 10 9 8 7 6 5 4 3 2

002-342947-Oct/2024

A CIP catalog record for this book is available from the British Library.

A catalog record for this book is available from the Library of Congress.

ISBN: 978-0-2416-9585-2

Printed and bound in China

www.dk.com

The rate at which the world is changing is constantly keeping the DK team on our toes. While we've worked hard to ensure this book is accurate and up-to-date, things can change in an instant. Road conditions can worsen, gas stations can close, and weather can impact access to view points. Road closures often occur in winter months, so it's important to check ahead before embarking on your road trip. The publisher cannot accept responsibility for any consequences arising from the use of this book. If you notice we've got something wrong, we want to hear about it. Please get in touch at travelguides@dk.com

This book was made with Forest Stewardship Council™ certified paper – one small step in DK's commitment to a sustainable future.
Learn more at www.dk.com/uk/information/sustainability